INTELLIGENT INFORMATION SYSTEMS

INTELLIGENT INFORMATION SYSTEMS

Meeting the Challenge of the Knowledge Era

Alan J. Rowe
Sue Anne Davis

In Collaboration with Sushmita Vij

Quorum Books
Westport, Connecticut • London

Library of Congress Cataloging-in-Publication Data

Rowe, Alan J.
   Intelligent information systems: meeting the challenge of the knowledge era /
Alan J. Rowe, Sue Anne Davis ; in collaboration with Sushmita Vij.
      p.   cm.
   Includes bibliographical references and index.
   ISBN 0–89930–912–7 (alk. paper)
      1. Management information systems.   2. Decision support systems.
   3. Information storage and retrieval systems—Business.
   4. Information technology—Management.   I. Davis, Sue Anne.
   II. Title.
   HD30.213.R689   1996
   658.4′038′011—dc20   95–46277

British Library Cataloguing in Publication Data is available.

Library of Congress Catalog Card Number: 95–46277
ISBN: 0–89930–912–7

First published in 1996

Quorum Books, 88 Post Road West, Westport, CT 06881
An imprint of Greenwood Publishing Group, Inc.

Printed in the United States of America

(∞)™

The paper used in this book complies with the
Permanent Paper Standard issued by the National
Information Standards Organization (Z39.48–1984).

10 9 8 7 6 5 4 3 2 1

□ □ □
CONTENTS

❑ ❑ ❑
TABLES AND FIGURES

TABLES

FIGURES

□ □ □
PREFACE

Intelligent Information Technology Systems link management to the reengineering of an organization.

Because of rapid change and increasing chaos in the environment, decision makers are increasingly dependent on intelligent information in order to perform effectively. Every facet of modern life from airplane navigation to open heart surgery to multimedia systems to teleconferencing to rapid response systems points in the direction in which information technology will be used. Powerful computers, possibly using light waves and thousands of parallel processors, intelligent software, smart manufacturing systems, and multifunction office devices tied to ubiquitous communications networks, are a few of the emerging technologies that will sweep factories and offices around the world into the twenty-first century. The infrastructure of technology resources will be widely dispersed at corporations, universities, and other organizations around the world and will be used to expand business and create new competitors. It is no longer sufficient to pursue the evolving nature of information technology. What is required is radical innovation in the way work is performed and how intelligent information is accessed across and beyond organizational boundaries. New approaches will have to be "invented" to cope with this information revolution. A company must be prepared with an organizational infrastructure which is able to respond to threats in real-time. In today's turbulent business environment, strategies will have to be implemented in tactical time frames. Rather than investing in isolated information technology systems, a company's top-level management must be prepared to invest in intelligent technology capabilities that will need to be managed on an enterprise-wide model representing the operations of their entire business. Based on this model, intelligent-based systems, data bases, software objects, and other technical components are integrated to do the equivalent of using computer systems to augment a manager's ability to assimilate and react to rapidly changing environmental information. No longer will reengineering suffice; a whole new perspective is needed where "if it ain't being fixed continuously, it is broke!"

Examples and cases are used to show how to achieve these objectives. Software and hardware considerations are included when required, in addition to issues such as whether to outsource or how to handle client server distributed computing. Intelligent Information Systems should be viewed as matching the style of decision makers with information requirements based on advanced technology. Important and effective tools for making organizations more competitive and for more effective utilization of both human and physical resources are explored.

THE URGENCY IN USING INTELLIGENT INFORMATION SYSTEMS

New machines permit revolutions but they do not start them. The changes going on in the world of information technology are not about machines, but their rate and nature are influenced by the extraordinary range of new technologies now available. A new economy is here, challenging us with a brave new world—informed and empowered by the distribution and power of a technology that even science fiction fantasists have had trouble anticipating. We are in the beginnings of the "real digital" revolution now. This is one of those historic points that changes the way that all society is going to work forever. It is as dramatic a change as the Industrial Revolution was to farmers. It is not about quality, flexibility, or time, but is a revolution about the availability and use of information and expertise. That is where the revolutionaries and visionaries are looking.

"We have spent hundreds of billions of dollars developing computer power that has set us adrift in a sea of data," says Thomas P. Kehler, Chief Executive Officer (CEO) of IntelliCorp., a California software company. Intelligent Information Systems hold the promise of putting that information to work in a way that truly supports managerial decision making. Intelligent Information Systems can assist decision makers with the ambiguity and judgment involved in complex decisions that conventional data processing cannot handle. This difference is attributable to the increased use of symbolic reasoning, such as in expert systems computer programs, rather than the pure number crunching that has characterized past practices. Intelligent Information Systems go beyond decision support systems because of the focus on the decision maker's reasoning ability and how decisions meet the needs of the organization.

It is forecasted that the next software revolution will be a transition from text-based computer programs to graphic operating systems and from application-based computing to document-oriented computing. The need for such enhancements are clear when one considers that the fall of many executives has been blamed on their limited use of information. Furthermore, executives who think that they can rely on authority or experience rather than information are clearly headed for problems. In an information-oriented society, information is power. However, one out of every four corporate executives who has relied on historical data as the bases for decision support often makes unrealistic decisions. Poor or wrong decisions are the most common cause for removal of executives. Knowledge of how decision makers think, reason, judge, and solve problems provides a foundation for the design of flexible and adaptive information systems that accommodate any user's needs. A test instrument is described that measures decision styles and information usage.

MEANS FOR IMPROVING DECISION MAKING

How does one know when a good decision has been made or how to improve decision making? Decision makers need a "frame of reference" from which to examine and understand a complex environment. Intelligent Information Systems can help provide this framework because they relate decision making to the style of the decision maker.

In a dynamic and rapidly changing business environment, decision makers should be able to scan events in order to understand what is happening and what actions are needed to cope with the situation. In a study of thirty-seven chief executives in small- to medium-sized high-technology firms, El Sawy found that they do scan systematically. However, they use limited sources for their information. Intelligent strategic scanning requires that the information is customized to meet the individual needs of the executives and their organization. General reports that rely on conventional information systems tend to be ignored. Intelligent information needs to be personalized for use by the chief executive and other decision makers in the organization.

Scanning provides valuable early warning signals. Intelligent Information Systems are used to monitor trends, identify critical events, determine threats, or obtain other information that would provide clues as to what might affect an organization's strategic posture. El Sawy's findings of the external sources of data used by the CEOs he studied are shown in Table P.1.

An examination of Table P.1 reveals that a computer-based information system would be used to supplement the chief executive's information needs for strategic scanning. A hybrid system can be used to provide the executive information which the computer can interpret and store in a knowledge base. Intelligent Information Systems utilize expert systems to develop trends and correlations for the data stored by the computer and to establish its significance for strategic scanning. Personal information systems show and

Table P.1
External Information Sources

External information source	Regularly used	Specific needs
Trade journals	17	10
Friends in industry	16	11
Customers	16	23
Other	31	25
Total external sources described	80	69
Personal sources	37	41
Impersonal sources	43	28

Source: Excerpt from Omar El Sawy, "Personal Information Systems for Strategic Scanning in Turbulent Environments: Can the CEO Go Online?" MIS Quarterly, March 1985.

capture how an executive reasons. Some use a bare minimum of information while others expect complete details and comprehensive analysis.

Increasingly, evaluation of an organization's performance is becoming more complex because of changes that are being made in organizational structures and decision-making responsibilities. Not only must decision makers of the future be variable leviathans capable of dealing with a multitude of different technologies, including computers, but they must also be aware of social and behavioral problems and must understand psychology, sociology, and political science.

The most important functions of the leaders will be to inspire by articulating a clear vision of the organization's values, strategies, and objectives and to know enough about the business to be the risk manager of risk takers. A better understanding of the role of leaders and managers in making effective decisions will have to emerge in order to assure that performance meets both the external as well as the internal organizational demands. Our objective is to provide the decision maker with a sound basis for understanding why Intelligent Information Systems are needed and for making the transition from current systems to more effective intelligent systems. It is precisely because of these considerations that Intelligent Information Systems, Heuristics, and Artificial Intelligence are becoming a normal part of the information environment. Coverage of these and other information-related topics, such as graphics and visualization, should ensure that the decision maker of the future has the tools to be effective.

□ ▫ ▫
ACKNOWLEDGMENTS

A book is a treasure, but it takes away from the precious time we would like to spend with our families. To those whom we desire to be with, we would like to express our sincere appreciation for their understanding and support, and trust that the effort justifies the sacrifice.

To our many friends and colleagues, we would like to express our thanks for the effort they extended on our behalf in reviewing the book and making helpful suggestions. We employed our network of colleagues to benefit from their many helpful suggestions. The ideas expressed in this book are solely our responsibility. For all their help, we would like to thank Jack Alcalay, John Basch, Warren Bennis, Richard Bernacci, Kent Bimson, Jim Boulgarides, Bob Canady, Dimitris Chorafas, Jessie Cox, Clifford Craft, Louis Davis, Richard Davis, Dorothy Dologite, Lance Eliot, Larry Fox, Michael Godfrey, Murdoch Heideman, Alex Jacobson, Matt Klempa, Tom Lincoln, Richard Mann, Richard Mason, Robert Mockler, Jim Paisley, Alan Patz, Alex Pinto, Howard Resnikoff, Clifford Robertson, Mel Salveson, Omar El Sawy, Hal Schutt, Inan Somers, Gene Starr, Joel Kurtzman, Ephrain Turban, and Ronnie Wells. For her secretarial help, we would like to thank Laura Wautemburg. Thanks also to the Greenwood staff for their support and encouragement.

AJR
SAD

Los Angeles
San Francisco

CHAPTER ONE
❏ ❏ ❏
DECISION MAKING IN THE 1990s AND BEYOND

There is no future for those who live in the past.

Today's economic climate makes old assumptions about decision making obsolete because of the complexity and increasing chaos that characterizes the world in which executives have to function. Bankruptcies are still a concern and, at the same time, mergers are leading to larger organizations while other organizations are downsizing, restructuring, or outsourcing. The current and projected economic environment gives rise to an urgent need for new tools and approaches to deal with an uncertain future and more complex decisions. Decisions confronting managers are illustrated by questions such as, should they cut dividends, reduce the level of research, spin off products, reduce the workforce, restructure the organization, or enter new markets? These are some of the issues that confront decision makers who live in our topsy-turvy world.

Most large companies still rely on a bureaucratic approach to decision making. However, to be successful, companies must follow a more flexible approach in which the organization is better able to respond to constant change. Adler (1994) states, "While we read every day about amazing new technologies that can revolutionize the way we work, most firms encounter difficulty translating even a fraction of the potential of these technologies into business advantages." Managers who have limited experience are often confronted with an intolerable level of ambiguity because of the difficulty that the human mind has in dealing with unstructured situations. These managers, who, on the one hand, must handle day to day problems but must also make far reaching and uncertain decisions, are ideal candidates for the use of Intelligent Information Systems.

Technological advances in telecommunications and in computers have radically changed the flows of information throughout the world. As a result of the expansive use of fiber-optic cables, satellites, radio, television, and phone lines, it is possible for people and computers—either large-scale "supercomputers" or "micro" personal computers—to communicate with one another in seconds, wherever they are located in the world. Modern computer networks allow data, video, and voice communications to flow among companies and organizations in order to share technological resources, such as laser printers and mainframe computers. They also enable organizations to extend the size and scope of their operations by collapsing time and distance. We have witnessed computer systems shifting from storing and reporting data to more intelligent utilization of available information and knowledge-based systems. Current systems are being replaced by those that include local and wide area networking, group decision making using shared data, interactive simulation models for strategy communication, integration of heterogeneous data bases, and expert system applications.

A proactive approach to job satisfaction and job design has resulted in radical change, such as General Electric's "work out" sessions, which evoke a sense of enthusiasm because workers are able to introduce meaningful change. Jack Welch, the key decision maker at General Electric (GE), has been the driving force for introducing change. He believes in a lean workforce, less bureaucracy, more innovation, and more commitment. Participation is achieved by a "work out" approach in which workers meet to correct problems that they have. Welch is intent on introducing an entrepreneurial spirit into the once stodgy GE. The result is that GE's stock was worth $131.7 billion in early 1996, compared with $62 billion when Welch took over the reins of the company. This kind of radical change can only be achieved by effective decision making.

Organizations that remain effective will be the ones that rely increasingly on Intelligent Information Systems. American Express could not process the number of inquiries they receive or make the credit decisions as quickly as they do without an expert system developed by Inference Corporation (Integrating Case-Based Reasoning, 1992). Whirlpool has a data-processing system that periodically searches customer-call data to identify troubled products that may end up in recalls or in million-dollar lawsuits. AT&T's Network Service tracks all service activities to ensure job satisfaction. Advanced companies have applied artificial intelligence-based systems to help solve customer shipments by using a parallel-processing computer. How are these systems different from the current systems in place? What features do such systems have that provide the element of intelligence? Answers to these questions arise from an examination of the decision maker using such systems, the technology used, and the decision-making environment.

CURRENT CORPORATE ENVIRONMENT

There are three major forces that affect the role of the decision maker and make corporate environments more complex. The first is the increasingly competitive nature of business that exists in our global environment. The second is a paradigm shift in the structure of organizations that will affect the way in which individuals function. The third force is the explosive growth of computer technology—exemplified by the number of personal computers and workstations that are estimated to reach a mark over 200 million. These dramatic forces portend a new generation of decision makers who will need to be more than computer literate and who are able to cope with the radical changes in organizational structures that emphasize team effort and group decision making. The new organization that is emerging is flat and provides "empowerment" to individuals who will increasingly be in a position to make significant decisions in their organizations. The kind of information needed at the operational level will, undoubtedly, require greater reliance on "expert assistance." These requirements can only be fulfilled effectively by a new generation of Intelligent Information Systems.

In addition to technical considerations, there is a growing recognition of the need to understand the role of perception, cognition, reasoning, and value judgments in decision making. For example, decision styles can now be used to determine the kind and amount of information preferred by managers. Multimedia displays may be the perfect answer for an individual with a high cognitive complexity style; an individual with a low cognitive complexity style would find a comprehensive display confusing. When designing Intelligent Information Systems, considerations, such as the mind's ability to perceive and process input data (information overload), become important because they determine the kind of information that can be utilized and the best manner in which to present it to the decision maker.

It has been projected that the world is on the verge of an economic boom. As economic interdependence increases, there is a growing need in developing countries for support—meaning the disintegration of barriers to the flow of information, money, and technology across borders. The trend toward global market integration means a shift to higher value-added production and tailored services. Cooperation, alliance, sharing, services, and innovation are characterizing the new look of global business. It is indicative of the rapidly changing environment of business and the need for more effective information systems.

Information is critical for sustaining a strategic competitive advantage and for the survival of the firm. Increasingly, decision makers will have to rely on information technology to achieve strategic competitiveness. For example, the airline industry depends as much on information technology as it does on its aircraft or repair facilities. There is no question that industry is entering a new era where only those who have the ability to compete effectively by utilizing Information Technology (IT) to support decision making will survive. Thus, Intelligent Information Systems will have to consider not only the decisions that managers make but the competitive environment in which the decisions have to be employed.

Computer-based information systems are increasingly vital to business success. Eliminating inefficiencies, meeting fierce competition, and the falling prices of computer technology will help stimulate the application of IT to improve business functions. Computer-based information systems rarely fail because of technology. They fail when managers do not accept that changing a computer-based information system will ultimately change the organization.

THE NEW DESIGN OF WORK

Businesses everywhere have become concerned about how to organize themselves so that they can deliver products on time, offer services that consistently satisfy customers, build market credibility and reputation and introduce new products faster and services faster than competitors. However, the more they have turned to information technology as a medium in which to do business and with which to manage business, the more serious these organizational problems have become.

The problem is not technology. The problem is the design of closed loop processes for conducting business. Inherent in these processes is a network of performers and customers who work toward the fulfillment of an original request. Such a network of workflows is called a business process or organizational process. Because of the growing concern in organizations for management of workflows, operating system technology is being drawn into the management of organizations. This will produce major structural changes within organizations and in the field of operating systems. As organizations and markets have been nurtured by information and communications technology, failures to see and manage human processes have grown into crisis proportions. Redesigning workflows for closure and simplicity is not a simple technological problem. The workflows are "the way things are done around here" and are part of the culture of the organization. This will have to shift toward "the way things should be done around here." Redesigning these processes means altering the culture of the organization. Technology by itself is not sufficient to bring this about. The gap between the interpretation of operating systems and the concerns of organizations has been brought into sharp focus by the widening realization that computers are for *communications*, not just for recording or processing. The connections will be complete when the boundary between the computer systems and the organization has disappeared—when they are seamless and ubiquitous.

This trend toward distributed processing is both an organizational and technological concept, with its premise being that hardware (micros and minis), data, and software need to be closer physically to the people who use them, and that the network needs to be designed around a combination of geographical and functional considerations. As the new Intelligent Information Technologies and Services find increasing use, they may usher in a dramatic social transformation. The possibility of conducting most social functions electronically means that there will cease to be any good reason why one cannot locate an office, home, school, or other facility virtually anywhere. Family life may also be revolutionized as education, shopping, work, and other activities are brought into the home. The home may recover its traditional role as a center of product, a role it played during the agricultural era. This may result in a resurgence of cohesive family lives, neighborhoods, and cities, as people devote more time and interest in their local communities. At the same time, these workers would be connected to the outside through powerful information networks.

Another important change is that electronic relationships are beginning to shift the locus of power in organizations. Authority figures can always use computers to dominate subordinates, but Intelligent Information Systems naturally tend to drive power, initiative, and control down to the bottom of large institutions. This transformation of power can be seen in large corporations which have decentralized into small, semiautonomous units, each collaborating among its employees, suppliers, stakeholders, and even competitors.

There appears to be an air of desperation regarding the concept of learning organizations and use of knowledge as market power. To turn a company into a learning organization requires that firms concentrate on developing their core competencies—the flexible skills that allow them to produce a stream of distinctive products that cannot be easily imitated by a rival. Older examples include miniaturization by Sony, optics by Canon, or timely delivery by Federal Express. However, the missing link is putting efforts into recruiting and training of selected employees. Core competencies also lie in plant layout and logistics design, as well as in the core vision statement or desired state of the company, for the next several years. After the determining of core competencies, the next dimension of the learning organization is removal of internal barriers to the flow of information. Knowledge engineers are needed to keep members of the organization up to date with what is going on in the industry and to act as mentors to guide and train younger members of the organization. An additional dimension is determining how people use information and reason by using tools such as the Decision Style Inventory, presented to evaluate the proper mix of people with differing skills or personalities. Companies look for employees with "T-shaped" skills—employees with deep expertise in one discipline combined with enough breadth to see its connections to others.

These decentralized corporations will require better technology structures, better work processes, and fewer but better people. This new organization structure is based on the postulate that the typical business of the future will be knowledge and intelligence based, and that the organizations will be composed largely of specialists who direct and discipline their own performance through organized feedback from colleagues, customers, and corporate headquarters. The key components in preparing for this change will be education and training. We are in the midst of a repolarization of work, using fewer and fewer, but better and better, educated and trained people. Figure 1.1 examines the elements to be addressed in redesigning business practices.

This Intelligent Information Age encourages the creative use of knowledge because the need to solve tough new problems is becoming the central function of a high-tech, global economy. This Intelligent Information Revolution offers enormous promise, but new technologies always introduce dangers as well as gains. As we become deeply reliant upon Intelligent Information Systems that are so powerful, controlling, and complex as to almost defy comprehension, great costs may be paid on the human side of the organization. For example, ensuring computer security, personal privacy, and protection against destructive intrusions such as viruses will require far greater care and ingenuity as Intelligent Information Systems become more pervasive. Perhaps the toughest challenge will be to develop effective means for finding our way through the avalanche of data that even now threatens to engulf us. It is ironic that people living in this information age feel more, rather than less, ignorant. An overabundance of intelligence may leave us with a heightened awareness of all that is unknown. The challenge will be for management to harness the power of that intelligence. Furthermore, the trend of moving toward free access to this intelligence and information across an organization eliminates the need for the hierarchical management systems that used to exist.

In the emerging knowledge era, we will have to reexamine jobs, managers, and work processes because knowledge will form the foundation of the successful future enterprise. Knowledge built on intelligent information will allow these organizations to be more flexible and better able to adapt to the continuously changing, and often chaotic, environment. Savage (1994) has identified three critical components of organizations that will need to be redesigned to meet new requirements:

Figure 1.1
Elements of an Intelligent Information System

INTELLIGENCE ADDING MODULE	DATA SOURCES MODULE	DECISION MAKER MODULE
1. Causal models 2. Expert systems 3. Simulation models 4. Case-based reasoning 5. Rules objects 6. Neural nets 7. Semantic nets	1. Experts 2. Graphic-user interface 3. Internet 4. Knowledge engineers 5. Case-based knowledge 6. Group knowledge	1. Perception 2. Cognitive complexity 3. Reasoning judgment 4. Expertise 5. Creativity 6. Conceptual maps 7. Leadership

	DATA KNOWLEDGE MODULE	DECISION OUTPUT MODULE
	1. Integrated heterogenous data bases 2. Data storage and retrieval 3. Knowledge bases 4. Client servers 5. World wide web access	1. Managerial decision making 2. Team group effort 3. Value judgment 4. Restructuring downsizing 5. Enhanced knowledge

1. *Business processes redesign.* This will lead to lean, agile, and robust enterprises based on dynamic teaming.

2. *Business network redesign.* A new electronic marketplace will mean that the enterprise will have to serve customers any place and at any time.

3. *Business scopes redesign.* Enterprises of the future will increasingly become virtual organizations that depend on networking to maintain a competitive position.

Instead of organization charts, the knowledge era enterprise will become ever-changing clusters of capable teams. Functional areas such as engineering, human resources, or financial activities will focus on incorporating customers and suppliers as stakeholders. Learning will help to cement teams into more cohesive entities, and the organization's real assets will be a combination of knowledge, expertise, experience, and empowered teams. The challenge confronting the new managers will be formidable and will require significant external expertise to help in the transition.

System Dynamics and Strategic Planning Simulation Models

Strategic planning is the organizational forum for expanding the company's knowledge base and management's thinking skills. Virtually every organization sets on a course with an intention to pursue that course until information indicates that they are off course. Then, the system attempts to self correct and get back on course. This behavior illustrates a goal-seeking feedback loop and is one that many organizations use to conduct business. Most managers are still trained to look for signals of differences and will make small course corrections. For many, this is the only solution, especially when policies and processes are not structured to produce the desired goal. If this is the case, the goal remains unattained and the gap between expectations and performance continues to widen. When the goals, practices, and processes of the system are not aligned, no amount of effort can cause the desired changes and results. Thompson and Weiner (1995) postulate that the use of system dynamics simulation models as part of the strategic planning process is fundamental to the learning organization; and in order to increase learning capacity, the organization must first see a need to improve. Goals, and the policies to achieve those goals, must be examined and aligned. The process for critical thinking and learning in an organization is strategic planning.

Strategic planning groups are often expected to make accurate predictions of events in the distant future which, today, is an impossible task. However, when managers expect planning to help improve the organization's adaptability—that is, to increase the learning capacity of the organization—it is possible to meet the expectations.

When incorporated into strategy formation, system dynamics can provide powerful insights into how and why structure determines organizational behavior. Testing alternate strategies in a system dynamic software model provides a management group with a common framework for proposed changes in the organization. The model may be used to capture and simulate organizational behavior and to serve as a learning laboratory for testing potential changes. Skills and learning are acquired by remembering and using solutions to previously solved problems and by remembering and avoiding previous mistakes or traps. When proposed changes produce an unintended consequence, the management team can trace the cause of the side effect and see why it occurred. For the learning organization, planning should provide techniques for checking whether the organization is meeting its goals. Learning the "why" can take the manager beyond the modeling process into the implementation processes: the mobilization of an organization and alignment with the corporate vision. It is an action step that helps to complete one learning cycle and opens up thinking for the next.

People are good at knowing the relationships between people, departments, companies, and competitors, whereas system dynamic modeling is good at tracing out the dynamic implications of those relationships in terms of growing or falling customer interest, changing market share, and increasing product functionality. System dynamics tries to make it easy for people to see how the relationships that they know about can produce the behavior they are concerned with. It can do so in the following ways:

- System dynamic software focuses on how social systems (like businesses or markets) can generate their own behavior. Examples of business behavior include rapid growth of sales, fluctuating levels of inventory, or falling morale.

- System dynamics synthesizes the experiences of system participants, as well as organizational structures, processes, and managerial decision styles.

- System dynamics recognizes that causality is often circular and that this circularity gives rise to the characteristic behavior of markets. An example is called the "word-of-mouth" growth loop in which as more customers buy a product, there are more people who talk about the product and consequently, more people who will hear about the product. The assumption is that when people like what they hear about the product, they will seek out that specific product, providing even more customers who can talk about its virtues. This self-reinforcing process, one of the market's thousands of feedback loops, can be a strong contributor to sales growth.

- System dynamics can provide you with a computer simulation model that can function as a laboratory for investigating how markets may behave based on your input and theories you may want to test. (In this book, tools such as STRATMAP are presented to evaluate frameworks for competitive strategies.)

THE NEW EXECUTIVE

If one looks at the new breed of executives entering the scene, it is quite obvious that those who will be running corporate America in the future will be quite different from those at the helm today. The new executives will tend to be younger, in the range of fifty-two years old; current top executives average sixty-one years old. Current executives have grown up with television and jet travel, and many have spent their entire careers in a single corporation or in a single industry. In the evolving knowledge society, managers will have to be prepared to forget much of what they learned previously because the rules have changed. It is clear that executives who cannot change will become "yesterday's managers," as witnessed at General Motors, IBM, Westinghouse, Digital Equipment, and American Express.

Another characteristic of the 1990s is the networking among individuals as a result of joint ventures, strategic alliances, and cooperative efforts among companies. This will become increasingly important because of global competition, as will the number of strategic options in terms of products, technologies, resources, distribution channels, and markets available to future managers. To be successful, executives will have to utilize imaginative and unconventional strategies. They will have to focus their attention on a positive vision in order to achieve meaningful communication and gain employee trust. They will also need to have a positive self-regard as leaders so that they can change the direction of their organization. Other qualities they will need are as follows:

1. Special abilities to stretch the organization's horizons and to apply vigorous communications which create an attitude of commitment and risk taking that builds on trust and teamwork. Also, they will empower members of the organization to assume responsibility.

2. Personal attributes will include high cognitive complexity, high ethical values, and high self-esteem.

3. Broad knowledge and experience in a given industry. They will also need education that includes an extended understanding of information technologies and the ability to use sophisticated, knowledge-based decision tools.

Technology advances have allowed cost reductions and productivity improvements. These are manifested through organizational changes and have generally affected middle management. Middle management jobs have all but disappeared and will not be coming back. These "middles" were created because we did not have sophisticated systems to manage all the information floating around the organization. They were necessary to filter, collate, summarize, forward, and act on information. New technology does many of these functions for us now. However, business-process definition tools relating to computer application development commonly have used a programming paradigm rather than a people-management paradigm. They focus on procedures and data, and their primary objective is to show the relationships between procedural elements (i.e., programs or manual activities) and the use of data. People in the enterprise appear as data records, merely input–output mechanisms, or as substitutes for software programs. Considering people and their accountabilities in an organization adds another dimension. What we have to consider are the following current organizational extremes (Scherr, 1993):

- *An organization that has completely defined procedures but no defined accountabilities for its employees.* This structure is usually found in well-established bureaucracies and will rarely create well-defined accountabilities.

- *An organization with well-defined accountabilities but few defined procedures.* This structure is usually found in start-up companies that will probably develop procedures as a natural way of doing business.

Organized bodies that embody both paradigms include an orchestra, surgical teams, and sports teams.

Contemporary managers generally say that people make the difference,—that intelligence is a kind of asset, more valuable than such traditional sources of wealth as raw materials, land, money, or technology. How is it, then, that public corporations lay off thousands of employees even as their CEO's declare that their employees are their most important asset?

Special abilities are important for executives to be successful. Adler (1994) emphasizes that executives will have to adjust to the following leadership of major changes if American industries are to overcome organizational and human hurdles and assure a more effective implementation of these technologies:

1. The effective implementation of these new technologies will require training at even the lowest levels in organizations in the understanding of the 'why' behind technology. Furthermore, a more cooperative working relationship needs to be developed between the technology users and technology development specialists.

2. In order for the necessary prerequisite skills to be in place to optimize the power behind the technology, a higher level of training investment will be required. In order to begin the building process for improved levels of company loyalty, larger investments in training in core prerequisite skills will also be required.

3. Firms will need to involve the workforce, blue and white collar alike, in the technological change process; the employees must be involved in helping plan new technology investments and in helping to solve American paranoia around union and employee involvement in technological change.

4. Organizations must weave together strategies across levels and functions. In today's environment, change is so rapid and so multiform, that any organization that restricts the tasks of strategic management to a handful of people at the top will find those people swamped by information overload. People at all levels of the organization must be mobilized in the strategy process, must be alert to opportunities and threats in the environment, must be aware of strengths and weaknesses of the subunit relative to benchmarking practices, and must be empowered to interject into the strategy process with new ideas and concerns.

There is a common thread to these four elements of the implementation challenge: business organizations must become knowledge-based organizations. Firms will need to create broader jobs that encourage employees to identify improvement opportunities in both processes and technologies. That will require better education and training and more cooperative employee relations. For an organization to learn, the capacity of installed Intelligent Information Technology is a starting point. This places an important requirement on the design of Intelligent Information Systems. Not only must such systems be technically sound, but they must be able to accommodate the personality needs of the executives in the organization responsible for performance.

Decision aids will become critical because information by itself rarely solves a problem. Decision aids are needed by upper-level management to assist them in analyzing data, evaluating business opportunities, recommending solutions, and documenting the decisions that are made. Executive Information Systems (EIS) are developed around performance measures based on critical success factors and stakeholder expectations. Then, they link these measures across functions to show how progress is being made on strategic goals. Feedback from EIS informs strategy formulation, business-plan development, and operational activities.

BEYOND CURRENT INFORMATION SYSTEMS

Progressive companies cannot ignore recent projections that estimate the information technology field could exceed $11 billion in the 1990s. Pacific Telesis and Nynex are using a management flight simulator to teach systems managers about the fast-changing telecommunications marketplace and the implications of their actions in the strategic planning process. Schlumberger Inc. has used a geological-analysis expert system that enhances the professional's decision-making abilities. They have used the system to determine whether new oil wells would be valuable based on measurements taken during drilling. Petroleum geologists are the ones who normally perform these analyses, and they can cost the company large sums of money if a wrong decision is made.

From their inception, the objective of computer-based information systems has been to provide decision makers with reports in a more meaningful and useful form. Unfortunately, most current systems do not really "support" decision making. One of the ways in which to correct this situation is a program that was introduced by Lotus Development. They have used a personal information manager that allows decision makers to enter information into an "Agenda" data base in natural, free-form units, called *items*, without the structure required in a typical data base system. Lotus "Agenda" assists the user by applying intelligence to the decision maker's knowledge by using contextual cues and historic information to help to draw inferences about the data.

Looking ahead, there are startling possibilities in the application of Intelligent Information Systems to support decision making. We will see a drastic change in the way computers are built, in their architectures, and in the kind of software they will use. In particular, parallel architecture, that allows programs to process a large number of electronic routes, provides an enhanced ability to do things more efficiently. This capability will enhance processing speed and introduce interesting, new, and untested potential. The impact on decision makers and management has yet to be determined. However, its potential is evident as more powerful systems are introduced.

Neural networks provide a frontier that may change the way managers look at decision making and at support systems. Neural networks have been used in Japan for a variety of applications that try to simulate human behavior. They also incorporate the concept of "fuzzy logic." This logic does not deal with precise values but is based on concepts with a range of values, thereby allowing fuzziness. The Japanese have applied it to washing machines, where the water can be determined as being dirty or not dirty, which is a fuzzy concept.

One of the most valuable assets a company has is its expertise. The potential loss of an expert can be devastating. When Campbell Soup Company was confronted with the fact that the expert in repairing "cookers" for sterilizing cans was about to retire, they decided to build an expert system to translate the expert's knowledge into computer rules. Using interviews and analyzing the expert's trouble-shooting heuristics, they developed a computerized adviser called "Cooker." This expert system now solves almost all of the company's cooker malfunctions.

The use of an expert's knowledge introduces an important new dimension in information technology. If a decision maker's knowledge is used, it creates a feeling of ownership for the organization which is critical when introducing a new information system. The interactive capability of information systems helps to incorporate insights and judgment into problem solving. Interactive computer technology can truly augment the manager's ability to make better decisions by building on his or her creativity and intelligence.

A successful expert-system application was developed by American Express Company to support its credit authorization staff, who used thirteen different data bases to determine what level of credit each customer should be given. If a customer makes a large purchase that is outside the normal buying pattern, the Authorizer's Expert Assistant makes a recommendation regarding the level of credit in a matter of seconds. A major advantage of the system is that expertise can be readily communicated. Experts often know how they arrived at a particular decision and they can readily identify the critical factors. An important benefit in the use of expert systems is that once knowledge has been put into the computer, it is available for use by others in the organization.

NEED FOR NEW INFORMATION SYSTEM DESIGN

One failing bank, in response to mounting economic pressures, relied on information technology to redesign the business to fit multiple decision needs. They had a limited amount of time to cut costs, increase profitability, and restructure the branch network. Information technology was critical for accomplishing this task in the short time available. To overcome obstacles to accelerated change, the bank introduced new work roles. Workstation computers were used to support the effort, and the information technology system was redesigned. Computer support tools made possible the meeting of the overall design objectives as projected (Heygate, 1990). These decisions are considered strategic decisions because they affect the future of the firm. They have far-reaching, long-term effects on performance, require an interdisciplinary perspective, and require consideration of both the internal and the external environments of the organization. Strategic decisions focus on opportunities and challenges anywhere in the world. These decisions determine when and how to restructure organizations and to develop vision statements and goals.

Senior managers are the ones who typically make strategic decisions. Middle managers are typically concerned with performance. These decisions require performance reports, clearly defined by objectives and the evaluation of objectives, and they rely on computer analysis. At the next level, the operational level, supervisors and team leaders make decisions that deal with worker satisfaction, working conditions, job design, and rewards for performance.

Effective distribution and application of these decisions is a key element in meeting customer expectations. External to the firm, a distribution revolution driven by computer technology is emerging as a response to the required time to deliver goods; time which is constantly shrinking. The question is no longer whether better information systems are needed, but rather how best to design and implement such systems.

INTELLIGENT KNOWLEDGE-BASED DESIGN

In all branches of industry, there are experiments going on to see how fast-changing technology can improve fast-changing work practices. Finding the right match of technology for the right business application is not easy. One of the Intelligent Information Technology tools that is appearing in multiple business arenas is knowledge-based expert systems, a subset of artificial intelligence. Knowledge-based system technology is a special kind of computer programming, significantly different from conventional algorithmic programming. To understand the differences and to see where intelligent knowledge-based systems fit into an organizational structure, it is useful to conceive of the organization's intellectual assets—the facts, figures, and know-how resident in its computers and in the minds of its human resources—as a series of interrelated layers of a four-layer pyramid (Williamson, 1989).

- *The Bottom Layer.* Corporate data, customer names, addresses and credit balances, inventories, and receipts and expenditures reside here. This is the level of data processing systems. Though vital, data alone are useless.

- *The Second Layer.* Traditional application programs work on data to produce the pyramid's second layer, information. To do this, applications use a set of algorithms that contain instructions for the organization of data in ways that are precisely described. The tasks they perform and the data on which they operate are specified in explicit detail in the program's code. Management information systems and executive information systems occupy this level of the pyramid.

- *The Third Layer.* Traditional application programs can change raw data into organized information but they cannot explain the significance of that information. Artificial intelligence technology provides the means for turning information into knowledge, the third layer of the pyramid. Knowledge-based systems reside here. Information becomes knowledge when intelligence is applied. It takes intelligence to form inferences and reach conclusions. Solutions to problems are often found by combining information in new ways, which algorithmic programs, by their nature, cannot do. Examples of existing knowledge-based systems being used effectively in organizations throughout the world are exemplified in Appendix A at the end of Chapter 5.

- *The Fourth Layer.* With the application of techniques such as heuristic search (the rules of thumb and educated guesses that make human experts more efficient than their colleagues), knowledge becomes intelligent expertise, the peak of the pyramid and the realm of Intelligent Information Systems.

In today's complex environment, many companies are trying to reinvent themselves to take advantage of the opportunities for change. Procedures that have been around for many years are being modified because the workforce is better educated, new communications media exist, and economies of scale are decreasing in importance. One insurance company estimated that it took almost twenty-two days to approve a policy, even though the actual work required to complete the process was only seventeen minutes. By sharing information, new technology highlights showed that most insurance policies only need occasional consultation with specialists. Using the new system, specialists can be consulted quickly, and most policies can be handled by a single person. The new system was a result of the reengineering of the process used for policy approval.

WHAT IS AN INTELLIGENT INFORMATION SYSTEM?

Intelligent systems help to identify relevant causes of problems, evaluate the benefit of proposed solutions, and document them even where they involve vagueness and uncertainty. These systems use current information to predict consequences of future action. To overcome the magnitude of the task of providing useful information, one needs to utilize data and knowledge more intelligently. Answers are needed for many questions: How valuable is increasing the amount of information available to managers? When would aggregate data be more appropriate for decision making compared with using elemental or detail data? When should graphics and visualization be employed? How can expert systems provide meaningful advice? How is access improved using an English language interface? How does groupware affect the way that managers make decisions? Unfortunately, most decision makers are inundated with mountains of details that send them into "information overload." Intelligent systems focus on how to achieve "desired results" rather than simply providing data or reports that are required.

One of the primary roles of an Intelligent Information System is to provide managers with knowledge-based expertise to make more effective decisions. In this role, the system serves as an "expert advisor" that can provide the support needed to cope with today's turbulent environment. In addition to managerial considerations, there are a number of technical aspects that need to be taken into account. Hardware and software are available to design effective decision systems. The ability to organize information in a form that is user-friendly, readily accessible, and decision oriented is needed.

An Intelligent Information System should provide support for decision makers, with an emphasis on semi-structured and unstructured decisions. It should support managers at all levels and provide integration between levels. Intelligence will have to be added to available data to adequately support complex decisions that require interpretation and evaluation of potential consequences and outcomes. Finally, a more friendly computer interface, including visualization and multimedia, will need to be incorporated.

Nonaka's (1991) theory of knowledge creation is useful for comparing Intelligent Information Systems with current information systems (see Table 1.1). Knowledge in an organization is explicit or tacit. Explicit knowledge describes what can be coded, stored, accessed, and easily reproduced. Tacit knowledge only exists within individual's cognitive frame of reference. Cognitive knowledge is the basis for the mental models that managers use consciously or unconsciously. Technical knowledge that managers have, in contrast to cognitive or tactic knowledge, includes "know-how" and procedures that are learned from experience. Current information systems focus on availability and communication of explicit knowledge and ignore the need enhancing the use of manager's tacit knowledge.

Mental models can be fallible and contribute to slow response and poor decisions. Yet, current information systems have not provided the much needed support for tactic knowledge. Information systems are still in the growth stage and have provided useful operational data. Better alignment

Table 1.1
Role of Information Systems in Knowledge Creation

	Explicit Knowledge	Tacit Knowledge
Current systems	Technical information -Technology	Tactical information -Decision support systems
Futuristic systems	Experience -Expert systems	Cognition and learning -Intelligent information systems

with the rapid developments in technology and the new structures of organization requiring a change in who makes decisions is needed.

As shown in Table 1.1, current methodology has focused primarily on explicit knowledge. Expert systems deal with explicit knowledge and have focused on the technical side of tacit knowledge. Cognition has been ignored. Group Support Systems generally move from articulating tacit knowledge, to make it explicit to its group members, to possibly making it tacit knowledge. Communication between and among individuals is needed in order to disperse and increase this tacit knowledge. Intelligent Information Systems incorporate features of Group Support Systems by emphasizing shared knowledge creation. At the level of an individual decision maker, Intelligent Information Systems must focus on tacit knowledge of managers in order to amplify, rectify, and disperse it to the organization.

ELEMENTS OF AN INTELLIGENT INFORMATION SYSTEM

Figure 1.1 contains four basic modules which constitute the elements of an Intelligent Information System. The major components of intelligent systems include the following: Decision Maker Module, Data Source Module, Intelligence Adding Module, and the Data Knowledge Module. Decision makers are at the heart of these systems because they form the kernel of how decisions are made. In turn, decision makers' cognitive complexity determines how they interact with and use the Intelligent Information System.

Technology is reflected in the computer systems and software used to operate the system. Natural language interfaces, graphics, and visualization provide access to the data and knowledge bases. Inquiry or access can be done in a number of ways. TransAmerica Insurance Company uses an English-language query system that works with system query language (SQL) which relies on an expert system to interpret the meaning of the inputs and then queries the knowledge base. The result is an output that can readily be used by decision makers to cope with the multitude of problems confronting the organization.

Decision makers rely on their own heuristics and input from experts. They also use creative approaches for finding solutions to complex problems. Various methodologies, such as object-oriented data bases, model-based reasoning, or simulations, are included in the intelligence adding module. The components of Figure 1.1 are covered along with related material to provide an understanding of how Intelligent Information Systems can be used. From this perspective, a primary objective is to show how to blend traditional information systems with enhanced knowledge-based systems using the intelligence adding module.

INTELLIGENT INFORMATION SYSTEMS

There are a number of successful applications of Intelligent Information Systems that rely on expert systems to help managers solve complex problems. At Rockwell International, engineers have been using object-oriented expert systems to design payloads for NASA's space shuttle. Engineers are enthusiastic about the program because it saves them considerable time and effort. In many cases, companies have been able to use Intelligent Information Systems to help build barriers to competitors by increasing the cost of customer switching. This helps to keep competition off balance. Business Insight is a computerized support system used at Dynatel Systems Division of 3M to explore strategic options. The program operates in an interactive mode and starts by asking questions such as, "How likely is it that a competitor will retaliate?" The value of the program is that it forces a systematic evaluation of the factors that need to be considered when introducing new products.

An Intelligent Information System can provide early warning signals, timely information, and in-depth analysis to alert managers to important events. Other ways that Intelligent Information Systems can improve decision making include the following:

- *Increased Effectiveness.* Definitive representation of the requirements of the business and its customers.
- *First Mover Advantage.* Introducing improvement in computer-based decision support systems will create higher costs for competitors who try to keep up.
- *Leveraged Resources.* Adding value to information systems prevents competitors from being able to respond effectively to new requirements.

- *Organizational Restructuring.* Relying on strategic alliances, networking, and a modular corporate structure sustains a competitive advantage.

An Intelligent Information System requires the technical capabilities of data base management, model-based software, and dialogue-generation software. The data subsystem should be able to combine a variety of data, add and delete data quickly and easily, provide logical data structures, and permit personal judgment entries. A model subsystem should have the capability of creating new models quickly, maintain existing models, interrelate models, and access an integrated model, if required. Also, these intelligent systems can be used to do the following:

- Determine whether information technology investments can significantly alter or leverage other elements of the business to create a competitive advantage. Careful selection, timing, and execution are needed to avoid information technology projects that have limited benefits.
- Determine whether information technology could be used to leverage resources to produce economics of scale or product differentiation. An assured payoff on the IT investment can improve performance and competitive position. This often requires integrating activities across products, business functions, or geographic locations.
- Determine whether information technology can fundamentally change the business. Investments in IT are generally accompanied by major business changes or process reengineering to produce a new competitive position.

SUMMARY

Intelligent Information Systems are the path to the future of information technology for supporting more effective business decisions. These will have to be moderated by the changes in technology, new software, and a new organizational paradigm. Recognizing that there will be vast differences in the way that information will be used in the future, Intelligent Information Systems provide us with a road map that can guide managers in the design and application of these new systems. This will assure a leading edge in maintaining a sustainable competitive position.

Intelligent Information Systems provide a framework that can be used to achieve improved decision making and assist in determining required organizational changes which encourage a culture of learning (Figure 1.2). Effective decision making is needed to achieve customer-oriented performance that produces high-quality products and finds new and better ways of doing work. Decision makers will have to look beyond transactional reporting systems to systems that provide intelligent information.

Figure 1.2
Intelligent Information Systems Framework for Design

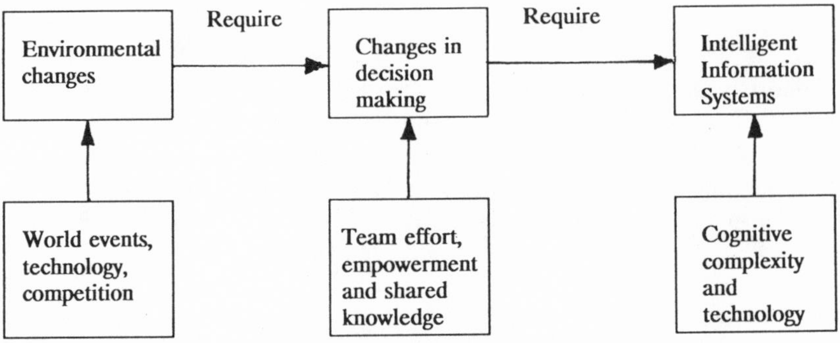

BIBLIOGRAPHY

Adler, Paul S. 1994. The Long & Short of Technology Investment. *USC Business* 2(Fall/Winter): 47–49.

Burn, John A. 1993. Requiem for Yesterday's CEO. *Business Week* (February 15): 32–33.

Crockett, Fess. 1992. Revitalizing Executive Information Systems. *Sloan Management Review* (Summer): 39–47.

Dent, Harry S. 1993. Global Alliances. *Fortune* (August 23, Special Advertising Section): S2–S19.

El Sawy, Omar A. 1985. Personal Information Systems for Strategic Scanning in Turbulent Environments. *MIS Quarterly*, March.

Grant, Linda. 1993. The Management Model that Jack Built. *Los Angeles Times Magazine* (May 9): 20–36.

Haeckel, Stephan H., and Richard Nolan. 1993. Managing by Wire. *Harvard Business Review* (September): 122–132.

Hamilton, Judith. 1994. Rate of Change Grows Ever Faster. *San Francisco Chronicle* (April 20, Section C): B1.

Heygate, Richard. 1990. Memo to a CEO. *The McKinsey Quarterly* (Autumn; 4): 68.

Hof, Robert D. 1993. Big-Game Hunter Bill Gates. *Business Week* (May 31): 84–86.

Humpert, B. 1988. Expert-System Applications in Finance Planning. Paper presented at Second Conference on Advances in Communications-Based Information Systems for Financial Institutions, April 11–13, London.

Integrating Case-Based Reasoning in Manufacturing Design. 1992. *Art Lines* 1 (7; Winter/Spring): 4–5.

Jacobson, Alexander D. 1989. FAIM Speech, unpublished.

Kleinschrod, Walter A. 1993. What Keeps Technology Managers Awake at Night? *Beyond Computing* (March/April): 23–28.

The Knowledge. 1995. *The Economist* (November): 63.

Lederer, Albert L., and Raghu Nath. 1990. Making Strategic Information Systems Happen. *Academy of Management Executive* 4(3): 76–83.

Miller, Michael J. 1993. The Next Software Revolution. *PC Magazine* (March 30): 81–82.

Millet, Ido, and Charles H. McWhinney. 1992. Executive Information Systems. *Information and Management* (August): 83–91.

Moy, Sandy. 1992. Open Systems: How to Survive the Revolution. *Beyond Computing* (June): 62–63.

Needleman, Raphael. 1992. No One Is Safe. *Corporate Computing* (June/July): 27.

Nonaka, Ikujiro. 1991. The Knowledge-Creating Company. *Harvard Business Review* (November/December): 96–104.

Nulty, Peter. 1987. How Managers Will Manage. *Fortune* (June): 47–50.

Powell, Bill. 1993. Eyes on the Future. *Newsweek* (May 31): 39–41.

Rowe, Alan J., and James D. Boulgarides. 1992. *Managerial Decision Making*. New York: Macmillan.

Savage, Charles M. 1994. The Dawn of the Knowledge Era. *OR/MS Today* (December): 18.

Scherr, A. L. 1993. A New Approach to Business Processes. *IBM Systems Journal* 32(1): 80–98.

Simon, Herbert A. 1987. Decision Making and Problem Solving. *Interfaces* 17(5; September/October): 23.

Smart, Tim. 1992. How Jack Welch Brought GE to Life. *Business Week* (October 26): 13–15.

Spayd, Michael K. 1993. The Psychology of Re-Engineering. *EDMS Journal* (March): 24–27.

Tapscott, Don. 1991. Open Systems, Managing the Transition. *Business Week* (October 14, Special Insert).

Thompson, James P., and Joan Weiner. 1995. Strategic Planning as a Tool for Building Learning Capacity. March. Unpublished Paper: 1–35.

Turban, Efraim. 1993. *Decision Support and Expert Systems*. New York: Macmillan.

What Technologies Will Have the Greatest Impact on Enterprise Computing Environments in 1993? *PC Week* (December 28/January 4): 93.

Williamson, Mickey. 1989. User Developed Expert Systems—Expert Systems for the Rest of Us. *AI Magazine* (March/April): 11–15.

CHAPTER TWO
□ □ □
REASONING AND INTELLIGENT INFORMATION SUPPORT

Imagination and creativity are often more important than intelligence.

A decision depends on the information perceived and how well it is understood. Managers, as decision makers, rely on their perceptions and cognitive abilities when using information. Where perception or cognition limits their effectiveness, an Intelligent Information System can supplement their abilities. An effective manager is one who perceives problems correctly and knows how to respond to a situation using analytic techniques, when required, and exercising judgment to find good solutions.

Perception and cognition are being recognized increasingly as critical elements of effective decision making. Intelligent Information Systems will incorporate these elements along with expert systems that act as decision advisors. Human reasoning underlies Intelligent Information Systems because such systems will have to be sensitive to the manager's cognitive ability.

Reasoning has been shown to be a critical aspect of decision making. It forms the basis for evaluation and judging information that has been received. Reasoning can be described as either deductive (logical) or inductive (intuitive). Barr and Feigenbaum (1981) suggest the following four categories to describe reasoning:

1. *Formal Reasoning.* This describes the manipulation of data structures using specified rules which allow the person to "deduce" new rules with which to draw inferences about the data perceived.

2. *Procedural Reasoning*. This category examines heuristic approaches decision makers use for answering questions and solving problems.

3. *Analogical Reasoning*. This approach compares objects or behaviors that are similar to ones already known in order to predict behavior of unknown events.

4. *Abstract*. This technique incorporates an ability to recognize cues, hints, or data which are used to draw conclusions. The accuracy of perception depends on an individual's understanding of cues or inferences based on an individual's cognitive complexity.

These four categories provide a useful framework for understanding the ways that managers reason about problems. Knowing the information that decision makers need and the ways in which they reason about that information is crucial for development of an Intelligent Information System.

From a different perspective, Andriole (1985) described *antecedent reasoning* as using rules that the computer uses for search, and *consequent reasoning* as a strategy that searches for actions which can achieve a specified goal. A diagnostic reasoning process is used to examine information to determine which activities should be sought. Other approaches to reasoning that are explored include case-based reasoning, heuristic reasoning, and analogical reasoning. The purpose for reviewing approaches to reasoning is to understand how humans make decisions to design Intelligent Information Systems.

PERCEPTION AND COGNITIVE COMPLEXITY

Human reasoning is related to cognitive complexity, perceptions, limits of judgment, and inference capability. Cognitive complexity determines an individual's ability to recognize or interpret the meaning of various cues or data. Complexity describes the number and type of the cues, whether they are complex or simple, and how the cues are acquired. Cognition also reflects an ability to extract imbedded information or gain insights from cue patterns, and reflects how these reinforce prior knowledge or experience. Perception relates to the meaning of cues and data which contribute to the human's ability to understand, reason, and make judgments about information that is available. For example, a genius is able to permute mental images that cover phrases, memory, abstract concepts, sounds, and rhymes. Intelligent people can form novel combinations of ideas, images, or symbols.

Decision makers respond to a perceived stimuli based on experience and cognitive complexity. Perception acts as the filter, allowing in only certain information. The way people respond to stimuli is called *perceptual attitude structure*. Managers who exhibit rigid attitudes are described as authoritarian and have a concrete attitude structure that is insensitive to change or to new information. This leads to a persistent bias in decisions even when there is contrary information. Individuals who have a highly flexible attitude structure relate well to varied perceptual stimuli. These individuals are comfortable consulting with others and are willing to search for new information. They also can handle highly complex situations and are able to resolve conflicting inputs. The difference in attitude structure can be related to an individual's degree of tolerance for ambiguity as it relates to their decision style.

Approaches, such as Graphical-User Interface, help to facilitate perception and provide meaningful information. User-friendliness will be enhanced by Intelligent Information Systems that recognize and interpret what the user is trying to do with the data received. The amount and type of information will be matched with the level of cognitive complexity of the user in order to provide more meaningful data. Managers with low cognitive complexity are susceptible to information overload; persons who have higher levels of cognitive complexity and are thinking-oriented tend to prefer either graphic information or numeric data. From a decision making point of view, the purpose for which information is used determines what to display, how to display it, and how the user can best interact with the information. Computer programs increasingly are using icons rather than symbols or keys as the means for entering data or running programs.

Sprague and Watson (1986) describe cognitive complexity as the following:

1. Ability to search for and use considerable information
2. Ablility to work with complex information and to derive meaningful conclusions
3. Ability to generate many alternatives from the information perceived
4. Ability to correctly perceive meaning in complex or field dependent situations

Anderson (1983) developed a theory of cognition which he proposes for computational purposes that could also be used as a framework to study the human mind. This approach is called Adaptive Control of Thought (ACT). It provides a general architecture with specifications for computational purposes. This architecture can represent knowledge structures that reside in working computer memory and their functional consequences. The approach depends on the nature of the storage process, the retrieval process, and the program application. The computation requires a mechanism for pattern matching and a process that enters the results in working memory which, in turn, affects productive memory.

Anderson's approach to cognition is a computational procedure primarily designed for use in artificial intelligence. To be useful for decision making, information depends on an individual's frame of reference. This allows relevant facts to be distinguished from randomly structured data.

Cognition also deals with both short- and long-term memory. Short-term memory depends on the transitory nature of the information, the mind's capacity, and whether information is chunked into units. On the other hand, long-term memory involves many functions that are normally associated with thinking, such as retrieval of information, concept formulation, or recall. The importance of cognition for information systems design is not limited to any specific applications. Rather, the decision-maker's attention span, ability to identify patterns, and willingness to use a holistic approach to a given situation would be integrated in Intelligent Information Systems.

BRAIN SIDEDNESS

The left and right hemispheres of the brain have been used to describe how people make decisions. The left hemisphere has been associated with analytic and deductive thinking and processing of information serially. The right hemisphere is considered the creative half that perceives problems as a whole and processes information in parallel. The right brain is also considered more intuitive, in contrast to the left brain which is considered more rational.

Differences between the right and left brain have been used to explain why some individuals can master complex mental tasks and others cannot. For example, a scientist who is very capable in his or her field may not be able to handle the problem of dealing with people. Also, differences help to explain why some executives favor verbal information while others rely on judgment or analysis as the basis for making decisions. Basically, the right brain is used to search for information; the left brain is used to formulate and evaluate options.

The anatomy of the brain reveals individual differences. The pattern of convolutions, the tissue in the major areas of the brain, and the corpus callosum—the bundle of nerves connecting the two hemispheres of the brain and which has 200 million fibers—are different for each individual. Variations in the intra-cell interaction influence how we think and account for different nerve functions. Conductivity of electrical impulses and the time it takes to cross synapses appear to be determined genetically and affect the speed of responding to stimuli. While synapse formation may be preprogrammed, specific experiences "select" which synapse will be strengthened. Although major connections are genetically determined, the environment is a major factor that influences human behavior and decisions. Long-term memory is associated with permanent structural changes in the synaptic connections.

Understanding the physical structure of the brain is not sufficient to understanding thinking. The chemistry of the brain is a means of understanding our thought processes. The cells of the brain that are involved in conscious activity, awareness, or emotion are different from any other living cells. The brain uses amine pathways that have a great deal to do with setting the level of activities of brain cells and with guiding them toward goal-oriented tasks. Emotions are considered the basis for long-term memory, affecting access and retrieval. Fear, anger, love, and sadness are complicated mixtures of feeling and physical response and are labeled emotions. Recent research shows that the experience of emotion depends on the complicated circuitry that interconnects the emotions as well as the patterns of nerve impulses. Half the neurons in the brain are dedicated to visual processing of information so that graphics can provide the widest mental bandwidth. Visualization that provides a picture of data and its relationships can be understood more easily by managers. An important challenge facing visualization is determining what is the most meaningful way to represent data. Color, animation, and sound reinforce visualization, which is extremely valuable for multidimensional data.

DECISION STYLE

The way in which the mind views problems that involve discovery and judgment is referred to as *decision style*. Decision style provides a means for understanding the way that the human mind operates in making decisions. Two key elements that define decision style are cognitive complexity and personal values. The way that a manager makes decisions depends on a number of factors, including the context in which a decision is made, the decision maker's way of perceiving and understanding cues, and what an individual values or judges as important. Decision style reflects the manner that a decision maker reacts to a given situation— "how" he or she interprets and understands cues, "what" the individual believes is important, and "how" the individual responds to external stimuli.

The Decision Style Inventory has been found useful in determining an individual's cognitive complexity (Rowe and Mason, 1987). The Decision Style Inventory considers also the individual's preference for solving problems in contrast to spatial visualization, and reflects a person's preference for technical versus social values (Figure 2.1). Decision style is measured using a test instrument called the Decision Style Inventory. The inventory helps to probe the psychological structure of one's mind to define both cognitive complexity and values. Decision styles show that each individual thinks differently depending on his or her cognition and values. The Decision Style Inventory provides a unique frame of reference that identifies the mind-set of each individual and reflects the decision maker's subjective rationality (see pages 50–51).

Decision styles are the scores one enters when answering the questions on the Decision Style Inventory. Decision style distinguishes the "way"

Figure 2.1
Decision Style Model

	LEFT BRAIN (Logical hemisphere)	RIGHT BRAIN (Relational hemisphere)
Has a high tolerance for ambiguity	ANALYTIC (relies on thinking) • Enjoys problem solving • Wants the best answer • Wants control • Uses considerable data • Enjoys variety • Is innovative • Uses careful analysis • Needs challenges	CONCEPTUAL (relies on thinking) • Has a broad outlook • Is creative • Looks for important goals • Is humanistic/artistic • Initiates new ideas • Is future oriented • Is independent • Needs recognition
COGNITIVE COMPLEXITY Need for Structure	DIRECTIVE (prefers action) • Expects results • Is aggressive • Is verbal • Acts rapidly • Uses rules • Relies on intuition • Meets objectives • Needs power	BEHAVIORAL (prefers action) • Is supportive • Uses persuasion • Is emphatic • Enjoys working with others • Communicates easily • Prefers meetings • Uses limited data • Needs affiliation
	Task/Technical	People/Social

VALUES ORIENTATION

in which style is used in decision-making situations. Effective decision makers are generally those individuals whose style matches the requirements of the decision situation. Also, decision styles describe the most likely way in which a manager perceives information and will mentally process that information to arrive at decisions.

Psychological tests are now being introduced into the information technology (IT) environment. They can be considered equivalent to benchmarking that is used to compare performance among computer programs or business enterprises. Using tests such as the Decision Style Inventory, the IT manager is better able to predict whether a prospective employee is psychologically suited for a specific task, such as a systems analyst or programmer. A research study done by Baumgartner, Jacobson, and Batchelor (1992) showed that an individual with a predominantly left brain, or analytic style, would not do as well as an individual who had a right brain, or conceptual style.

HUMAN REASONING

To understand the human mind, we often make assumptions regarding how facts are perceived, how judgments are made, and how preference will affect decisions. In the book *The Emperor's New Mind*, Penrose (1989) deals with consciousness and shows that the human mind is constantly coming up with questions for which there are no general answers. This finding is supported by the chaos in brain wave patterns following activities, such as inhaling new smells or having periods of severe concentration. Given the difficulty in describing thinking, the question arises whether it is possible to represent human thinking on a computer which does not have intuition, imagination, emotion, common sense, or the power to exercise judgment.

Successful managers know how to adapt to new or unknown situations by using intuition and "creating" meaningful solutions to complex problems. In order for information systems to contribute to this mental process, we need to explore how cognitive complexity relates to the way in which we reason with information in the brain. When computer capability is matched with human intelligence, we can achieve the best of both worlds—the power and structure imposed by the computer and the intuitive, creative, and heuristic capability of the mind. The computer becomes an assistant that utilizes the knowledge and expertise of managers and specialists to form a true information system that can effectively support decision making.

Using the decision style model in Figure 2.1, one can determine the relationship between decision style, cognitive complexity, and reasoning. This model provides a frame of reference for identifying an individual's reasoning ability and approach to problem solving. An extension of the decision style model leads directly to the reasoning model shown in Figure 2.2. The model shown in Figure 2.2 shows the relationship of cognitive complexity to the way humans reason. The model indicates the differences in problem solving and decision making as a function of cognitive complexity. Because cognition influences the way managers perceive and reason about problems, the Decision Styles Inventory can be used to determine the kinds of decision support that would best fit each style.

Figure 2.2
Cognitive Model of Reasoning

	LEFT BRAIN (Logical)	**RIGHT BRAIN** (Relational)

Has a high
tolerance for
ambiguity
	ANALYTIC
	(Prefers thinking)
	
	• Uses formal or
	  abstract reasoning
	• Relies on
	  inferential
	  logic
		CONCEPTUAL
		(Prefers thinking)
		
		• Uses analogical
		  reasoning
		• Relies on judgment,
		  values, and
		  beliefs

COGNITIVE **COMPLEXITY**		

Has a need
for structure
	DIRECTIVE
	(Prefers action)
	
	• Uses procedural
	  and antecedent
	  reasoning
	• Relies on intuition
	  and experience
		BEHAVIORAL
		(Prefers action)
		
		• Uses consequent
		  reasoning
		• Relies on
		  instinct and
		  feelings

	Task/Technical	People/Social

VALUES ORIENTATION

MEASURING DECISION STYLES

The Decision Style Inventory has been used with many groups and has a very high face validity and reliability, as shown by the number of people who agree that their styles are a correct description of how they make decisions. The scores on the Decision Style Inventory measure the relative intensity of each of the four basic style categories. The Decision Style Inventory is included at the end of this chapter.

The decision style model in Figure 2.1 has two key factors: cognitive complexity and values orientation. The lower half of the model indicates that the directive and behavioral styles prefer structure; the styles in the upper half prefer complexity. The cognitive complexity dimension separates the upper and lower halves. Also, styles describe the individual's personality, situational awareness, and problem-solving capability. Each of the basic four styles has four possible levels of intensity that determine to what extent the style is used. The level of intensity of each style is determined from the score on the Decision Style Inventory. Table 2.1 shows the scores for a large number of individuals. One would not expect managers to fit neatly into only one category; the typical manager has at least one dominant style with at least one, and often two, back-up styles.

Table 2.2 shows the Decision Style Inventory scores for a diverse sample of managers. Notice that none of the groups had a dominant level of intensity for the directive style. Top executives and senior military officers typically have a dominant score for the conceptual style. The scores shown for middle and upper managers is most representative of managers. The senior executives had a dominant conceptual style. The foreign executives had a dominant conceptual style and show the cultural differences for that particular country. When scores fall into more than one style category, they form a style pattern. While any decision style categorization is approximate, knowledge of the manager's dominant styles or style patterns provides useful information about decision making and the type of decision support the manager would find useful.

The individual's decision style forms the backbone of effective decision making. As Drucker (1966) says, "Effective executives do not make a great many decisions. They concentrate on what is important. They try to make the few important decisions on the highest level of understanding. They try to find the constants in a situation, to think through what is strategic and generic rather than to solve problems."

Decision styles can be used to provide clues to which behavior one might expect for an individual. They offer a useful basis for determining how to relate information systems to an individual's decision style. A hard-

Table 2.1
Intensity of Decision Style

| Decision Style | Level of intensity | | | |
	Least preferred	Back up	Dominant	Very dominant
DIRECTIVE	below 68	68 to 82	83 to 90	over 90
ANALYTIC	below 83	83 to 97	90 to 104	over 104
CONCEPTUAL	below 73	73 to 87	88 to 94	over 94
BEHAVIORAL	below 48	48 to 62	63 to 70	over 70

Table 2.2
Typical Decision Style Scores

	Sample Size	Directive	Analytic	Conceptual	Behavioral
Managers					
Male	194	74 (B)	89 (B)	83 (B)	54 (B)
Technical	54	71 (B)	94 (B)	74 (B)	61 (B)
Female	93	74 (B)	88 (B)	74 (B)	64 (D)
Senior U.S. Executives	80	70 (B)	90 (B)	93 (D)	47 (B)
Foreign Executives	110	73 (B)	87 (B)	85 (B)	55 (B)

Notes: B = Back up; D = Dominant.

driving executive wants information that provides control and generally prefers short, bottom-line data. A sophisticated information system does not appeal to these individuals. Yet, executives such as Harold Geneen or Lee Iococca were extremely successful in building enterprises. Table 2.3 shows a comparison of styles for entrepreneurs and managers. Entrepreneurs build enterprises and require both detailed information (directive style) and broad information (conceptual style), whereas managers prefer planning documents which show considerable analysis.

INTELLIGENT SUPPORT

Human reasoning is based on the decision maker's ability to process what they know, whether they learn by example or create new approaches. Reasoning is used by managers to discover patterns in data, facilitate visualizing objects from abstract or ill-defined information, help to infer multiple meanings from a single input, and generalize from diverse inputs. These are precisely the areas where Intelligent Information Systems can have a significant impact. This is only possible if the systems relate to human reasoning.

Human reasoning can be fallible, evidenced by the difficulties encountered when dealing with situations such as the following:

• Tradeoffs between two factors, such as cost–benefit
• Effect of delays on scheduling or capacity constraints

Table 2.3
Comparison of Entrepreneurs and Managers

Basic Style	Entrepreneurs	Managers
Directive	83	75
Analytic	76	90
Conceptual	97	80
Behavioral	44	55

- The impact of risk and uncertainty on decisions
- The effect of rates of change or cycles
- Effects of interdependencies among organizational units
- Predicting causality among variables
- Ability to handle combinatorial and sequencing problems
- Understanding the effect of time lags and interruptions

Intelligent Information Systems can provide analyses and advice which allow decision makers to be more effective despite the difficulties described. These problems point to the need to articulate mental models prior to evaluation and decision making. This can form the basis for correcting existing models, leading to faster and lower-risk knowledge creation.

Intelligent Information Systems can aid and enhance decision making by applying specific reasoning tools. This can help managers correct possible errors and provide them with a new perspective with which they may not be aware. Figure 2.3 categorizes the computer-based reasoning tools that would best accomplish this task for each decision style and reasoning orientation. Descriptions of the computer-based reasoning tools are covered in detail in the following section.

CONCEPTUAL MAPS

Today's world requires that managers have the ability to work with ideas, images, information, and knowledge. The role of managers has changed with easier access to minicomputers, workstations, and very powerful personal computers. As these computers are linked to form local or wide-area networks as part of client–server networks, they reflect the more complex reality in which managers will have to operate. Conceptual maps can support the manager's cognitive reflection of the world.

Figure 2.3
Intelligent Support for Human Reasoning

	LEFT BRAIN (Logical)	RIGHT BRAIN (Relational)
Has a high tolerance for ambiguity	ANALYTIC (Thinking) • Uses model-based reasoning • Relies on abstract reasoning (inference)	CONCEPTUAL (Thinking) • Uses conceptual maps • Relies on analogical reasoning (judgment)
Has a need for structure	DIRECTIVE (Action) • Uses heuristic reasoning • Relies on procedural reasoning (intuition)	BEHAVIORAL (Action) • Uses case-based reasoning • Relies on a personal frame of reference (instinct)

COGNITIVE
COMPLEXITY

Technical   People

VALUES ORIENTATION

Notes: Technical describes the left-brain individual's logical focus and social describes the
right-brain individual's relational or people-oriented focus.

The conceptual map reflects the way in which managers interpret the
reality of the situations in which they function. The maps are based on a
manager's perceptual acuteness, cognitive complexity, personal values,
and past experiences. A map becomes a means for adding structure to an
otherwise chaotic situation. Imaging is a means for creating a mental picture of what has been seen. Mental images are used for problem solving
based on information that has been scanned. Maps or diagrams preserve
representations of knowledge. However, visual architecture can be difficult when trying to compare complex shapes to standard images.

The mind maps situations and events continuously. This is comparable
to how a computer program is used to create order out of ambiguity.
Cognitive maps are relevant for decision making because they deal with

problems such as organizational change, operational problems, strategic decisions, and complex problem solving. Conceptual decision makers can readily "map" the ambiguity, disorder, or asymmetry that exists in many problems. They use visual information that includes images, maps, spatial relations, color, and texture. Also, pattern recognition fits into the realm of conceptual maps.

Diagrammatic reasoning is another way of describing conceptual maps used for representing visual knowledge. The visual diagrams are used by participants in meetings for reasoning with the knowledge presented and for problem solving. Traditional symbolic representations are being combined increasingly with iconic representations to help managers form more meaningful mental images of a problem.

HEURISTIC REASONING

There have been many definitions of heuristics, ranging from trial and error to intuitive logic. Heuristics describe the way we think, reason, and perceive problems. Polya (1957) describes heuristics as, "The study of methods and rules of discovery and invention. Heuristic reasoning has as its purpose the discovery of a plausible or provisional solution to a problem. If you cannot solve the problem at hand then solve some related problem." Pearl (1990) considers heuristics as rules of thumb to guide actions based on specific criteria, methods, or principles for deciding which alternative will achieve a defined goal. Heuristics applied to computer programs provide intelligent search strategies for problem solving.

The term *heuristic* is derived from the Greek *heuriskein*, which means to invent or discover. It involves exploring and probing in order to gain knowledge. The knowledge is then fed back and used to modify the search. Many heuristic approaches use rules that either help to find intermediate solutions or help to find the most promising paths in the search for a solution. Heuristics may require finding and interpreting information that leads to a solution. Heuristic reasoning is not final but is helpful in discovering a good solution and interpreting results. Heuristic search is used to provide feedback based on information obtained from previous attempts. The initial problem formulation changes as new information is obtained regarding possible solutions.

When decision makers use heuristics for the solution of complex problems, they rely on both their analytic and intuitive reasoning capability. Reasoning about problems uses the analytic properties of the left hemisphere along with the intuitive and creative capability of the right hemisphere to find good solutions to what might seem to be unsolvable problems.

Finding a workable solution to most problems requires that a number of factors be taken into account. For example, managers are generally aware that a small percentage of customers account for most of their sales and a small percentage of workers have most of the accidents. This approach to heuristics is based on the Pareto Law which separates items into two categories of payoff. The Pareto curve shows how it is possible to reduce the search to a small number of alternatives which contribute the maximum payoff.

Abductive reasoning is described as a method for developing cognitively plausible heuristics. This kind of reasoning is a means for drawing inferences regarding a hypothesis used to explain a set of data. An illustration of the use of abductive reasoning is the identification of antibodies. To better understand the medical protocol used in the analyses of blood, experts were asked to describe blood patterns using a simplified set of assumptions. This was needed to reduce the problem of how to separate a single antibody from multiple-antibody data. Using symbolic reasoning, the experts were able to choose candidates from the data observed based on the assumption that their solution was the correct explanation of observed data. This approach found a solution by dividing the data into two categories and then generating hypotheses for a specific antibody or group of antibodies. Using abductive reasoning, the definition of an antibody did not depend on reference to a specific antibody. This greatly simplified the process and the accuracy of the findings.

Heuristic reasoning has a number of advantages for management problem solving. Heuristic reasoning not only builds on the intuition of the decision maker but it provides an approach that allows the decision maker to find solutions to complex problems in a reasonably short time. In many cases, heuristic reasoning provides an equivalent solution to a mathematical optimization. Heuristic problem solving is intimately intertwined with the way in which we think and the way in which the mind operates on new subject matter. Heuristics are more acceptable by managers because they can understand what is being proposed. They are also more willing to implement solutions with which they are comfortable.

It Is Not Just Show Business for the Entertainment Industry

It is becoming increasingly important for companies such as Colombia Pictures to use heuristics in the development of decision-support tools, allowing them to predict the probable return on investment before investing millions in a film. Two Wharton School professors, Drs. Eliashberg and Sawhney, have designed a decision-making model that has the ability to forecast a movie's box-office results before the film has opened. The model includes values for multiple parameters, such as a movie's "decay parameter" for word-of-mouth spreading activity (or how quickly people who have seen the film will stop talking about it). Also, it includes the "forgetting parameter," which measures the likelihood that consumers interested in seeing a film will let it slip their minds. This is a management tool that allows studios to plan their advertising and distribution on a more scientific basis rather than on a "gut feeling" or intuition.

The value of heuristics, when used by persons knowledgeable about a problem under study, is described by Talbot (1986). The experts compared a total of twenty-four heuristic decision rules that had been reported in the literature with the optimal solution to the "line balancing problem." These heuristic rules were not developed by managers but by researchers who were exploring alternative heuristic rules. Using "computer output" time "per line balance" as the objective function, the best heuristic rule increased the run time by only 4 percent over the optimum solution. When "results" were used as the objective function, the heuristic rule was only 2 percent higher in balancing the line than the optimum solution.

Boeing developed a scheduling methodology called DockPlan to combine a planner's knowledge and experience in overhaul scheduling with a simple, computerized, scheduling heuristic algorithm. The heuristic scheduling model relies on human judgment that provides an innovative approach to a problem that was complicated by dynamic interactions. The process is interactive, linking an experienced planner with a schedule-generating model. The heuristic was based on the interaction between the planner and computer model and was able to achieve good solutions.

The DockPlan system was installed at American Airlines and had a number of benefits, including productivity improvement, maintenance cost reduction, and a better identification of revenue opportunities. These results came from reengineering the existing dock plan. Turnaround time to develop a new schedule for maintenance and component removals takes from one to eight minutes only (Integrating Case-Based Reasoning, 1992). Many successful applications of heuristics include the following: scheduling of jobs, airlines, and salesmen; location of warehouses; delivery routes for trucks; new product introduction; design of electric motors and transformers; and the layout of cutting patterns to reduce scrap (Hinkle and Kuehn, 1992).

Intellistore is an in-store computer system currently being used in the food industry by Boston Chicken. In-store point-of-sale (POS) terminals are being used for multimedia educational programs as well as for assisting store managers in scheduling, tracking inventory, and managing production. Also, Intellistore incorporates forecasting functions that help the manager use heuristics to estimate purchasing requirements, how much of each side dish to prepare, and staffing needs. The system allows its managers to forecast eighteen to twenty-four months ahead to see how they could use technology in their stores, as well as enabling them to receive real-time feedback on how they are doing now. Transforming the system into a dynamic system and adding intelligence to the forecasting model is the next challenge facing this food chain, expected by Wall Street to have 250 stores opening this year. Boston Chicken has required that all of its units use the same technology and collect data in a standardized format to facilitate comparisons.

There have been many other applications of heuristics to solve problems. For example, the optimum assignment of jobs to machines normally used linear programming to find a solution. The computer program that executed this method required several million calculations to find the optimum solution. The same problem was solved manually in a little over one minute by applying a heuristic rule. This solution involved organizing the data so that a small percentage of the assignments were seen to be far better than the others. Examining the problem in a logical manner was sufficient to find the optimum solution.

Although heuristics have been used for many years to solve complex problems, there are some shortcomings that Geoffrian and Van Roy (1979) describe. If the heuristic requires too many iterations, it is seldom used. When dealing with sequential decisions, managers can fail to anticipate future consequences because heuristics do not provide a global perspective. Furthermore, interdependencies within a system can have profound influence on the system as a whole. Goeffrian and Van Roy state, "Common sense approaches and heuristics sometimes fail because they are *arbitrary*. They are arbitrary in the choice of a starting point, in the sequence in which assignments or other decision choices are made, in the resolution of ties, in the choice of criteria for specifying the procedure, in the level of effort expended to demonstrate that the final solution is in fact best or very nearly so." The result can be erratic with good performance only in some specific applications. While concerns may be expressed about using heuristics, they almost always assure workable solutions, and they do reflect the manner in which most managers make their decisions.

MODEL-BASED REASONING

In general, model-based reasoning requires heuristic reasoning applied to well-structured problems with clearly defined objectives. In most complex problems, models by themselves are not sufficiently robust to cover all aspects of the problem. While heuristics can be used without models, the converse is generally not true for managerial problems. A question often raised is whether heuristic reasoning is based on the intuition and knowledge of experts. Approaches, such as the Pareto Law for partitioning problems or steepest ascent (highest priority), help formulate heuristic rules that can be based on experience; or they can be a combination of experience and formal approaches, such as linear programming. Where applicable, the combining of heuristics with formal methods offers the most powerful constructs and the greatest likelihood of finding useful solutions.

Model-based reasoning has a number of advantages over other approaches. Model-based reasoning can aggregate information by using one or more equations that closely approximate actual conditions. Model-based reasoning requires less time and fewer constraints, and assures greater consistency from one application to the next. Interpretation of results is easier because the process starts with knowledge about the models used. Development of heuristic rules is also facilitated because of models such as the Pareto Law, which helps to categorize the relative importance of items. Bimson and Burris (1987) have used conceptual model-based reasoning as a basic methodology for developing heuristic rules.

Many of the critical issues facing acquisition managers are a result of the inability to predict the future in the face of unknown variables. This uncertainty, in addition to environmental constraints, has significant consequences on cost overruns, schedule delays, and inadequate technical performance. A study by Martin identified the major causes of cost overruns and cost growth as poor-cost estimation, inadequate research and development specifications, impact of external environmental factors, significant internal environmental factors, inadequate management practices, and technological considerations (Dean and Owens, 1985). Acquisition managers have used many approaches in their attempt to control the problems identified. Tools such as model-based reasoning, however, have provided a means for improving acquisition decisions.

A Causal Integrative Model was developed to assist the acquisition process that included basic elements that have causal relationships and to show how they related to uncertainty. The elements that were included in the Causal Model of the acquisition process included the following:

- *Environmental Uncertainty.* This element included those variables and factors exogenous to the project that directly affects performance.
- *Technological Uncertainty.* This dealt with the determining state of the art and the interdependencies that cause delays or cost overruns.
- *Contract Urgency.* This covered the priority, time compression, stretch out, concurrence, or change in scope of the project.
- *Managerial Performance.* This covered the organization's ability to carry out a given project and included expertise, quality, prior experience, available resources, and manpower.

Although the model was extremely complex, it proved to be a very useful means for evaluating the most likely causes of cost overruns and project delays. It was tested initially on a program that involved state-of-the-art hardware development. Data from the project were used to determine the impact of direct effects as well as second- and third-order effects on cost, technical performance, and scheduled delivery.

Prior to using the model, the project manager underestimated the cost of labor by 40 percent. Without a model, the project manager was unable to comprehend the interaction of the many factors involved or their causal relationship. The model was able to predict accurately the impact of changes in labor content and labor availability on all three measures of project performance: cost, schedule, and technical quality. The model has since been applied by the project manager using the computer program as a knowledge base to deal with the complex interactions that otherwise were not tractable.

Knowledge acquisition and engineering techniques are being used for the redesign of the decision-making activities and the knowledge flows among organizational entities and processes. These techniques, including interviewing, protocol analysis, and concept modeling, quantify how decisions contribute to processes and what knowledge is required to support decision making. Process management tools and techniques then track the substance, sources, destinations, influences, and use of knowledge. Canon U.S.A. worked with Inference Corporation in the redesign of their sales processes for independent dealers of Canon Copier Products. The sales process at Canon is notably complex because it consists of a decentralized product distribution network composed of company- and noncompany-owned dealers and representatives. Their network consists of approximately 500 independent office equipment dealers, five subsidiaries, and sixty Canon representatives involved in selling Canon copiers. This decentralized distribution network is impacted by regional demographics, economic and competitive influences, as well as different philosophies of noncompany-owned dealers and representatives. This diversity demands flexibility on the part of Canon in their sales philosophy, strategies, and tactics. It included a knowledge repository containing knowledge about successful sales experiences, products, and specific accounts, vulnerability within the marketplace, and Canon business goals. Canon decided to represent and implement the redesigned knowledge flows with Inference Corporation's ART*Enterprise and CBRExpress. The system is called SAMS (Strategic Account Management System) and is now in nationwide use.

In another application, NASA had been utilizing Intelligent Information Systems at their Kennedy Space Center in Florida to diagnose failures and to recommend corrective action. They found that a rule-based expert system could not provide comprehensive coverage when it was confronted with a vast amount of data that required diagnosis. Confronted with this situation, NASA built a model of the system. The principal difference between the rule-based and model-based system was that the latter used a model that simulated the structure and function of the machinery under observation. The model of the equipment's internal functioning and processes allowed them to determine better the probable causes of a malfunction and how to correct it. In contrast, the rule-based system required an elaborate set of rules relating information received from the sensors to the internal state of the equipment.

In diagnosing a failure, the NASA model-based system determined what could happen in the simulated model that would give the same results as observed with the sensors. The system provided aggregate data to determine the probable cause of a failure. NASA is using the model-based approach for diagnosing faults within the liquid oxygen loading system and for the environmental control unit. A major advantage of the model-based reasoning approach has been the system's ability to detect problems that were not considered initially. Using a rule-based system, the unknown failures could not be diagnosed.

Model-based reasoning provides an effective decision-aiding tool that allows managers to interact with the models and enables them to view the results on-line. "Smart" modeling systems can be designed for users that support technical advances in knowledge engineering and expert systems. To avoid the limitations of modeling systems, the emphasis can be on developing useful, rather than more powerful, systems.

The management at Shell Oil Company has defined *organizational learning* as the process through which management teams change their mental models of the company, its market, and its competitors. This model is an integrative set of ideas and practices that shape the ways people view and interact with the world. One of the information and communication tools that Shell uses is scenario planning, a process that creates hypothetical alternative futures. Rather than looking toward the future as if there is only one possibility, scenario planners formulate and define multiple alternatives.

Shell is well known for its pioneering work in scenario planning, which started in the late 1960s. At that time, they made no correlation between scenario planning and organizational learning. This connection was discovered through trial and error when scenario planners realized that they had to change the existing mental models of managers in the company, removing them from one way of thinking, based on their experiences, to a way in which they would envision situations under different scenarios. They had to bring their assumptions—their mental models—to the table so they could be challenged and revised.

Perhaps the most important value of model-based reasoning is its ability to augment the reasoning power of an expert. Managers often rely on intuition or experience and tend to use simple solutions. Because managers have different levels of cognitive complexity, they approach problems in different ways. Model-based reasoning can overcome some of these limitations by adding intelligence to aid in the solution of complex problems.

In order to deal with most real-world problems, Pearl (1990) has shown that managers use qualitative approaches. Using a qualitative approach, one can develop a "qualitative" causal model. Qualitative causal reasoning about physical systems is required where a model may not be available. At best, a model is an approximation of a real system. Development of a model of a physical system requires simplification because the level of detail and computation would become too complex. For example, systems are built on well-defined models which are not designed to accommodate new conditions when required. Different models are often applied even for a single task. Thus, model-based reasoning is a powerful approach where it is applicable. Otherwise, heuristic reasoning can be used to solve intractable problems.

ANALOGICAL REASONING

Analogical reasoning is considered a very powerful approach that is used by managers to solve problems based on prior experience. Eliot (1986) suggests that the analogical process is used for learning by example or by specifics when observing events that can lead to the discovery of new ideas. A concept introduced by Clough (1984), called the Representativeness Heuristic, deals with similarity or resemblance. An event is represented by a collection of features, and similarity is described as a feature-matching process that can be used to categorize the information. The Representativeness Heuristic relies on intuitive judgment. Analogical reasoning uses judgment to determine in which category an object belongs and whether an observed event is significant or merely random. For example, a loan officer relies on judgment to project general characteristics and features about an individual based on prior observed experience.

The Representativeness Heuristic varies with each individual because of cognitive complexity. Individuals make judgments intuitively based on their recall regarding the proportion of objects in a given category. Tversky and Kahneman (1973) describe the concepts of Judgmental Fixation and Anchoring, which describes how people make estimates when given an initial value. People tend to resist new information even when the data show that a previous conclusion was wrong. Initial choices have a disproportionate impact on judgment and decisions. To avoid this predisposition, Intelligent Information Systems can provide advice to preclude premature judgment using limited information.

Reasoning by analogy starts with a mental process. In the early twentieth century, Steinmetz was considered a genius because he had the ability to explain solutions to problems based on analogy. A major problem with analogical models is the large number of ways one could use them to represent a problem. Also, the manager must have the ability to recognize the mental model that best describes a given situation. The analogical representation should include necessary descriptive information and relationships among elements in a system or problem.

CASE-BASED REASONING

Case-based reasoning is an effective tool for solving problems based on the use of past experience. A case-based reasoning program starts with a rough design, which identifies the critical requirements and then searches for the closest similar example from past experience to determine operating specifications. Using an expert-system design based on past case histories, one can readily determine the feasibility of a given solution. Alternative designs can be examined in order to find an ideal solution. An expert system can quickly examine many cases until a satisfactory conclusion is reached.

Using the case-based approach, Nippon Steel was able to explore a scheduling cycle which permitted an 85 percent shorter design time so they could respond to customers more quickly. Also, it allowed better designs at lowered material costs of 30 percent, while at the same time was able to raise quality. The result was a $200,000-per-year improvement, using case-based reasoning in all of its locations. Nippon Steel relied on input from their customers for increasingly complex products requiring the highest possible quality. This, in turn, put their quality-design experts under severe pressure to turn out designs in less time. Using the case-based approach, Nippon Steel was able to be more responsive to the needs of their customers. They tried to solve this problem with a conventional data base retrieval system. However, it lacked any reasoning power. In desperation, they turned to a knowledge-based system and case-based reasoning to develop a Quality-Design Expert System. The quality expert system has two interconnected systems and used an expert system shell, the Automated Reasoning Tool (ART), to integrate and accelerate the design cycle. The first step was to determine whether a product could be produced at all. If it could, the expert system would provide a design and would plan the operational requirements and costs.

Many people solve problems by using an equivalent of case-based reasoning. Attorneys and arbitrators use cases as precedents. Doctors rely on cases to explain an unusual combination of symptoms. Using the old case and diagnosis, a doctor can find a solution to the seemingly new problem. Case-based reasoning offers significant time savings and can be used either to solve problems or for evaluation of proposed solutions. In the problem-solving mode, cases are used as a guide to help prevent mistakes. New situations can be evaluated by comparison with old situations. Interpretive case-based reasoning is used to evaluate a proposed solution by providing justification, interpretation, and projection of the possible effects of a decision.

Case-based reasoning can also be integrated with model-based reasoning. Case-based reasoning is a design approach based on the reuse of prior knowledge to solve similar problems, starting with a conceptual design and using parameters to modify the design. Case-based logic can incorporate functional models of physical devices in order to facilitate the content, organization, indexing, and modification of cases. Combining this with model-based reasoning helps to retrieve, adapt, and evaluate design cases dealing with functional models.

REASONING USED IN MANAGERIAL PROBLEM SOLVING

Effective managers solve problems rather than make excuses. For example, a computer plotter was being developed at Hughes Aircraft Company for producing large, inked drawings. The Air Force requested sixteen-foot drawings but the computer program was designed only to process eight-foot drawings. The department manager suggested that the computer program link two eight-foot drawings to produce the sixteen-foot ones that the Air Force wanted. Because of a tight time schedule, this approach solved the problem. The alternative was to rewrite the entire computer program, which would have entailed considerable time and money.

Current approaches to solving managerial problems rely typically on intuition, judgment, creativity, inductive reasoning, inference, assumptions, and implicit treatment of risk. DeBono (1994) applied what he calls "lateral think" as the means for breaking away from deductive logic when finding solutions to managerial problems. Other approaches, such as Synectics, nominal group technique, or brainstorming, attempt to find solutions by relying on creative vision generated by human interaction. However, these approaches seldom incorporate a systematic analysis of data or careful problem formulation such as is done in the knowledge representation used in expert systems.

Managers structure problems based on their perception of what needs to be done. In the problem-formulation process, decision criteria are used to determine what is important, how an information search will be done, whether deviations signify a problem, and what data are needed to determine cause and effect relations. This process is heavily dependent on available data and on people's motives, power struggles, and tensions. Data do not always represent the facts because they depend on how an individual reasons. The real value of decision-aiding tools is that they can assist in the analysis of problems and reduce the ambiguity resulting from human interpretation.

When structuring a problem, considerable judgment is used to determine what is an appropriate answer. Both problem finding and problem solving rely on managerial judgment to arrive at an acceptable solution. Where there are complex interrelationships, the outcome of a possible solution is hard to predict. Complex problems have many dimensions and they are not always known in advance. What is relevant at one point in time may not be relevant for future periods. For example, protection of inventory stockouts may be more important at some points in time than profit, or might depend on the possibility of a labor strike.

To be useful for problem solving, an Intelligent Information System must be flexible and interactive. Flexibility is needed in order to structure problem solutions for many different outputs. Interactive capability is needed to reduce the time to examine alternatives. In addition, interaction must be easy enough to facilitate problem analysis and to examine results. This capability is especially important when there is a high level of interdependency among elements in a system. Therefore, an interactive system should be able to operate in a flexible mode in order to provide the maximum decision support.

IBM Case

An example of an extremely complex decision is the one that faced IBM in the late 1980s. The once-proud computer company was humbled by the losses that were being sustained. A question that was being asked was "What went wrong at IBM?" There were many conjectures, such as top management was unable to develop a viable strategy without a major restructuring. Some people questioned whether it was a failure of leadership on the part of the previous Chief Executive Officer, John F. Akers. Could an appropriate course of action or strategy have been determined with a suitable decision-support system? Asking these kinds of questions is generally a good way to begin the design of an Intelligent Information System.

Considering that the market for mainframes is mature, fragmented, and price sensitive, IBM could have foreseen that it would have to take forceful measures to counter the adverse situation it faced. For example, competitors such as DEC had been striving to beat IBM in the mid-sized computer market. DEC relied on an open system architecture to help restore profits and market share. As a retaliatory measure to compete in this market segment, IBM announced a cheaper minicomputer, dropping the price from $16,000 to $12,000. Using a "sizzling" RISC system (reduced instruction set computer), IBM hoped that it could competitively position itself in the workstation segment. IBM had a major triumph with their AS/400 when most companies had given up on the minicomputer. IBM defied conventional wisdom and built a $14 billion business.

IBM's Silverlake Project developed the AS/400 relying on a major transformation in operating procedures in the Rochester, Minnesota, facility. For many years, IBM focused on products rather than being customer-driven. Against all odds, and using an unorthodox approach to development, the Silverlake Project was completed in two years, even though it involved thirty-seven different suppliers on three continents. It used the RISC technology that required 10 million individual parts and 2,500 applications programs. The power of an empowered team was an underlying force that drove the Silverlake Project.

When a company ignores what is happening in the external environment, problems such as those confronted by IBM arise. Beginning in 1981, IBM decided to use outsourcing for its PCs. Intel supplied the main chip, Microsoft the software, and hundreds of suppliers and developers designed applications and accessories. By 1985, IBM had 40 percent of the PC market. However, within a decade, IBM's position eroded to the point that in 1996 it had only an 8-percent share of the market. What caused this radical decline? They lost control because all the outsourcing partners did not have the same interests as IBM, and there was nothing they could do at that time (Stone, 1996).

For many years, IBM dominated the mainframe computer market. In a valiant effort to retain the mainframe as an important element of the computer industry, IBM took a bold step to incorporate it as a key element of networking (Verity, 1991). Although IBM had been the dominant player in the mainframe business, controlling almost two-thirds of the market, it was in a state of crisis.

IBM has been striving to return to its former competitive position. One of its newer products, for example, is a redesigned processor for the IBM PCs. To increase the sales of its PCs, IBM has been willing to sell clones made in Europe by an Asian firm. They have started selling PCs by mail order. For a period of time, the demand was so overwhelming that there was up to a two-month wait (Carroll, 1992). IBM has also been trying to convince Time–Warner to develop a system for transmitting video relying heavily on IBM's "interactive" video and using current cable television.

In an attempt to depart from the prevailing IBM culture, Lucie Fjeldstad was appointed the manager of the multimedia business. For the first time at IBM, she is bringing in executives from outside of the computer industry. She was given the opportunity to manage the multimedia business quite independently. James Cannavino, in charge of IBM's personal computers and workstations, also refused to conform to IBM's previous bureaucratic approach by satisfying customer demand for price and quality. These are the kinds of actions that IBM intended to use in order to reinvent itself.

Strategic alternatives that IBM might have considered prior to its debacle include the following:

1. Expand its telecommunications, multimedia, networks, and interactive television. The efforts with Time–Warner show the merits of this recommendation.

2. Further the development of their sizzling RISC chips. (This is now underway.)

3. Acquire companies that round out required technical competence in the above areas. Acquisition of Lotus Notes is an attempt to proceed in that direction.

4. Expand the marketing of clones by subsidiaries using mail order or telemarketing. This has been underway for some time.

5. Restructure the organization into independent strategic business units to provide flexibility and a greater entrepreneurial spirit. In a number of instances, individual entrepreneurial managers have taken the bit and are running their own shows.

6. Provide training support to help the organizational transition and to help foster a more open structure that emphasizes creativity, entrepreneurial spirit, and teamwork. The Silverlake Project shows the merits of this recommendation.

7. Expand their strategic alliances in the United States and abroad. Position themselves for a European Common Market and exploit the opportunities in developing areas such as Eastern Europe and Southeast Asia. They are now in a joint venture with Siemans and Toshiba to develop the next generation RISC chip.

8. Provide superior service to users and consider entering the outsourcing business. Timeliness, quality, value, and pricing need to be brought into line with competition. The new Ambra PC follows this recommendation exactly.

9. Reduce the emphasis on the mainframe segment and focus on the AS/6000 and related machines. (They are now emphasizing the mainframe as a network support system.)

Louis Gerstner, IBM's chief executive, was confronted with the need to demonstrate the value of a careful strategy based on an industry analysis and supported by expert systems in evolving the options. Although Gerstner has been moving cautiously in changing the organization, he feels very strongly that IBM should change from a customer–vendor relationship to one that is more of a client–advisor relationship. He is concerned that IBM has not obtained more value from its $6.5 billion in research and development spending by introducing more new products.

He wants to focus on the minicomputer and mainframe business and is willing to let others produce the PC. A recent example of a need to shift to a transaction-oriented workstation environment involves an installation of IBM's High-Performance Transaction System, an established software package that normally runs on a mainframe. Michigan National Bank knew they needed to employ more advanced technology for routing paperwork (i.e., processing checks from remote sites). Today, 60 billion checks are processed annually by U.S. banks but only 5 percent of all checks are processed by check-imaging systems. The major reason for this is that many banks must process checks at sites other than where their mainframes are located and remote processing is too costly and time consuming. Michigan National solved their problem in the last quarter of 1995 by installing IBM's High-Performance Transaction System on an RS/6000 workstation at remote bank locations without the mainframe. Mainframes at the bank's central data center are equipped with RS/6000 check sorting and imaging equipment. Michigan National has used a strategy whereby their main office and data centers are in high-rent locations and their check-processing capabilities are in lower-rent locations. Michigan National found that it took more than one minute to enter data and send a single readable image. Using imaging processing, they were able to transmit contained images over MICR lines almost instantly. The RS/6000 convinced IBM that they needed a major restructuring of the sales function in order to introduce a product-oriented organization in contrast to a sales organization organized by geographic region where there would be overlap of product responsibility.

Gerstner's new view for IBM is called Network-Centric (Sager, 1995). In part, this was promoted by the departure of Lotus's Jim Manzi, who could not accept the bureaucratic approach at IBM. Looking for a long-term growth niche, IBM sees the driving force of the future as the integrated digital networks that will carry a whole new host of applications. Gerstner feels that the coming communications revolution will change IBM even more than the semiconductors did. Having lost its position in the PC market and the fight against Microsoft, IBM is now poised to move forward with electronic commerce that will serve the consumer in many ways. As IBM moves into the latter part of the 1990s, with the semiconductor industry continuing its explosive growth and a projected worldwide growth in sales from $260 billion in 1995 to $261 billion by 1998, a push toward commercial chip manufacturing and the embedded controller chip market has phenomenal potential. Embedded controllers are specialized microprocessors that are responsible for functions in such products as telephone answering machines, microwave ovens, and the electrical systems in automobiles. Even now, many cars contain dedicated computer chips that use satellite technology to direct a repair vehicle to a car that has broken down, as well as sensors and controls for power steering systems. Thompson Consumer Electronics has entered into an agreement with IBM for a new interactive television set-top box, which uses a multichannel television service using satellite and microwave distribution before its planned fiber-optic network is completed. This effort on the part of IBM is part of their three-year-old strategy to realize a profit from its huge investment and core competencies in semiconductor manufacturing. Some strategic alternatives for the remainder of this century may include supplying memory, logic, and microprocessor chips to commercial customers, as well as industrial customers such as Hewlett-Packard and Silicon Graphics; expansion of memory chip production capacity with strategic partners; advancing development of controller chips to enhance time to market for the Power PC; and concentrating on marketing and servicing to the commercial market.

In the future, IBM sees customers buying computer power just as they buy electricity today. Can IBM succeed in its new direction? Does Gerstner have the information and vision needed to make correct strategic decisions? Answers to these questions will be addressed in this book and will show that by providing intelligent decision support, companies such as IBM can improve the odds of achieving their goals.

SUMMARY

A critical problem facing managers is how to switch intuitive reasoning to a more systematic approach. Several ways of tackling this problem have been explored. Starting with a clearer understanding of the way that managers reason about problems and examining the importance of value judgment and use of interactive terminals to facilitate problem solving are two ways discussed in this chapter.

The relationship of reasoning and judgment to the manager's decision style and cognitive complexity are also described. Using this knowledge, one is in a position to determine which individuals are best suited to tackle a given problem. If the problem is purely technical, then an analytic thinker is preferred; if the problem is organizational or involves an extremely complex situation, then the creative thinker (the conceptual style) would best fit the requirement.

Recognizing which problems need to be solved does not automatically assure that they will be solved. Each individual has creative capabilities, and given the right environment, is able to perform more effectively than in the bureaucratic structures that many companies still employ. This chapter articulates means with which Intelligent Information Systems can be developed to enhance the problem solving used by different styles of managers. Intelligent Information Systems can assure more workable solutions than managers who rely solely on intuition or experience.

APPENDIX: DECISION STYLE INVENTORY IIIA—QUESTIONNAIRE AND INSTRUCTIONS

DECISION STYLE INVENTORY III-A ©
Alan J. Rowe, Ph. D., 1981, rev. 1988
IDEATION Div. HRA, inc.
384 Bonhill Rd., Suite 101
Los Angeles, CA 90049-2322

The Decision Style Inventory has twenty statements. Each statement has a set of four responses. You are required to enter the numbers 1, 2, 4 or 8 in the space provided for each response. The significance of these numbers is as follows:

> 8 is the response that you consider is <u>most</u> like you
> 4 is the response that you consider is <u>moderately</u> like you
> 2 is the response that you consider is <u>somewhat</u> like you
> 1 is the response that you consider is <u>least</u> like you

The numbers that you enter reflect how you feel about each response that you have ranked. A sample set of possible responses is shown below:

My prime objective is to:

have a position with status	4
be the best in my field	2
achieve recognition for my work	8
feel secure in my job	1

Note that each number can be used only once.

The responses you make to each of the twenty statements reflect how you normally act in your work situation. The number you enter shows how you believe each response describes you, not what you think is right. There are no correct answers. There is no time limit in answering these statements. Enter the number that first comes to your mind. This is probably how you really feel about the response. However, you can change you mind and replace a number at any time.

Computer printouts for the Decision Style Inventory or further information can be obtained by contacting IDEATION at the address shown above.

DECISION STYLE INVENTORY III-A ©

For each statement below, enter one of the following responses:
8 for **most** like you. **4** for **moderately** like you. **2** for **slightly** like you. and **1** for what is **least** like you.

1. **My prime objective in life is to:**
   ___have a position with status
   ___be the best in whatever I do
   ___be recognized for what I achieve
   ___feel secure in my work
2. **I enjoy work that:**
   ___allows independent action
   ___is technical and well defined
   ___involves people
   ___has variety and challenge
3. **I expect people to be:**
   ___highly capable
   ___productive and fast
   ___receptive to suggestions
   ___committed and responsive
4. **In my work, I look for:**
   ___a good environment
   ___new approaches or ideas
   ___the best solutions to problems
   ___practical results
5. **I communicate best with others:**
   ___by having a group discussion
   ___in a formal meeting
   ___on a direct one-to-one basis
   ___in writing
6. **When I plan, the emphasis is on:**
   ___current problems
   ___meeting objectives
   ___future goals
   ___team effort
7. **When faced with solving a problem, I:**
   ___look for creative solutions
   ___rely on proven approaches
   ___rely on my feelings
   ___use careful analysis
8. **I prefer information that is:**
   ___accurate and complete
   ___provides specific facts
   ___is easily understood
   ___broad and covers many alternatives
9. **When I'm not sure what to do, I:**
   ___try not to do anything
   ___look for a way to compromise
   ___search for as many facts as possible
   ___rely on my intuition
10. **Whenever possible, I avoid:**
    ___using numbers and formulas
    ___conflict with others
    ___long debates
    ___incomplete work

11. **I am especially good at:**
    ___remembering dates and facts
    ___solving difficult problems
    ___seeing many possibilities
    ___interacting with others
12. **When time is important, I:**
    ___refused to be pressured
    ___decide and act quickly
    ___seek guidance and support
    ___follow plans or priorities
13. **In social settings, I generally:**
    ___Think about what is being said
    ___speak with others
    ___listen to the conversation
    ___observe what is going on
14. **I am good at remembering:**
    ___people's personalities
    ___people's faces
    ___places I have been
    ___people's names
15. **I prefer work that provides me:**
    ___achievement of my personal goals
    ___acceptance by the group
    ___the power to influence others
    ___challenging assignments
16. **I work well with people who are:**
    ___energetic and ambitious
    ___self confident
    ___open minded
    ___polite and trusting
17. **When under stress, I:**
    ___become frustrated
    ___become anxious
    ___tend to be forgetful
    ___am able to concentrate on work
18. **Others consider me:**
    ___disciplined
    ___aggressive
    ___supportive
    ___imaginative
19. **My decisions typically are:**
    ___sensitive to the needs of others
    ___broad and flexible
    ___systematic and careful
    ___realistic and direct
20. **I dislike:**
    ___following rules
    ___being rejected
    ___losing control
    ___boring work

BIBLIOGRAPHY

Anderson, Alan. 1988. Macintosh Memory Management. *Byte* (April): 249.

Anderson, J. R. 1983. *The Architecture of Cognition*. Cambridge: Harvard University Press.

Andriole, S. J. 1985. *Applications in Artificial Intelligence*. Princeton: Petrocelli Books.

Barr, A., and E. A. Feigenbaum. 1981. *The Handbook of Artificial Intelligence*. Los Altos, Calif.: William Kaufmann.

Bartholomew, Doug. 1995. Shooting Checks Off-Site. *Information Week* (October 2): 88.

Baumgartner, Stephen J., M. A. Batchelor, and G. H. Jacobson. 1992. Integrating Conceptual and Analytical Decision Styles into Computer Information Systems Coursework. *The Journal of Computer Information Systems* (Winter): 56–58.

Begley, S., and K. Springen. 1986. Memory. *Newsweek* (September 29): 48–49.

Benbasset, I., and R. N. Taylor. 1978. The Impact of Congitive Styles on Information. *MIS Quarterly* (June): 43–54.

Bimson, Kent D., and Linda Boehm Burris. 1987. Conceptual Model-Based Reasoning for Software Project Management. *Lockheed Software Technology Center* (July): 1–15.

Blanchard, Ken. 1991. Managing: Different Styles for Different People. *Today's Office* (August): 20.

Carrol, Paul. 1992. IBM to See PC Clone Made by Asian Firm. *Wall Street Journal* (March 11): B1.

Chandrasekaran, B., N. Hari Narayanan, and Yumi Iwasaki. 1993. Reasoning with Diagrammatic Representations. *AI Magazine* (Summer): 49–56.

Clough, D. J. 1984. *Decisions in Public & Private Sectors*. Englewood Cliffs, N.J.: Prentice-Hall.

Cohen, Joel E. 1988. The Counterintuitive in Conflict and Cooperation. *American Scientist* (November/December): 577–584.

Complexity of Abductive Reasoning. *AI Magazine* (Summer): 46–49.

Day, George S. 1986. *Analysis for Strategic Market Decisions*. San Francisco: West Publishing.

Dean, M., and Stephan D. Owens. 1985. Essential Attributes for Project Success. *Project Management Institute Proceedings*, October: 7–9.

DeBono, Edward. 1994. *DeBono's Thinking Course*. New York: The author.

Doktor, Robert. 1976. Cognitive Style and the Use of Computers and Management Information Systems. *Management Datamatics* 5(2): 83–88.

Drucker, Peter. 1966. *The Effective Executive*. New York: Harper and Row.

Dwinnell, B. 1987. Extending Expert Systems: Model Based Reasoning. *AI Expert* (March).

Early, Michael D. 1993. Which Way to Client/Server Land? *Beyond Computing* (May/June): 45–48.

Eliot, Lance B. 1993. Case-Based Reasoning in Estimation. *AI Expert* (May): 9–11.

Eliot, Lance B. 1986. Analogical Problem-Solving and Expert Systems. *IEEE Expert* (Summer): 17–28.

England, G. W. 1967. Personal Value Systems of American Managers. *Academy of Management Journal* 10: 53–68.

Fatsis, Stefan. 1993. A New IBM Shows It Too Can Be Nimble. *Los Angeles Times* (May 23): D7.

Fefer, Mark. 1993. Forecast Boffo. *Fortune* (September 20): 12–13.

Fulton, Steven L., and Charles O. Pepe. 1990. An Introduction to Model-Based Reasoning. *AI Expert* (January): 48–55.

Gardner, Howard. 1986. The Mind's New Science: A History of the Cognitive Revolution. Boston: Basic Books.

Gazzaniga, M. 1988. *Mind Matters*. Boston: Houghton Mifflin.

Geoffrion, A. M., and T. J. Van Roy. 1979. Caution: Common Sense Planning Methods Can Be Hazardous to Your Corporate Health. *Sloan Management Review* (Summer): 41.

Goel, Ashok K. 1992. Integrating Case-Based and Model-Based Reasoning. *AI Magazine* (Summer): 50–53.

Goldsmith, Timothy Eugene. 1991. Assessing Structural Knowledge. *Journal of Educational Psychology* (March): 88.

Haley, Paul V. 1987. A Search Strategy for Commonsense Logic Programming. *Byte* (October): 173–175.

Hedberg, Sara. 1993. New Knowledge Tools. *Byte* (July): 106–113.

Heintz, Timothy J., and William Acar. 1992. Toward Computerizing a Causal Modeling Approach to Strategic Problem Framing. *Decision Sciences* 23: 1220–1230.

Hertz, D. B. 1985. That World Out There: Models and Knowledge Representation. *TIMS/ORSA Annual Meeting*, Atlanta.

Hertz, David Bendel. 1988. *The Expert Executive*. New York: John Wiley & Sons.

Heygate, Richard. 1990. IT for CEOs. *The McKinsey Quarterly* (Winter): 54–63.

Hinkle, David, and D. Kuehn. 1992. Applying Case-Based Reasoning to Autoclave Loading. *IEEE Expert* (October): 21.

Hof, Robert D. 1993. Ed Zschau Doesn't Fit Big Blue's Mold—And That's the Point. *Business Week* (May 10): 28.

Hogarth, R. 1980. *Judgment and Choice*. New York: John Wiley & Sons.

IBMP2P: Solid Base for Collaborative Computing. 1993. *PC Week* (March 22): 96–99.

IBM the Axeman. 1993. *The Economist* (July 31): 59–60.

IBM Will Test Selling Its PCs by Mail Order. 1992. *Wall Street Journal* (June 29): B1, B5.

Integrating Case-Based Reasoning in Manufacturing Design. 1992. *Art Lines* 1 (7; Winter/Spring): 4–5.

Jeffreys, William H., and James O. Berger. 1992. Ockham's Razor and Bayesian Analysis. *American Scientist* 80(January/February): 64–72.

Keeney, Ralph L., and Detlof von Winterfeldt. 1989. On the Uses of Expert Judgment on Complex Technical Problems. *IEEE Expert* (May): 83–86.

Kelves, Daniel J. 1986. Brain Teasers, The Mind's New Science: A History of the Cognitive Revolution by Howard Gardner. *The New Republic* (February): 38.

Ketonen, Jussi A. 1989. Toward Reasoning. *AI Expert* (February): 44–58.

Kolodner, Janet L. 1991. Improving Human Decision Making through Case-Based Decision Aiding. *AI Magazine* (Summer): 52–67.

Lavigne, Meg. 1983. The Secret Mind of the Brain. *Columbia Magazine* (December): 16.

Levinson, Marc. 1992. IBM, Please Call AT&T. *Newsweek* (December 28): 44–45.

Liu, Zheng-Yang. 1993. Qualitative Reasoning about Physical Systems with Multiple Perspectives. *AI Magazine* (Spring): 77–79.

Lou Gerstner's First 30 Days. 1993. *Fortune* (May 31): 57–62.

Lou Gerstner's "Vision" for IBM? Making Money Again. 1993. *Newsweek* (August).

Mapping the Brain. 1992. *Newsweek* (April 20): 66–70.

McGeer, Patrick J. 1995. Multivalued Diagrams Show the Way. *Electronic Engineering* (September 25): 60–61.

McGeer, Patrick J. 1971. The Chemistry of the Mind. *American Scientist* 59: 221–289.

McCarroll, Thomas. 1993. IBM's Unruly Kids. *Time* (February 1): 54–55.

Mind Works. 1986. *Science AAAS*, 25–31.

Montazemi, A. R., and D. W. Conrath. 1986. The Use of Cognitive Mapping for Information Requirements Analysis. *MIS Quarterly* (March): 45–56.

Morton, Michael S. Scott. 1987. Interactive Visual Display Systems and Management Problem Solving. *IMR* (Fall): 69–81.

Patz, Alan L. 1992. Personality Bias in Total Enterprise Simulations. *Simulation and Gaming* (March): 45–76.

Pearl, J. 1988. *Heuristics*. Reading, Mass.: Addison-Wessley.

Pearl, Judea. 1990. Reasoning with Belief Functions: An Analysis of Compatibility. *International Journal of Approximate Reasoning*. 1: 363–389.

Penrose, Roger. 1989. *The Emperor's New Mind, Concerning Computers*. New York: Oxford University Press.

Polovina, Simon, and John Heaton. 1992. An Introduction to Conceptual Graphs. *AI Expert* (May): 37–43.

Polya, George. 1957. *How to Solve It*. Anchor Books.

Professor POS. 1994. *Restaurant Business* (July 20): 48–50.

Pylyshyn, Zenon W. 1986. *Computation and Cognition*. Cambridge, Mass.: Bradford Books.

Rettig, M. 1987. Heuristic State Space Search. *AI Expert* (March): 5.

Rockart, John F. 1979. Chief Executives Define Their Own Data Needs. *Harvard Business Review* (March/April): 81–93.

Rokeach, Milton. 1973. *The Nature of Human Values*. New York: Free Press.

Rosch, Elenor, and Barbara B. Lloyd. 1978. *Cognition and Categorization*. New York: John Wiley & Sons.

Rowe, Alan J. 1987. A Modeling Approach to Developing Heuristic Decision Rules for Use in Expert Systems. Proceedings, First International Conference on Artificial Intelligence and Expert Systems, June, AMK Berlin.

Rowe, Alan J., and Fred Bahr 1977. A Heuristic Approach to Complex Problem Solving. *Journal of Business and Economics* (Fall): 159–163.

Rowe, Alan J., and James D. Boulgarides. 1992. *Managerial Decision Making*. New York: Macmillan.

Rowe, Alan J., and James D. Boulgarides. 1983. Decision Styles—A Perspective. *LODJ* 4(4): 3–9.

Rowe, Alan J., and Paul R. Watkins. 1992. Beyond Expert Systems—Reasoning, Judgment and Wisdom. *Expert Systems with Applications* 4: 1–10.

Rowe, Alan J., and Richard O. Mason. 1987. *Managing with Style*. San Francisco: Jossey-Bass.

Sager, Ira. 1995. The View from IBM. *Business Week* (October 30): 142–150.

Schank, Roger, and Larry Hunter. 1985. The Quest to Understand Thinking. *Byte* (April): 143–145.

Schlender, Brenton. 1992. How Sony Keeps the Magic Going. *Fortune* (February 24): 75–84.

Schrage, Michael. 1991. IBM Should Use Japan's Formula. *Los Angeles Times* (November 28): D1, D4.

Schwartz, Evan I. 1993. IBM: A Work in Progress. *Business Week* (August 9): 24–25.

Sellers, Patricia, and David Kirkpatrick. 1993. Can This Man Save IBM? *Fortune* (April 19): 63–67.

Senge, Peter M. 1994. Learning to Alter Mental Models. *Fortune* (October 17): 147.

Senn, James A. 1986. Myths vs. Facts about Graphics in Decision Making. *Spectrum Society for Information Management* (February): 1–4.

Seymour, Jim. 1994. Selling Imaging to Top Management: A Good Idea for Bad Times. *Beyond Computing* (January/February): 15–16.

Simon, Herbert A. 1987. Decision Making and Problem Solving. *Interfaces* 17(5; September/October): 11–31.

Spillman, Richard. 1990. Managing with Belief. *AI Expert* (May): 44–49.

Sprague, Ralph H., Jr., and Hugh J. Watson. 1986. *Decision Support Systems*. London: Prentice-Hall.

Springen, K. 1986. Memory. *Newsweek* (September 29): 48–49.

Sterling, Leon. 1987. Mathematical Reasoning. *Byte* (October): 177–180.

Stone, Nan. 1996. Second Looks. *Harvard Business Review* (January/February): 14.

Stottler, Dick. 1992. Case-Based Bid Preparation. *AI Magazine* (March).

Taggart, W., and Daniel Robey. Minds and Managers: On the Dual Nature of Human Information Processing and Management. *Academy of Management Review*, 187–195.

Talbot, F. B. 1986. A Comparative Evaluation of Heuristic Time Balancing Techniques. *Management Science* (April): 68.

Thinking Looks Like This. 1991. *Newsweek* (November 25): 67.

Turban, Efraim. 1992. Seminar: Intelligent Decision Support Systems (IDSS) and their Impact on Knowledge Workers. Rand Operations Research Group, June 18: Santa Monica, California.

Tversky, Amos, and Daniel Kahneman. 1973. Availability: A Heuristic for Judging Frequency and Probability. *Cognitive Psychology* 5: 207–232.

Verity, John W., and Evan Schwartz. 1991. Software Made Simple. *Business Week* (July 31): 80–81.

Vose, G. Michael. 1987. Introduction, Heuristic Algorithms. *Byte* (October): 148.

Wakins, Edward. 1993. "Mindstorming": Thinking the Unthinkable. *Beyond Computing* (May/June): 57–59.

Weber, Jack. 1993. Visualization: Seeing Is Believing. *Byte* (April): 121–128.

Wiler, Clinton. 1992. Value Judgement. *Computerworld* (March 2): 69–70.

Wohl, Amy D. 1993. Multimedia: Toy or Tool? *Beyond Computing* (January/February): 57–59.

CHAPTER THREE
□ ☐ □
KNOWLEDGE ENHANCEMENT

Attitude is the key to using new ideas.

There is little doubt that computers can be made to behave in increasingly "intelligent" ways. Because problem solving is often ill defined and highly intuitive, the structure required by computer systems has improved problem formulation. Because we can incorporate "expertise" into computer programs, they can specify decision alternatives that are generally superior to what individuals can do who have little expertise. Expert systems are one of the tools that are becoming increasingly useful in many applications, but their ultimate potential can be enhanced considerably if used to augment the reasoning power of decision makers. The challenge is how to couple the reasoning and judgment of the human mind with the power, speed, and capability of the computer.

In an era of increasingly complex problems, knowledge-enhancement tools are needed to aid decision makers. However, managers often need to be convinced that they should use new tools because, in many cases, tools can be overwhelming. Managers will not risk using something unknown or not tested. Although there is considerable evidence to show that complex methods can aid in the solution of difficult decisions, a gap still exists between their application and what the practicing manager is willing to try.

On the other hand, technical specialists are not proficient at explaining what they are doing and why it is necessary. There is the question of whether advanced methods are useful in all cases, or are simplified approaches just as useful. As one might expect, there are two answers to this question. In many instances, using advanced approaches is an exercise in futility if they are neither suitable nor cost effective. In other cases, the difference between a correct or incorrect decision can mean the survival of a company.

ASSISTING DECISION MAKING

In order to understand where and how new approaches can aid decision making, one can examine the following classification of the problems:

1. *Task Environment*
   - *Certain.* This is where the consequences for given alternatives are known.
   - *Risky.* The likelihood of the consequences occurring can be assumed.
   - *Uncertain.* The likelihood of the consequences and all possible consequences are generally not known.

2. *Problem Characteristics*
   - *Structured.* The goals and the procedures of the situation facing the decision maker are clear, although the goals may be competing.
   - *Semistructured.* The goals are clear but there are many competing procedures that can lead to the goals. The benefits derived from any procedure are not necessarily visible, as the procedures contain several complex steps and levels.
   - *Unstructured.* Here specific goals may be difficult to articulate and a fundamental understanding of the source of difficulties may be unclear. These decisions are often nonrepetitive and may be value enhancing as opposed to problem solving.

This classification of the kinds of problems confronting decision makers is arbitrary because categories are never completely unique. The classification scheme should be viewed as a continuum, with the decreasing levels of information available in one category eventually leading to the next.

Intelligent computer-based information is one of the tools that can help management make more effective decisions. For example, ratios and averages were used for many years as the basis for determining profit, return on investment, and cost measurement. However, with the ability to track hourly, daily, and weekly data for each profit center or product line, the role of information has changed. Today, multiple measures, along with projections or trends, can show market share, product life cycle, profitability, competitor strength, product mix, or percentage return on investment.

If information is current and presented in a meaningful form, it can provide a better basis for decision making. This capability will permit managers to examine, in as much detail as desired, the relationship between the actions taken and performance. Rather than looking at performance after the fact, managers can look at current information in order to prevent problems before they occur. The ability to monitor trends and to determine the direction an activity is headed provides useful information.

An Intelligent Information System would incorporate cost-effective tools. Can such systems be developed economically? The answer is that economics is a critical consideration that must be taken into account. However, with the power and availability of personal computers and low-priced workstations, it is projected that the use of computers will become as commonplace as the telephone and the jet, and that system-design criteria will determine effectiveness. What is needed is the intelligent use of information and knowledge that can enhance the effectiveness of decision making and the performance of the organization.

To examine the ways computers can aid decision making, a classification of available systems is shown in Figure 3.1. On the horizontal axis, structured problems are differentiated from unstructured problems that require reasoning and judgment. On the vertical axis, levels of uncertainty

Figure 3.1
Classification of Information Systems

PROBLEM TYPE

DECISION TYPE	Structured	Semi-Structured	Unstructured
Uncertain	Simulation	Neural Nets	Chaos Theory
Risky	Decision Support Systems	Expert Systems	Fuzzy Logic
Uncertain	Cost/Benefit Analysis	Case-Based Reasoning	Causal Models

are differentiated from an uncertain environment where all possible consequences are unknown. Many of the capabilities shown in Figure 3.1 should be used as components of an Intelligent Information System and can be accessed appropriately through the user interface.

Based on this classification, we can show the ways in which computer systems can support decision making. The lower left section represents the more conventional applications of computers. These provide managers with information but seldom provide solutions. Decision support systems are used to provide more meaningful information and to focus on decision implications. A review of current applications of expert systems indicates that they fall, along with decision support systems, into the structured problem type. Semistructured problems require enhanced support, such as model-based reasoning, causal models, simulation, and neural nets.

The final section deals with unstructured and extremely complex problems. This is where the potential is greatest for adding intelligence to aid in solving the complex and uncertain problems confronting organizations. This class of problems will require a deeper understanding of the decision maker and an extension of knowledge representation to more complex problems. However, the payoff from such broad systems is significant. The new architecture of organizations will bring such decisions down from executive levels to the operating levels of an organization. They will become pervasive throughout the organization. Their coordination, knowledge sharing, and knowledge accumulation are prerequisites for the design of Intelligent Information Systems.

USE OF DECISION-AIDING TOOLS

Current decision-aiding techniques that could improve experts' reasoning often rely on unrealistic approaches, such as linear models, rather than more realistic nonlinear models or heuristic decision rules. Some quantitative approaches are too restrictive, such as utility theory or econometric models. Analytical approaches are most appropriate for problems that require statistical decision analysis or model-based reasoning. Analytic methods have limitations, but so do experts. Experts are prone to two types of errors: (1) errors due to missing concepts or knowledge and (2) errors due to expert's cognitive bias. Given the same conditions, experts tend to repeat these errors. Urgency and stress contribute to errors also. Where there are multiple or simultaneous errors, there could be a "chain" effect of gross errors. In order to avoid some of these errors, heuristics and knowledge should be treated separately. An Intelligent Information System should do the following:

• Differentiate between knowledge and heuristics, an ability which an expert hones with years of experience. Deep, substantive knowledge can avoid the use of shallow heuristics.

- Recognize the value of the Psychological Decision Theory, which deals with cognition and bias in applying statistical approaches.
- Replace simplified models with heuristics in order to predict and support human judgment.

An example of an Intelligent Information System is one used by ARCO, in which the company applied computer simulation in the operation of one of their oil refineries. When a major unit broke down, the computer program was able to rebalance the mix of products to be run in the refinery within one day. On a manual basis, this rebalancing required as much as thirty days. At the cost of oil, one can imagine the value of twenty-nine additional days of operation. This was well worth the cost of a decision simulation model that could be used as the basis to supporting management in a complex decision.

International Utilities used a decision model as the basis for evaluating its investments when contemplating acquisitions. The model provided executives with "information" that they could review on a timely basis for identifying the most likely return on investment, the risks involved, and the impact on earnings. These approaches to decision support undoubtedly will receive increased emphasis.

Expert systems will become integral to Intelligent Information Systems where the expertise can be communicated. Experts often know how they arrived at a particular decision, and they can readily identify the critical factors. An additional benefit in the use of expert systems is that once knowledge has been programmed and is in the computer, it can be shared and used as a training tool or as an expert advisor.

VALUE CONTRIBUTED ANALYSIS

Although not new, a tradeoff of value contributed versus cost is needed for companies to rationally allocate limited resources. A value analysis requires that the decision maker identify what the costs and the value contributed are before making a decision. Basically, a value analysis is applied to problems where one can readily identify two competing factors. For example, when trying to evaluate the cost of an investment, the manager balances the benefits to be derived from the investment with the outlay of funds. This approach can also be used to find the value contributed when trying to solve a problem by balancing the expected value or gain for alternative solutions with the potential consequences or loss. Many managerial decisions can be viewed in this manner, including the benefit of carrying a large inventory compared with the cost of shortage. The value of additional information can be compared with errors caused by lack of information, and the value of improved quality can be compared with the effect of losing customers because of defects or inadequate service.

The number of visits a salesperson should make to customers can be evaluated based on the number of sales expected. There are very few managerial decisions that do not have this general characteristic of both value contributed and cost, or other effects. Value incorporates all the direct and indirect benefits of actions taken compared with the consequences of those actions.

From an Intelligent Information Systems perspective, this approach can be extended to key management decisions, such as, what capacity is needed to adequately match customer demand? A value-contributed analysis is shown in Figure 3.2. It illustrates how increasing the accuracy or availability of information reaches a point of diminishing returns. Achieving 100-percent accuracy or availability is not possible because of the rapid increase in delays, system stress, and rapid increase in costs.

The value-contributed approach is similar to a cost–benefit analysis approach, used extensively by the government in their procurement of military hardware. It has also been used by companies such as IBM and GE in evaluating new projects to determine whether the value or benefit achieved was worth the resources expended. The calculation of the net value contributed is straightforward. For example, IBM includes both tangible and intangible value and costs. It includes the urgency of projects, the acceptance of solutions, and the likelihood that the project will succeed. This provides managers with an intelligent approach to justify large expenditures for projects.

Figure 3.2
Value Contributed

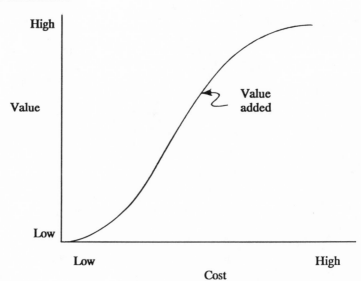

DECISION ANALYSIS

Decision analysis has been used for many years to examine decisions involving risk and uncertainty. Decision analysis includes decision trees, influence diagrams, probability theory, utility theory, and multiple-attribute decision analysis. The assumption on which decision analysis is built is that a rational decision maker will maximize the expected utility of an action taken.

Decision analysis has been used as part of decision conferencing in Australia to assist in the formulation of strategic decisions and other complex problems. Decision analysis has spawned the development of new methodologies for evaluating risk in order to make more informed decisions. General Motors has used decision analysis in an environment where there are multiple decision makers. The result is a higher level of consensus within the group. This contributes to making the best possible decision with the information available and with a better understanding of the risk involved in the decision.

International Minerals Corporation (IMC), one of the world's largest producers of fertilizers, was concerned with the problem of determining the maximum level of debt they could sustain for a given investment so that equity capital would be at a desired level of risk. The funds required were in excess of the amount that was available to the company, and factors, such as the cost of capital, tax saving, interest deductions, and a possible boost in earnings per share, had to be taken into account. A mathematical model was developed including all the factors that affected income (sales volume, prices, costs); this model took into account the estimates of possible levels of profitability or loss covering various debt-to-equity ratios based on IMC's financial structure and an estimate of the chances or risks of each occurrence. The result was that executives based their decision on the value added by incurring debt, rather than on an arbitrary approach such as the amount of funds available.

Decision and risk analysis has been used by Du Pont's business teams to explore creative strategy alternatives and evaluate them. Those with the greatest expected value were selected for implementation. Du Pont applies risk analysis to the resources in several business processes. The result in one of the Du Pont divisions that used risk analysis for selecting a strategy was an increase in the division's value by $175 million. Du Pont's decision and risk analysis application required an implementation plan based on the following elements:

1. Defining the major activities that were needed to make key events happen.
2. Finding ways to minimize risk based on the cost or other resources needed.
3. Developing a contingency plan for the strategy chosen.
4. Measuring progress in the changes required by the recommended strategy.
5. Changing the corporate culture by empowering small teams.

For decision makers to behave in a consistent, rational manner, a utility function is useful to rank possible outcomes by preference. Consequences need to be determined for alternatives that are chosen, and Bayes's theorem, which relies on subjective probability, can be used when using incomplete information. Because human decisions involve choices, uncertainty and inconsistency are typically based on incomplete information, and new or additional information is generally ignored in favor of using incomplete data. These are precisely the conditions that favor the use of Intelligent Information Systems; they maintain accessible knowledge bases and utilize generic heuristics to aid decision making.

DECISION TABLES

Decision tables are another tool that has been used for many years because they can assist in computer programming and in defining decision rules in expert systems. VP Expert is an example of an expert-system shell that accepts decision-table input to formulate the heuristic decision rules in its forward chaining program. Table 3.1 is an example of a decision table used for making insurance decisions. This application shows the relationship between conditions for insurance, the decision rules, and actions specified for each decision rule.

The decision maker or expert defines explicitly all the conditions that apply and what actions or decisions will be made for each set of conditions. Too often, simple rules such as age or number of accidents are used as the basis for a decision, which could lead to erroneous decisions. Table 3.1 helps to identify the relevant factors and how they are used as the basis for decisions. The rules can also be based on heuristic reasoning to help define the manner in which the decision maker should respond to a given set of inputs. Most of the data in this table are fuzzy in nature and would require fuzzy logic to supplement the use of the decision table. Fuzzy logic is described later in this chapter.

As shown in the decision table, a person who drives 15,000 miles per year, is thirty-five years old, has had two accidents in the last three years, and uses the car for business will pay $2.50/$1,000 for the insurance. Another 35-year-old who is a better driver and goes 10,000 miles per year will only pay $1.50/$1,000. While these rules appear simplistic, they reflect the heuristic judgment of a decision maker, along with actuarial data on accidents and costs.

EXPERT SYSTEMS

The explosive growth of expert systems and its myriad applications portend far-reaching implications for the way decisions will be made and managerial problems solved. Just as computers have influenced the processing of

Table 3.1
Decision Table—Insurance Decisions

Factors to Consider	Conditions			
Miles driven per year	10,000	10,000	15,000	15,000
Age of driver	25	35	25	35
Accidents in last three years	1	1	2	2
Major use	Pleasure	Business	Pleasure	Business
Decision rules				
Limit*	100/300	100/200	50/100	25/50
Rate per $1,000	1.12	1.50	1.75	2.50
Type Coverage	A	B	C	D

*In dollars.

data, expert systems can improve activities that require access to large knowledge bases which utilize rules of inference to control the use of that knowledge. A totally new generation of computers may be required for expert systems to reach their full potential. Model-based reasoning, simulation and theoretical knowledge, and cognitive aspects of decision making will be incorporated into emerging knowledge-based design. Indicative of the changes taking place is the position taken by Larry Guise, president and founder of Intelligent Technology Group, who has stated that successful computer system companies will have to focus on "solutions" rather than to be known simply as technology companies.

The integration of expert systems with managerial decision making means that there will have to be a closer matching of the decision-maker's style and specific decision requirements with the development and use of expert systems. Extremely complex problems require a problem-solving methodology that has embedded the semantics that are used to describe the situation. Successful application of computers for solving complex problems requires insight, imagination, and a deep understanding of both computers and the problem area. These considerations, and the need to better understand the cognitive process, help point the way for the development of large-scale, complex expert systems to tackle major decision problems.

In many cases, however, expert systems do not support decisions because of underlying assumptions that are made. Decision making needs to be flexible and adaptive in order to meet the changing conditions and needs of the decision maker. Expert systems are necessarily a component of Intelligent Information Systems.

Developing an Expert System

Dun & Bradstreet (D&B), working with Inference Corporation, developed an expert-systems program for protecting the Credit Clearing House (CCH) from customers who had bad credit risks. CCH is a product group within the Dun & Bradstreet Business Credit Services. CCH had decided to reduce the risk exposure of apparel-industry manufacturers, wholesalers, jobbers, and marketers. They started by assigning credit ratings and credit limit recommendations for the retail customers. D&B relied on their Information Technology Research (ITR) group to develop the application which would provide better credit analysis to CCH's 4,000 customers. ITR recommended expert systems as a solution for the problems, based on the following objectives:

1. Improve the quality of service provided
2. Improve productivity of personnel at CCH
3. Provide new customer information as soon as it became available
4. Improve the consistency of the ratings and recommendations to CCH clients
5. Provide a foundation for new and enhanced product development

Previous to the new system, CCH credit recommendations required a staff of trained analysts to review data from several different D&B business information reports, as well as the problem of maintaining and updating a data base covering credit ratings for approximately 200,000 businesses. The quality of this specialized service for apparel-industry customers depended not only on the staff's analytical skills but on ensuring that recommendations reflected the latest data base changes, as well as on the ability to respond quickly to customer requests. Meeting these criteria was extremely time consuming and affected D&B's ability to meet its customers' growing need for greater speed and accuracy.

D&B used Inference's expert system tool, ART-IM (Automated Reasoning Tool for Information Management), to develop the CCH Credit

Recommendation Expert System. According to a senior vice president of Data Resources for D&B, the expert-system application provided major benefits to CCH customers. This included increased quality and consistency in ratings, faster recommendations on new apparel business, and expanded coverage of the industry. The system accesses real-time information, stored in CCH's mainframe data bases, to provide specific dollar recommendations for its customers within seconds. By continually updating available information, the expert system improves CCH's accuracy and response time in handling requests. As a result of the credit recommendation expert system, CCH's customers are more confident when establishing credit lines for the retail stores with whom they do business.

Before going into full development, ITR developed a prototype of the expert system and demonstrated it to senior management upon completion. A conclusion was that many components of the CCH credit analysis were generic and could be reused for other products, which would significantly reduce development time using their knowledge-modeling approach. An initial review of the system's results showed that there was a 92-percent agreement between the rating done by experts with the expert system. After fine tuning the program, the agreement rate was raised to 98.5 percent. Certain "knockout" rules were defined; a "knockout" is a case for which a system decision cannot be accepted as completely accurate and is referred to an analyst for further review.

When making a recommendation, the system first receives the request from the CCH customer and accesses information residing in three different segments of the D&B mainframe data base. Then, it applies a selection of rules from over 800 rules in its knowledge base, makes a decision, and transfers that decision, with supporting information, back to the user. The time it takes the expert system to make a decision is less than half of a second.

The CCH application provided intelligence on a recommended dollar guideline, or a "no guideline" (knockout) decision, when the system was unable to offer a dollar amount. In the case of a "knockout," an analysis was completed by the expert system, giving a recommendation as well as an opposing decision. Then, an analyst decided whether to accept the expert system decision or to use the opposing decision.

An organization can create its own expert systems and save substantial sums of money. To do this, a program known as an "expert-system generator" or "expert-system shell" is used. For example, 1st Class Fusion is an expert-system generator that can be used by an expert without requiring computer experience. Fusion leads the expert through a series of screens that permit the expert to transfer his knowledge to the computer so it can be tapped by other people. In designing an expert system using Fusion, one would have to go through a series of steps that match the screens in Fusion. First, what are the different possible results of an advice session? For example, if it is a medical expert system, one might start with the list of diseases that an expert system will diagnose. Next, you would have to decide all the factors that go into making a decision. For a medical system, there might be dozens of such factors, including temperature, blood tests, and the results of the various blood tests. Finally, one would have to provide a series of examples that Fusion can use to determine its rules. An example might be as follows: "If the patient has a temperature and a sore throat, tell him to take an aspirin and call me in the morning."

Typically, one has to provide dozens, even hundreds, of examples. Fusion applies a mathematical artificial-intelligence algorithm, called "ID3," to these examples to come up with advice rules. It can display these rules in the form of a decision tree so one can see if the expert system makes sense. Then, the expert system is ready to give advice to your employees. It can be refined by adding more examples. It costs approximately $1,200 for 1st Class Fusion, which is capable of developing very large information bases. More modest expert systems can be developed using a lower-priced version that costs approximately $500.

One of the best selling expert-system shells today is VP Expert from Paperback Software, of Berkeley, California. However, there is a difference in the ease of use between the two programs. Whereas Fusion takes you through a series of screens that often look like a spreadsheet, VP Expert demands that one designs the expert system as a series of rules. The distinction is that VP Expert is much more likely than Fusion to require a programmer and a knowledge engineer to get the expert system developed. This will require interviews with experts and the translation of their expertise into rules that VP Expert can process.

Other Examples of Expert Systems

The primary role of an expert system is to provide an executive with the needed expertise to make intelligent decisions. In this role, the expert system serves as an "expert advisor." McFarlan (1981) describes Digital Equipment Corporation (DEC) as being severely hurt by its failure to compete in the personal computer field. However, for a period of time, DEC was able to outperform IBM, Apple, and other competitors by using an expert system to communicate directly with customers. When customers placed an order, DEC provided them with complete specifications and delivery dates. At the same time, the information was sent to the factory so that work could commence on the order.

American Express uses an expert system, the Credit Assistant, which helps to review credit accounts for credit risk and identify possible fraud.

The system has reduced transactions for review from twenty-two to one, while assuring worldwide consistency on credit policies. Estimates indicate that the Credit Assistant improved productivity by 20 percent and saved $1.4 million annually. American Express relied on thirteen data bases to determine the credit level for each customer. With the Authorizer's Assistant, if a customer made a large purchase that was outside of the normal buying pattern, the expert system recommended a credit limit in a matter of seconds. Did this replace the decision maker? Not really, because the decision-maker's expertise was embedded in the computer program. Furthermore, the advice could be overridden when necessary.

An interesting expert-system application in financial planning was developed by Humpert (1988). It is called the Underwriting/Lending Advisor System. He describes how bank loan officers and insurance underwriters approach risk assessment. They apply their specialized knowledge by using both qualitative and quantitative reasoning to analyze a particular application. Because they have limited time, they tend to be incomplete and inaccurate in their risk assessment. They often rely on judgment regarding management inputs that cover how to cope with specific problems. Their decisions can be described as multiattribute assessments involving interdependent factors, such as financial terms, previous financial performance, and related information. Reference information, such as ratings for different occupations and financial reports, are also used when available and as time permits. The Underwriting/Lending Advisor has been used to assist the underwriting of commercial insurance covering worker's compensation, inland marine, commercial auto loans, and computer facilities.

In still another application, Humpert (1988) developed an expert system for Programmed Evaluation of Personnel (PEOPL). Evaluation of personnel can be an expensive procedure, and objective measures contribute only a small part to prediction of success. Supervisor ratings are often biased. The PEOPL project is also used to improve the selection and assignment of personnel. PEOPL facilitates predictive and evaluative measures within selected occupations. Experts use heuristic shortcuts to avoid inappropriate decisions, but complex organizational decisions need reasoning to clarify alternatives and reduce conflict. PEOPL is an example of an advisor that is based on expert input.

Westinghouse Electric Corporation had a major problem with turbine failure and resorted to using an expert system to monitor the turbines. Turbine failure can cause thousands of dollars worth of damage, as well as idle time for the turbine. The system developed by Westinghouse diagnoses data continuously from monitors on the turbines and makes recommendations for maintenance. Another example of a successful application of expert systems was developed by Coopers & Lybrand, called ExperTAX, which is used to help accountants provide better tax advice. It makes expert's knowledge and experience available to junior accountants to help them perform more accurate tax planning.

Utilizing Marketing Systems

Utilizing knowledge-based expert systems, managers are able to build more effective strategic marketing systems. The knowledge-based methods facilitate the application of heuristics, judgment, and intuition to problems such as resource allocation, new product development and evaluation, brand development, pricing, customer service, and distribution channel management. Expert systems improve the odds for marketing success by utilizing learned knowledge of past successes and failures. Expert and knowledge-based systems are used on desktop computers, and there are a number of low-cost, easy-to-use shells available. Examples of current, strategic-marketing expert-system applications in commercial use include the following:

1. *ADCAD*. This expert system employs detailed, multifaceted, and substantiated knowledge about advertising to help managers choose appropriate television campaign approaches.
2. *Brand Managers Assistant*. This represents a knowledge-based system approach to the brand management function. The four phases of brand management—analysis, planning, execution, and control—provide the framework for modeling the brand management process.
3. *Business Insight*. This is an expert system designed to help businesses find the best strategies for introducing a new product.
4. *Innovator*. An expert system for new product planning, evaluating new financial services, screening of ideas, and provision of an approve, reevaluate, or reject recommendation.

The projected use of expert systems in marketing shows a continued emphasis on automated data analysis and more expertise being applied at the point of purchase. The proliferation of expert systems for marketing gives rise to the importance of creativity and expertise when making these decisions. The potential of applications of expert systems in marketing is shown in Table 3.2.

Enhanced Expert Systems

Knowledge acquisition and representation depend on the expert's ability to exercise judgment, which depends on cognition, values, and beliefs.

Table 3.2
Potential Areas for Expert Systems in Marketing

AREA	APPLICATION
STRATEGY AND CONTROL	Market Planning
	Target Marketing
PRODUCT MANAGEMENT	Product Portfolio Analysis
	New Product Development
	Product Launch
	Product Performance
	Ongoing Product Support
RETAILING AND DISTRIBUTION	Distribution Planning
	Transportation Planning
	Space Management
	Merchandising Support
	Expert Replenishment Systems
	Direct Marketing Support
PROMOTIONS	Promotion Budgeting
	Media Planning
	Promotion Evaluation
	Sales Territory Design and Assignment
	Sales Force Support
PRICING	Pricing Expert Systems
	Expert Yield Management Systems
SERVICES	Service Quality Advisor
	Service Design Advisor
	Automated Service Dispatch
MARKET RESEARCH	Market Research Advisor
	Demand Forecasting
	Market Monitoring

Heuristics depend on these same factors. To develop meaningful expert systems for complex management problems, we need not only to know how managers think (cognition), but how to extend the manager's reasoning power by incorporating both analytic reasoning and intuitive problem solving in the development of heuristic decision rules.

If we examine approaches used by knowledge engineers, we find that they rely on structuring their heuristics based on forward chaining, using "if–then" logic. The value of using the "if–then" logic is that there is a direct and clear basis for establishing the rules to be used in expert system computer programs. Furthermore, these rules can be tested by an inference engine for consistency or violation of logical procedures. However, developers of successful expert systems that incorporate heuristic rules need not be constrained by only one structure. The following approaches can also be used:

- Where theoretical knowledge is available, such as queuing theory, it can be incorporated into the knowledge representation.
- Simulation models can be utilized when variables are time dependent and there must be simultaneous consideration of multiple variables. Heuristic rules can be more robust and provide useful insights into system functions.
- Alternative representation of knowledge, such as model-based reasoning, can be used to replace if–then logic. The use of model-based reasoning reduces significantly the number of rules needed to represent a problem.

Because rules can be quite numerous when dealing with complex problems, sometimes running into the thousands, a means for grouping rules is provided by frames. Semantic nets, which are a subset of frames, show semantic relationships, inheritance, and object relations. Although most experts think in a linear fashion, their knowledge is often in the form of relationships, or networks, of objects, concepts, or activities.

A basic problem in developed expert systems is the knowledge acquisition and representation process. Brule (1986) indicates that one of the central issues facing the designer of an expert system is how best to "extract the expertise from a human expert." This problem stems from not knowing the source of a person's expertise. Also, he raises questions regarding the limitations on the acquisition of knowledge because of the methods used. Knowledge engineers often are restricted by the knowledge representation schema chosen. Fortunately, more robust approaches are replacing the use of rule and frame-based representation schema. The potential disadvantage of these broader schema is that there is no single formal approach comparable to rule-based "if–then" logic. This becomes a critical issue for knowledge engineers who need to decide which schema is most appropriate.

SIMULATION USED TO SOLVE COMPLEX PROBLEMS

Simulation can be used for problems that involve many factors which interact in ways that are difficult to determine ahead of time. The assignment of personnel is an example of what are called "combinatorial" problems because of the large number of combinations of the factors involved. Strategic problems are another example of such complex problems where, in many instances, managers rely on heuristic rules to find a solution. On the other hand, computer simulation can incorporate these rules using a model that describes the problem under consideration. This approach requires a clear understanding of a problem and determination of what is a satisfactory solution. Testing alternative strategies in a model provides a management group with a common framework for proposed changes in the organization. The model may be used to capture and simulate organizational behavior, as well as serve as a learning laboratory for testing potential changes. Skills and learning are acquired by remembering and using solutions to previously solved problems, and by remembering and avoiding previous mistakes or traps. When proposed changes produce an unintended consequence, the management team can trace the cause of the side effect and see why it occurred. For the learning organization, planning should provide techniques for checking how well the organization is doing to meet its goals. Learning the *why* can take the manager beyond the modeling process into the implementation process—the mobilization of an organization and alignment with corporate vision. It is an action step that helps to complete one learning cycle and open up thinking for the next. Simulations are good at tracing out the dynamic implications of those relationships in terms of growing or falling customer interest, changing market share, or increasing product functionality. Systems-dynamics simulation modeling tries to make it easy for people to see how the relationships about which they know can produce the behavior with which they are concerned. For example, they can accomplish the following:

- Focus on how social systems (like businesses or markets) can generate their own behavior. Examples of business behavior include rapid growth of sales, fluctuating levels of inventory, or falling morale.

- Synthesize the experiences of system participants as well as organizational structures, processes, and managerial decision styles.

- Recognize that causality is often circular and that this circularity gives rise to the characteristic behavior of markets. An example of this is called the word-of-mouth growth loop: As more customers buy a product, there are more people who talk about the product. Consequently, more people will hear about the product. The assumption is that when people like what they hear about the product, they will seek out that specific product to buy, providing even more customers who can talk about the virtues of the product (or service). This self-reinforcing process, one of the market's thousands of feedback loops, can be a strong contributor to sales growth.

- Provide a computer simulation model that can offer a laboratory for investigating how market may behave based on your inputs and the theories that you may want to test.

An example of the use of simulation is the computer model for market analysis used by Carborundom Corp. It was based on a mathematical formulation that described their operations and was able to determine which salespeople, distributors, customers, markets, and products were the largest profit producers. The company used simulation to generate several scenarios to calculate return on investment from their promotions and to determine which were the profitable products. Also, it determined the effect of price adjustments, the projected cost for each item on gross margin, and the cost savings. In this sense, the simulation was behaving as an expert advisor.

An interesting example of the use of simulation was a model that the Borax Corporation developed. Management considered using the simulation model for establishing the profits that they wanted to achieve for the next five years and applied it to strategic planning, based on profit objectives which included a detailed one-year budget. The objective was to establish an intelligent system which would include an operational accounting system for the various operating divisions of the business. The result was a financial accounting system that was able to describe those parts of the business which would produce the desired level of profitability. This model permitted Borax to examine all major lines for the entire budget, and to do so every week. If manufacturing or marketing conditions changed sufficiently, the company was in a position to modify the budget accordingly because it was all computer based.

An important consideration in the application of simulation is the accuracy of the model used to describe the many interactions that exist in actual problems. If the problem is readily describable, then the level of confidence regarding how close the simulation represents the problem can be established. For example, counting the number of cars flowing through a tunnel is easier than estimating the potential response by customers to a new product. Normally, a simulation model includes the following:

1. A structure that describes the process and the environmental forces
2. A description of the physical aspects of the process (e.g., change, delays, capacity)
3. Determination of how elements of the process interact and affect each other
4. Determination of the heuristic decisions that need to be made
5. Specification of the desired outcomes

Although simulation has many advantages, the difficulty involved in developing a model, programming it on a computer, and utilizing the results cannot be overlooked. The problem of modeling is important because the results of simulation are no better than the data and the model used. Fortunately, a model need not duplicate exactly actual conditions in order to be useful. Rather, a model is designed to predict behavior resulting from system changes. Because models are used to test new ideas, the simpler the model is, the more effective it is for decision-making purposes. In general, the larger the number of factors included, the more difficult it is to draw meaningful conclusions. The number and range of the variables can be limited to ones that are of interest to the decision maker based on use of a sensitivity analysis of the variables.

NEURAL NETWORKS

Neural nets are linkages of nodes that are presumed to simulate brain functions by operating on an input pattern. This pattern is transformed in a hidden layer of nodes, which then produces an output on a third layer of nodes. Neural nets have been used for many years as the means for pattern recognition, such as the Perceptron, an early version of a neural net. Current usage of neural nets has been extended to cover many business, medical, and military requirements. For example, neural nets have been used successfully for screening loan applications at banks.

Neural networks can provide an important aid for decision making. The speed of neural networks is significantly greater than most current systems. For example, they are able to process information one billion times faster than conventional computers. Applications of neural nets include machine vision, design of robotics, and speech and handwriting recognition. They can also solve problems of pattern recognition and analysis of integrated computer circuitry. Neural nets have helped Chase Manhattan to detect credit card fraud and Security Pacific Bank to analyze loan risks. Also, they have been used in medicine to detect abnormal heart sounds and interpret electrical cardiographs. A neural-net electronic nose, which recognizes smells, is used in Japan to test the freshness of sushi. The Ford Motor Company is developing a network computer that simultaneously monitors all aspects of automotive operation, including the engine, the power train, suspension, electronic steering, brakes, and climate control.

Neural networks have been equated with the associative-memory capability of humans. It is this capability that makes them useful for tasks such as risk management, process control, direct marketing, optical character or pattern recognition, and financial forecasting. This capability is a result of a structure or set of layers of interconnected nodes. The summation of the electrical charges on the nodes gives a vector value that produces an output based on the charges that were input. An example of how a neural net transforms inputs to outputs is shown in Table 3.3. Entering the data in this simplified neural net produces an output that depends on the hidden layer connections shown in Table 3.3. One needs to know the bias data or the transfer function and how to interpret the meaning of the output. In this case, the data would not mean anything unless one knew what all the inputs, hidden layer, and output signify. As is true with many such systems, it is not vital that the decision maker know the details of the network; the decision maker must know that it produces the desired results. This is similar to the automatic transmission on a car. Few people know how it works. They simply know that when they put the car in drive, it will go forward. Managers need to be convinced that the results are meaningful and useful. The evidence is that neural networks are being used and are producing meaningful results.

Japan has used neural networks for a variety of applications that try to simulate human behavior and which incorporate fuzzy logic. Fuzzy logic does not deal with precise values but with concepts, such as a very bright finish. Because "bright" can have a range of values, it is called fuzzy. On the other hand, the Japanese have applied fuzzy logic to washing machines to determine whether the water is not dirty, which is a fuzzy concept. The final impact on decision making and management is yet to be determined.

FUZZY LOGIC

Fuzzy logic is an area of concentration in artificial intelligence based on determining whether information is neither true nor false but lies in between the two extremes. Humans use information in their everyday lives when making intuitive decisions. If they use general rules of thumb, fuzzy logic can and should be applied to the situations which confront them. Control software that utilizes fuzzy logic can apply a flexible set of "if–then" rules. Referring to Figure 3.3, values which are within the cross-hatched area can be considered definitely false, and those values within the shaded area can be considered definitely true. If the data fall on either side of the overlap area, fuzzy logic might not be useful in dealing with the situation. Information which is within the common area should be studied, then stored and used to classify the data (Dewey, 1995). The stored data structure can be used to make inferences regarding how best to solve a problem. For example, if fuzzy logic is used in a temperature control system, the blower can run continuously with small adjustments in speed. In contrast, current systems turn the blower on and off in order to maintain the desired temperature. This causes excessive use of energy and requires larger motors to achieve what a fuzzy logic approach can do at a lower cost.

Table 3.3
Interconnected Nodes

	Input Layer Connection			
Data Source 1	4.8	15.1	-6.4	-24.9
Data Source 2	-27.8	-4.2	-30.5	-11.2
Data Source 3	13.7	-7.6	-12.0	-11.4

	Hidden Layer Connections			
Hidden node 1				
Node bias	-3.3			
To	4.8	-27.6	13.7	
From	-3.2			
Hidden node 2				
Node Bias	-13.7			
To	15.1			
From	-2.7	-4.2	-7.6	
Hidden node 3				
Node Bias	3.7			
To	-6.4			
From	-2.7	-30.2	-12.0	
Hidden node 4				
Node bias	3.3			
To	-24.9			
From	-2.3	-11.2	-11.4	

	Output Layer Connections			
Bias	0.8			
To	-1.3	-2.7	-2.6	-2.3

Figure 3.3
Fuzzy Logic Values of Data

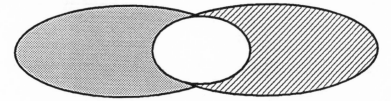

Almost every problem with which decision makers are confronted is essentially fuzzy in nature. There are seldom clear cut, unequivocal definitions, although one would think that this was possible. Most managerial problems involve judgment, which points up the problem of fuzziness. To deal with the kinds of decisions that executives make, fuzzy logic has been applied to describe how humans reason about solutions to problems which are fuzzy. Although fuzzy implies being imprecise, this is not the case. Fuzzy logic provides results that are simpler, more direct, and more reliable when used for problems related to computing and control. The initial stages of fuzzy-based system designs rely on the intuition used by the designer. Often a graphics interface and rules are used to present the design in textual form. By drawing graphs and stating a limited number of rules, the designer is able to achieve a level of rigor and precision that is not done easily using conventional approaches.

Fuzzy logic has also emerged as an important element of expert systems and in the knowledge representation used in such systems. Although a fairly new branch of study, fuzzy logic enjoys considerable popularity for the design of control systems and determining the possibilities of certain events occurring. Fuzzy logic is important because it reflects the reality of what managers do when they are confronted with complex decisions. Most decisions involve ambiguity, vagueness, and uncertainty; these are precisely the kinds of problems that fuzzy logic is best suited to handle. In turn, fuzzy engineering is the application of fuzzy logic in knowledge acquisition and for "defuzzifying" a problem, especially where there are multiple experts involved who have different opinions as to what is correct.

Fuzzy logic extends decision-making ability because it is closer to the reality of how things are described than is the simple yes–no or zero–one approach. Most descriptions indicate that something was or was not done; often what happens is that something is partially done. For example, if a car is parked in two spaces, we could say that it was mostly in one of them, and leave it at that. However, the reality is that the car is partially in both spaces. Fuzzy logic helps to reduce uncertainty because it can be used to describe more states of nature, especially where there are no precise answers. For example, if a person is described as young, how old would this be? The individual could be fifteen, twenty, twenty-five, or even thirty years old and still be considered young. Fuzzy logic describes the likelihood of each age being in the category called young. It helps to deal with the uncertainty of complex, ill-defined situations where there are no precise answers, such as what is a "good" profit? Also, fuzzy sets describe the distribution of answers to imprecise questions.

Kosko describes fuzzy thinking as the set of rules which deal with imprecise problems that are hard to define in classic terms. Reasoning deals with gray areas and rarely deals with a yes–no answer. Even well-defined states of a situation, such as, "Is the switch on or off?" can be misleading. A switch is on some of the time and off some of the time. We would have to say the switch is on whenever it is dark outside. But what about on rainy days when it is overcast but not dark? Kosko (1993) calls these "partial fits." It is interesting to note that adding information to a fuzzy set does not change the fuzziness. It merely helps to define the curve of inclusion in a fuzzy set. Kosko defines the fuzzy approximation theorem (FAT) as any curve that can be approximated by a series of patches. Fuzzy logic defines what these patches are, and fuzzy sets are the group of the fuzzy patches which define the shades of partial inclusion. Fuzzy systems can work in parallel and allow rules to fire at specified times.

CAUSAL MAPS

A map illustrated by Tufte (1990a) describes one of the best ways to display the losses suffered by Napoleon's army during the Russian campaign of 1812. When Napoleon left the Polish–Russian border, the size of the army was 442,000 men. The width of a drawn band indicates the change in the size of the army at each position as it invaded Russia. In September, the army finally reached Moscow with only 100,000 men. Napoleon's bitter retreat from Moscow in the cold winter is shown by another band which is related to temperature and time. The Grande Armee struggled out of Russia, with only 10,000 men returning home. Graphics portray a coherent story using multivariate data. Graphics provide a much more understandable portrayal of what happened than data that are displayed on a time line. In the Napoleon example, the variables are shown as follows: the size of the army, its location, the direction of the army's movement, and the temperature changes versus time during the retreat from Moscow. Tufte (1990b) claims, "It may well be the best statistical graphic ever drawn."

In his study of graphics, Senn (1986) showed that more effective analysis and decision making can be achieved when using graphics. Graphs facilitate reading presented information accurately, detecting trends, recalling facts, and understanding the message presented. Graphs proved superior in spotting trends, and they also were superior in helping to recall a large amount of detailed information presented. In general, however, the research failed to support the superiority of graphics in all business settings. The implication is that designers of information systems need better guidelines, such as cognitive complexity, when determining when to use graphic output.

Conceptual graphs rely on a projection for pattern-matching operations. Graphs help to increase the number of concepts and relations that can be understood. Graphs can have many specialized variations, and projection can be common to more that one graph. A key factor is that the projection of information is helpful in developing new knowledge by using conceptual graphs. Also, projection helps to combine small graphs into larger ones.

Causal mapping helps to frame strategic problems by speeding up the convergence of ideas. Casual mapping is useful for communicating problem situations because, typically, participants have different mental models. One approach to causal mapping is to use comprehensive situation mapping, which extends the mapping construct by assigning strengths and direction to links. Links can model the necessary causality requirements and help to model quantitative parameters describing complex situations.

When both data and objects are represented in causal maps, managing software systems require the following:

1. *Factor Identifier.* This is used to identify critical factors in a situation.
2. *Situation Mapper.* This uses causal maps for describing a situation.
3. *Scenario Simulator.* This is used to test implications of assumptions that have been made.
4. *Assumption Surfacer.* This explores differences in maps.
5. *Consensus Formulator.* Consensus on new maps is used to replace existing ones.

Individuals participating interactively in a situation form their own causal maps. The process is used to generate a map which can involve a number of new factors. Scenario simulation and assumption surfacing contribute also to modifying individual maps before consensus takes place. STELLA is a microcomputer-based software product that allows graphical construction of simulation models. STELLA was used in a learning laboratory at MIT, where simulation models are directly built from the causal maps created by managers working with this software.

Hanover Insurance is a medium-sized firm that was undergoing organizational upheaval when attempting to adapt to a changing external environment. They were attempting to discard the old, authoritarian management style and to encourage a shared vision, openness, and fast response. In a project at MIT, the managers individually mapped their mental models of the organization's core processes, which were collected to form a causal network of activities. The simulation that resulted from this shared model was later used as a training tool for incoming managers. The process of the modeling and the creation of a learning tool aided in improving communication skills, providing a shared experience, and creating a culture of learning at Hanover Insurance.

Today, if you call directory assistance, there is a chance that you will be speaking with a friendly voice—a computer-assisted friendly voice—that asks you for the city and the name of the person or company that you wish a telephone number for. Catalog orders may soon be handled by speech-recognizing computers. One of the companies that offers an innovative combination of computer voice recognition and telephone technologies is Wildfire Communications, Inc. Wildfire responds to spoken requests and is virtually tireless. The system will place calls, direct incoming calls to the number of your choice, place calls designated as important, and store messages for other calls. The system can also broadcast voice messages to groups of people with whom you wish to speak with one broadcast. However, time and training have to be invested to enable this technology. First, users will have to be trained to keep their commands simple and to use a language understood by the system. Second, a data base of contacts, names, and telephone numbers has to be created. This can be done by using the system; however, names may have to be spelled by using a dial pad or the "alpha-bravo-charlie" phonetic alphabet. This particular system is not inexpensive, but is within the reach of many mid-sized businesses.

Wal-Mart is an example of a corporation that has designed an enterprise-wide information model that its apparel suppliers use to replenish stock in its Wal-Mart stores. As an example, Wal-Mart transmits millions of characters of data about the day's sales to Wrangler, a supplier of blue jeans. The two companies share both the data and a model that interprets the meaning of the data. Also, they share software applications that act on that interpretation. They send specific quantities of sizes and colors of jeans, which simplifies logistics and inventory costs and leads to fewer stock outs. Each time the data model is changed to reflect a new fashion season or pricing pattern, both Wal-Mart and Wrangler learn to adapt for the next season or price change.

SUMMARY

The explosive growth of expert-systems applications is evidence of the significant potential for solving complex management problems. Heuristic methods can be used along with cognition and judgment to explore alternative representations or structures which can extend current applications. Bob Dwinnell, at Amphenol, strongly states his position regarding alternate structures: "I think model-based reasoning which can be used to model a system's structure and function and then reasoning about the model is even more valuable as a software programming technique than the classic expert-systems approach." When approaches such as this are combined with methods such as simulation and heuristics, interesting new possibilities arise. Alternative schema representations, including models of known phenomena, decision tables, and semantic networks, offer the opportunity to increase the accuracy and the effectiveness of knowledge representation, and can enhance their value in Intelligent Information Systems.

How can we tie the elements of expert systems and human decision making together? Augmented reasoning can come from the synergistic integration and support provided by expert systems. Better tools are being developed and will become an integral part of management expertise. We can anticipate expert systems that have a natural-language interface, that incorporate adaptive learning, that have complete and correct knowledge representation, and that relate the decision-maker's cognitive style to the computer. These expert systems will support unstructured decision making and will eventually lead to more Intelligent Information Systems.

The application of expert knowledge in Intelligent Information Systems will introduce an important change in future systems. By using the decision maker's knowledge, managers become part of the system. They have ownership which helps to motivate them to use the computer systems even if they are unfamiliar with the programs. If these information systems can provide information that discloses trends, forecasts, or whatever the decision makers want, then they are more likely to be used.

Causal maps and graphics can make computer interaction easier. Visualization will enable decision makers to incorporate many insights and judgments into evaluating problems. This can augment the manager's ability to make better decisions. Causal mapping can tap into the creativity and intelligence that manager's have and will allow them to enhance that creativity because it allows them to utilize available information more effectively.

BIBLIOGRAPHY

AI + Database = Personal Information Manager. 1988. *AIWEEK* (September 1): 9.

Amir, Shawn. 1989. Building Integrated Expert Systems. *AI Expert* (January): 27.

Bodily, Samuel E. 1992. Introduction: The Practice of Decision and Risk Analysis. *Interfaces* 22(November/December): 1–4.

Brule, James F. 1986. *Artificial Intelligence, Theory, Logic and Application*. Blue Ridge Summit, Pa.: Tab Books.

Davis, Sue Anne, and Rajendra S. Sisodia. 1993. *Expert Systems Applications in Marketing: Evolution and Prognosis*. Unpublished paper.

Dewey, Douglas. 1995. Everything You Ever Wanted to Know about Fuzzy Logic. *InfoWorld* (Spring): 7–8.

Fried, L. 1985. Expert Systems Enter the Corporate Domain. *Management Technology* (January): 59.

Harmon, Paul. 1988. *Expert Systems*. New York: John Wiley & Sons.

Hedburg, Sara. 1993. New Knowledge Tools. *Byte* (July): 106–112.

Hertz, David Bendel. 1988. *The Expert Executive*. New York: John Wiley & Sons.

Holsapple, C. W., and A. B. Whinston. 1995. Knowledge Management in Decision Making and Decision Support. *Knowledge Policy* (Spring): 5–23.

Humpert, B. 1988. Expert System Applications in Finance Planning. Paper presented at Second Conference on Advances in Communication-Based Information Systems for Financial Institutions, London, April 11–13.

Kakamoto, Gene. 1989. Business Strategy Advisor: An Expert Systems Implementation. *Journal of Information Systems Management* (Spring): 16–24.

Kosko, Bart. 1993. *Fuzzy Thinking: The New Scenario of Fuzzy Logic*. New York: New York Perion.

Kosko, Bart, and Satoru Isaka. 1993. Fuzzy Logic. *Scientific American* (July): 71–76.

Krumm, F. V. 1993. Management and Application of Decision and Risk Analysis in Du Pont (November/December): 84–93.

Leonard-Barton, Dorothy, and John J. Sviokl. 1988. Putting Expert Systems to Work. *Harvard Business Review* (March/April): 91–98.

McFarlan, F. Warren. 1981. Portfolio Approach to Information Systems. *Harvard Business Review* (September/October): 141–150.

Montalbano, Michael. 1974. *Decision Tables*. Chicago, Ill.: Science Research Associates.

Negoita, Constantin Virgil. 1984. Management Applications of Expert Systems. *Human Systems Management* 4(4; Autumn): 275–279.

Oxman, S. W. 1985. Expert Systems Represent Ultimate Goal of Strategic Decision Making. *Data Management* (April): 37.

Rowe, A. J. 1965. Computer Simulation—A Solution Technique for Management Problems. *Fall Joint Computer Conference* (Fall): 259–267.

Rowe, A. J., and Fred Bahr, eds. 1972. A Heuristic Approach to Managerial Problem Solving. *Journal of Economics and Business* (Fall): 159–163.

Rowe, A. J., Clifford Craft, and John F. Hermaun. 1977. A Heuristic Approach to Complex Problem Solving. *Journal of Business and Economics* (February): 16–19.

Rowe, Alan J., and Paul R. Watkins. 1992. Beyond Expert Systems—Reasoning, Judgment, and Wisdom. *Expert Systems with Applications* (4): 1–10.

Senn, James A., Sirka Jarvenpas, and Gary W. Dickenson. 1986. Myths vs. Facts about Graphics in Decision Making. *Spectrum Society for Information Management* 3(February): 1–4.

Shanteau, James. *Psychological Characteristics of Expert Decision Makers*. Manhattan, Kansas: Kansas State University.

Silverman, Barry G. 1992. Judgement Error and Expert Critics in Forecasting Tasks. *Decision Sciences* (23): 1199–1219.

Silverman, Barry G., and Arthur J. Murray. 1990. Full-Sized Knowledge-Based Systems Research Workshop. *AI Magazine* (Special Issue): 88.

Sprague, Ralph H. 1986. *Decision Support Systems*. New Jersey: Prentice-Hall.

Storey, Veda C., and Robert C. Goldstein. 1990. An Expert View Creation System For Database Design. *USC Expert System Review* 1: 19–45.

Tony, A. 1992. Designing Virtual Worlds. *AI Expert* (August): 23–35.

Tufte, Edward. 1990a. *Envisioning Information*. Cheshire, Conn.: Graphics Press.

Tufte, Edward. 1990b. *The Visual Display of Quantitative Information*. Cheshire, Conn.: Graphics Press.

Turban, Efraim. 1988. *Decision Support and Expert Systems*. New York: Macmillan.

Turban, Efraim, and Theodore J. Mock. 1985. Expert Systems: What They Mean to the Executive. *New Management* 3(1; Summer): 45–51.

Verity, John W., and Evan I. Schwartz. 1991. Software Made Simple. *Business Week* (September 30): 92–100.

Verso, Dave, and Steve E. Tice. 1990. Virtual Reality Technology for Product Development. *SimGraphics Position Paper* (May): 1–7.

Williamson, Mickey. 1989. User Developed Expert Systems—Expert Systems for the Rest of Us. *AI Magazine* (March/April): 11–15.

Zeichik, Alan L. 1992. Solutions, Not Tools. *AI Expert* (March): 5.

CHAPTER FOUR
❑ ❑ ❑
KNOWLEDGE SHARING

Sharing information can have greater impact than the quantity of data.

With changes taking place in computer technology, the way information is used in an organization will also change. Although knowledge and data are available in most organizations, an Intelligent Information System can make them more useful. While there is a growing fascination with sophisticated approaches, these may not address the real problems at hand. Rather, "smart" programs that apply "intelligence" to real world problems and aid decision making will provide meaningful support. When reviewing high-level computer tools for extracting or mining the contents of large data bases, concern should be on solutions, not tools.

Software can do more of the routine thinking and can assist decision making. Intelligent solutions and expert-system advice can help "augment" the decision maker's reasoning power, while leaving the drudgery to the computer. To accomplish this goal, we examine ways in which existing data and knowledge can be used more effectively to help achieve the full potential of computer-based and knowledge-based systems for group decision support.

The importance of intellectual capital should not be underestimated. Where managers have had the insight to utilize the ultimate intangible asset—knowledge—they have found a way to put real dollars on the bottom line. It is difficult to measure intellectual capital, professional skills, experience, and information. Where intellectual material has been identified and formalized, it can be used to produce a higher valued asset. It is estimated that three-fourths of the value added to a product is derived from the knowledge and information used (Losee, 1994).

The learning organization creates knowledge. Groupware, which includes shared data bases, Electronic Data Interchange (EDI), and conferencing, provides decision makers with the ultimate source of information. Using this capability, the learning organization becomes a knowledge-creating company. In a highly competitive economy, the only real advantage is knowledge. Customers change, products become obsolete, and competitors increase. Successful organizations create knowledge to counter these uncertain events. Where knowledge is widely disseminated throughout the company, the company is utilizing its brainpower or intellectual capital. Japanese companies have learned how to create new knowledge by using available knowledge and linking it to highly subjective information, insights, intuition, and hunches. To make this work, Japanese companies rely on commitment and a sense of identity by individuals with the overall company mission. The essence of their innovation is changing the way problems are perceived. They recreate the company continuously, and everyone is involved in the process (Nonaka, 1991).

INFORMATION REQUIREMENTS FOR ORGANIZATIONS

To determine how information can assist decision making, a good starting point is the examination of the kinds of decisions managers make at each level in the organization. At the operating level, most information concerns detailed transactions, such as payroll, accounting, inventory, or production status. These transactions are output in regularly scheduled reports that are used by operating managers for their day-to-day decisions.

At the middle-management level, information is generally summarized and used primarily for keeping managers informed. Top management is where strategic decisions and long-range considerations are critical. However, at that level of the organization, information is summarized even further, and reports are largely in response to special requests. Where strategic decisions cannot often deal with a rapidly changing environment, no matter how well conceived, responsiveness is needed to readjust forecasts as new information and new conditions arise. Information is needed, therefore, to more rapidly adjust projections and to provide the basis for new decisions. Because conditions change in rapid and erratic ways, adjustments are needed to cope adequately with the new situation.

In general, flexibility is required to meet ongoing changes in operations and to meet unanticipated problems. In the past, fixed approaches, such as budgets, schedules, and plans, were adequate. This is no longer the case. As new demands arise, the computer can play a major role in aiding decision making by providing more rapid and more accurate information. Management can no longer wait for something to go wrong; they must be in a position to anticipate problems and be able to take whatever corrective actions are needed. Fortunately, today's organizations are no longer as rigid as those in the past. The level of complexity and judgment required mean that each individual feels a sense of ownership in the job that they are performing. Appropriate information can assist in a better understanding of roles and performance requirements.

To be useful as a decision aid, information systems must be relevant to and understood by the managers who use them. Important decisions will increasingly require approaches, such as graphic-user interfaces, multimedia, or expert systems, that act as assistants. Because changes in information technology can be threatening to some managers, care must be exercised to avoid resistance by those who are affected by any redistribution of power. Argyris (1991) has shown that it is extremely difficult to build an integrated system in a place where departments have been locked in conflict and would be skeptical about being required to cooperate. In order for an Intelligent Information System to function effectively, an organizational culture of trust and confidence will also be necessary.

The value of information systems as decision aids depends ultimately on how managers use reasoning and judgment in their decisions. Computer-produced information is not a substitute for the intuition and judgment needed to assess organizational performance. Qualitative factors often provide more sensitive clues concerning operating units than numeric data. Many top executives would rather talk to the people who use computers to get their judgment than to use the computers themselves. Increasingly, organizational problems concern people-based issues which computer-based information systems cannot solve alone. One top executive interviewed said, "I simply do not want computer printouts on my desk, I won't read them." The consensus at the chief executive level is that subjective judgment is still a valuable asset. When desired, it can be augmented by computer information.

GROUP DECISION MAKING

A major paradigm shift is now taking place in how information technology is being used in organizations. There is a shift from individual to workgroup information, and from isolated technology islands to integrated systems. Another shift taking place is from internal to interenterprise computing. These technology shifts include the following:

1. Network computing that is microprocessor based and network based.
2. Open systems in which proprietary software is shifting to open standards that include Multimedia vendor–customer partnerships.
3. A software revolution where software development is shifting away from a craft, and where graphical and multiplatform user interface is being used, as well as increased integration in applications.

Network computing is important because it provides operational alignment, platform specialization, and cost savings. In 1992, mainframe costs for one million instructions per second (MIPS) was $70,000, whereas workstation costs were under $300 per MIPS. Networking has improved integration, flexibility, and innovation. Networking used in open systems can run software, share information, and communicate, regardless of which computer is used. These systems have significant potential but must deal with the following issues:

Portability. Software applications can be easily moved among computers, enabling people to be portable, also.

Interoperability. Different computers communicating with one another while readily sharing resources, information, and applications.

Open systems can help to achieve significant savings in the costs of hardware, software, managing information, and managing change. These systems create standards for hardware that have the characteristics of a commodity. This allows computers to be purchased based on performance rather than price. Open systems are critical for those organizations where technology is currently based on isolated systems that are costly, not integrated, hard to maintain, or difficult to change.

Network vendors are trying to deal with their current platforms while shifting to open, multivendor platforms. However, transition to multivendor products causes two problems: (1) how to create a suitable migration path and (2) how to protect market share and stay competitive in an open platform approach? The first problem, the migration path, is something vendors must deal with if they really intend to shift to more open systems. Quality is also critical when attempting to remain competitive in an open, multivendor environment. By and large, the shift toward open, multivendor network services creates a great opportunity for those who are able to either respond quickly or to enter the network arena and provide excellent solutions for industry's needs. The 1980s provided network companies a significant opportunity for growth. The 1990s will determine who benefits and who loses by the change.

Network users should benefit in the move toward better interoperability, but not without a price. The transition to open, multivendor platforms may mean that users are forced to accept new technology as vendors make the transition from where they have been in the past. Because traditional monolithic vendors are finding it difficult to adjust to new roles, vendors, such as IBM or DEC, are involved now in a much more open, multivendor system which shifts the vendor's role from a supplier to an agent serving customers' needs. Vendors will also have to become more integrative with systems, and sell or recommend hardware other than their own. Vendors who are able to meet this challenge will have the greatest opportunity for growth and profitability.

To facilitate this shift from individual to work-group decision making and problem solving, three approaches have been used.

Brainstorming. This approach is used to aid group decision making by having the group generate new ideas. Group brainstorming is most applicable when a problem is well defined. To encourage idea generation, criticism is prohibited. Free expression is encouraged so that radical ideas can be presented. The quantity of ideas generated is important because the larger the number of ideas, the greater the likelihood of finding a good one. Combinations of ideas are pursued to encourage the maximum participation and acceptance. Group brainstorming is a means to create an environment where people can think freely because inhibition, self-criticism, and criticism of others is eliminated.

The Nominal Group Technique. The Nominal Group Technique is a structured approach to problem solving. Discussion and interaction during the process is restricted. Group communications and interactions are structured during the silent generation of ideas, which are then written down and recorded without discussion. A preliminary vote on the importance of each idea is taken, and a discussion of the vote is used to resolve inconsistencies in ideas. A final vote is then taken which represents the group decision. This final vote gives group members a sense of accomplishment and documents the group's findings. The Nominal Group Technique facilitates group decision making by reducing conflict between members and the group leader. Also, it gives members social reinforcement while generating ideas, and it encourages commitment to future phases of the decision process.

Automated Decision Conferencing. This approach to group decision making is intended for use when there are urgent, important, and complex decisions and divergent opinions regarding the best course of action. Conferences may last several days depending on the complexity of the problem under consideration. The conferencing can include management science models and computer-support technology. When the process is completed, the solution is based on group consensus and it is documented. Automated decision conferences include six to fifteen group members, along with three staff members. One staff member aids the group decision-making process, one operates the computer, and one records the decision rationale. All key individuals in the organization who are involved in the decision should be present. Participants are not permitted to bring supporting records or written information, as they are a distraction in the conferencing process. The process usually starts by identifying the problem in written detail. The information is entered into a computer after the problem is described. The computer output is presented to the group, which subjects it to extensive examination and careful analysis. When a tentative solution is reached, it is refined until all participants are satisfied. Through this approach, decision conferencing incorporates the advantages of quantitative analysis, as well as behavioral considerations, to promote an open group process and resolve any conflict. It can deal with complex decisions involving large amounts of information, and it helps to encourage commitment by members of the group.

In general, a group or a team can make more effective decisions than an individual. Groups have more information and a more comprehensive perspective than a decision maker operating independently. Implementation is more effective if members have participated in making the decision. Also, understanding and acceptance of a decision by those involved in its implementation provides a sense of ownership in the decision.

On the other hand, group decision making usually consumes more time and is more difficult than individual decision making. Occasionally, groups make decisions that are not in accord with the goals of the organization. Members of the organization may come to expect involvement in all decisions. Groups may be unable to reach a decision because of disagreements among members or because of pressures for conformity. Nonetheless, the group decision-making process has been used increasingly to obtain potential benefits, while still allowing the manager to choose when to make a decision alone.

KNOWLEDGE SHARING

Groups are increasingly sharing information and participating in decision-making functions once reserved for professionals. Technology architects will replace system builders. The standards in hardware, software, and telecommunications will also change management roles. For example, American Airlines is looking forward to the day when they can buy hardware and software from third-party vendors.

Sharing knowledge cannot be forced on organizations, even where there are similar operations that are performed. Multiple and different knowledge-based systems have evolved, and now the problem is how to develop a willingness to share information. Common libraries can be developed that use knowledge from multiple, related applications. Corresponding software can be embedded in related applications so that knowledge can be used in common. To facilitate sharing, one can use a single knowledge base to extract user-interface requirements.

The major advantage of an information sharing partnership is that it helps to use data without incurring excessive financial or technological risk. In one case, eighteen mid-sized paper companies developed a global information system that linked them with their key customers and international sales offices. Although the system cost $50 million to develop, it provides speed and quality of response that could not be achieved by any of the individual offices. With sales of nearly $4 billion and the desire to compete effectively in a service business, they felt they should have an on-line, global data interchange with their key customers. Using the shared data system, customers had an instantaneous means of determining the status of their order, or they were able to place new orders which previously took twelve days. At first, the companies were uneasy about sharing proprietary information with big, global competitors. However, the choice is not whether to share data but whether to be left out, as happened in the airline industry.

Examples of Information Sharing

McDonald's Corporation has seized the use of future technology. This fits the image of the United States, where it is believed that new information technologies hold the potential to dramatically change the way their people work. A futuristic, perhaps realistic, scenario may look like this: It is Saturday afternoon. It is lunch time. Children-laden vehicles are pulling into the parking lot. As the car doors are opened and shut, imbedded sensors in the pavement below signal to the kitchen that sixty people have just arrived. A computer orders a robot to place fifty Big Macs onto the grill and place 100 orders of french fries into the fryers. Your order is taken by a computerized sound box (a voice recognition system) that understands dialects. After you have finished telling the machine what you want, an automated beverage-dispensing mechanism fetches your drink by lowering a cup, positioning it under the correct fountain, adding ice, filling it with liquid, and placing a lid on it. You pay for your meal with a debit or charge card and go to the dining room to watch, on a widescreen television, cartoons piped in via satellite.

Kraft USA, in its move toward relationship marketing and customer intimacy, has created the capacity to tailor its advertising, merchandising, and operations in a single store or in several stores within a supermarket chain to the needs of the stores' customers. To do this, Kraft has assembled a centralized information system that collects and integrates data from three sources. The the system collects data from individual stores by consumer purchases (category and product) and correlates these patterns by measuring the effect of displays, price reductions, and the like. Profiles of their customers who have bought specific products over the past several years and their rates of purchase are also provided. A second information data base contains demographic and buying-habit information of customers from 30,000 food stores nationwide. A third set of data, purchased from an outside vendor, contains geo–demographic data by zip code. At Kraft headquarters, the trade marketing team sorts and integrates the information from these data bases, and uses the results to supply sales teams with suggested promotional programs, new product ideas, value-added ideas, and selling tools. For example, the trade marketing team sorted all shoppers into distinct groups, with names such as full-margin shoppers, planners, dine-outs, and commodity shoppers.

DHL Worldwide Express has given their customers a way to track packages by using an interactive voice response (IVR) system based on software agents that let customers use their telephone keypad to instantly find out the status of their package. The IVR system is only one of the information-sharing tracking methods available to their customers. Currently some customers use a PC and a modem to dial into DHL's global tracking system and get the data electronically, using the telephone (or their fax machine) as a shipment tracking tool. The system also notes when a package is not delivered and can track international packages when they clear customs. At least 70 percent of the package-tracking calls received by DHL go through the IVR information management system instead of an agent.

Utilities such as PSE&G (the third largest combined utilities company in the United States) and the Southern California Gas Company face the significant challenge of increasing customer service while controlling costs. These companies have large and diverse customer bases, which make them ideal candidates for the rapid adoption of information-sharing software agent technology. To address this challenge, utilities are seeking information-sharing technologies that can cost-effectively automate information handling and communication tasks within functions such as customer service and human resources. Edify Corporation is a leading provider of agent-based software used to automate the handling, communication, and sharing of information for these companies. Southern California Gas Company, the largest natural gas distribution system in the country, has licensed Edify's Electronic Workforce system to manage the dissemination of critical gas volume notification to its largest customers. PSE&G, with 12,000 employees, uses the Electronic Workforce to automate its human resources function by giving employees easy access to human resource information. Commonwealth Gas serves over 230,000 customers across forty-nine communities in central and eastern Massachusetts. They use the system to access customer account balances, budget plan information, conservation information, credit payment plans, fuel assistance information, and payment location by zip code. In addition, Edify software agents are used to confirm service appointments automatically with customers or notify customers when a representative runs late for a scheduled service appointment.

The Ford Motor Company made major strides in design innovation using a program called Technical Information and Engineering Systems

(TIES). TIES is a highly interactive development environment that includes a customized graphics system, allowing users to create visual representations of customer preferences and other technical factors. The system enables users to view an unlimited number of operations. In addition to the graphics capability, TIES offers many important functions, including the ability to record relationships between requirements, engineering, and strategic competitive position.

Previously, information at Ford was aggregated when it was shared among users. The single most important factor contributing to the success of TIES was that it met the needs of users, had their enthusiastic support, and obtained an almost immediate productivity payback because of time and cost reduction. TIES has been in production a number of years and is considered an important, new process in an industry that traditionally has a long product life cycle. As new automobiles and their components are produced from TIES-assisted designs, Ford anticipates reductions in life-cycle times as well as improvements in product quality. The payoff to Ford is seen in the number of benefits they have achieved.

In another example of information sharing, hotels are considering a jointly-owned reservation system to reduce the high charges of airlines reservation systems. As a group, they expect to achieve significant reductions in charges per reservation. Although partnering is becoming critical to strategy, it will require the support of management. The technological advances in telecommunications have radically changed information flow around the world. With the expansion in the use of fiber-optic cables, satellites, radio, and television, it is possible for people and computers, whether large-scale or personal computers, to communicate with one another in seconds around the world. Modems and computer networks allow use of data, video, and voice communications so that organizations can share technological resources such as printers and computers. Also, they enable organizations to enlarge their operations by reducing time and distance.

The results of these breakthroughs facilitate interorganizational and globally distributed computer systems. These systems permit direct communication and information exchange across organizational and national boundaries. Electronic Data Interchange (EDI) among organizations and their customers, suppliers, and other business partners, is one outcome. Electronic Mail (E-Mail) and Electronic Funds Transfer (EFT) are other benefits. E-Mail allows messages to flow quickly between one point and another, while EFT enables the movement of funds between accounts wherever they are located.

The Society for Worldwide International Funds Transfers (SWIFT) is a long-established, worldwide electronic utility system that permits fully coupled, shared electronic business transactions to take place throughout the world. EFT has revolutionized the world's banking and financial services. Added technological tools, both domestic and worldwide, are accelerating information-product delivery services. For example, Dow Jones News Retrieval Service, Reuters, and McGraw-Hill electronically make news, commodity, financial quotes, and other information available worldwide as soon as it happens.

When Should Group Decision Making Be Used?

The objective of group decision support systems is to combine human intelligence with information technology in order to solve complex organizational problems. A group decision support system (GDSS), which recognizes both human and technical requirements, is best able to facilitate solution of unstructured problems. In addition, groups benefit from computer-based information systems which support electronic meetings. Information Technology can also contribute to achieving a sustainable, competitive market advantage, helping to extend or leverage a company's capability in the field by using scale advantage. Information sharing is becoming increasingly critical because of the cost of coordination and the need for flexibility and responsiveness in information intensive industries.

Organizational Considerations in Information Sharing

Social and group pressures directly affect decisions that are made in an organization. Therefore, the role of information technology is helpful in enhancing productivity and facilitating the use of transorganizational information. The emphasis for group support systems is on usage and not on technology. Given this perspective on information-sharing technologies, how should one go about the design and use of knowledge and data bases so that they can serve more effectively the role of Intelligent Information Support?

The first step in answering this question is to examine the ways that groups are involved in decision making. Managers can choose from a variety of alternative ways of involving groups in their decisions, or they can choose to make decisions alone. There are a number of ways in which managers can involve others in the decision making. The question of which alternative to choose depends on the circumstances related to the decision. What criteria should a manager use in deciding how to decide? The factors often suggested are: the importance or the quality of the decision, the acceptance of the decision by the group, and the time it takes to make the decision. Quality can depend on whether the decision is made alone or by the group. Acceptance of decisions affects the amount of time required or how it will impact on performance effectiveness.

Vroom and Yetton (1973) have suggested five ways in which managers can determine the best way to make a decision in a given situation. They are the following:

1. The manager decides to make the decision alone using the available information.
2. The manager obtains information from employees and then decides on how to solve the problem.
3. The manager shares the problem with employees or a group and obtains ideas and suggestions. The manager decides whether to incorporate employees' suggestions.
4. The manager involves employees as a group in a problem and obtains their collective ideas and suggestions. However, the manager makes the decision.
5. The manager shares the problem with employees as a group, and together they generate and evaluate alternatives and attempt to reach agreement or consensus on a solution.

The manager can then use the following factors to determine which method to employ:

1. The importance of the decision quality
2. The extent to which the manager possesses the information and expertise to make a high-quality decision
3. The extent to which employees have the necessary information to generate a high-quality decision
4. The extent to which the problem is structured
5. The extent to which acceptance or commitment on the part of the employees is critical to the effective implementation of the decision
6. The probability that the manager's decision will be accepted by employees
7. The extent to which employees are motivated to achieve the organizational goals
8. The extent to which employees are likely to be in conflict over preferred solutions

Based on these factors, a manager can use a decision table to determine which method would work best. An example of these rules is presented in Table 4.1. Under the first factor, "decide alone," the decision is not important, and the information or expertise of the leader and subordinates are not critical; the problem is relatively structured, and acceptance by employees is likely even if the manager makes the decision alone. The choice of decision mode can be selected from Table 4.1.

Under the fifth factor, "seek consensus," the manager does not posses sufficient information or expertise to make a high-quality decision alone; the employees possess collectively the necessary information and expertise. Acceptance and commitment, along with expertise, are critical to effective implementation, and employees would probably not accept a unilateral decision by the manager. Table 4.1 suggests that, under these circumstances, the manager should share the problem with employees and work as a group to generate and evaluate alternatives, while attempting to reach a consensus.

Table 4.1
Group Decision Approaches

FACTORS	Decide alone	Obtain Information	Share Problem	Subordinate Influence	Seek Consensus
Importance of decision		X	X	X	
Manager expertise	X				
Subordinate expertise		X	X	X	X
High decision structure	X	X	X		
Acceptance is critical			X		X
Acceptance is probable	X	X			
Subordinates are motivated					X
Potential conflict				X	

PROBLEMS IN GROUP DECISION MAKING

There are a number of problems and pitfalls associated with group decision making. We address this question and discuss the advantages and
disadvantages of using groups for decision making. We show how group
methods, including computer support, can improve the decision-making
process.

An important consideration in group decision making is group structure and how group members approach problems. For some decisions, it
is important for group members to have face-to-face interaction. In other
cases, the inclusion of groups in a decision may be too cumbersome. For
example, when negotiating with a customer about a project, it is generally preferable that an individual carries out the discussion. The size and

composition of the group can also determine whether there should be active participation or whether there is the potential for conflict. Teams or smaller groups are usually more cohesive than larger groups. If the time required to reach a decision is limited, groups may prove cumbersome. On the other hand, Japanese groups feel that time is not the critical element but that involvement and consensus are important in carrying out the decision. Where group members are similar in knowledge, attitudes, needs, and interests, the quality and acceptance of solutions will generally be higher.

Cohesiveness has been considered an important factor in group decision making because it determines how well the group works together. Both size and composition affect group cohesiveness. The larger the group, the more diverse its membership and the more likely that cliques will form, leading to lower the cohesiveness. Members of highly cohesive groups communicate more easily with one another. However, peer pressure can lead to conformity where the group does not allow opposing or unpopular opinions or viewpoints. The potentially negative consequences of conformity are an important consideration in group decision making. A classic instance of the impact of conformity is the Bay of Pigs invasion decision by President John F. Kennedy, in which he was strongly influenced by the opinion of his staff, and the consequence was the failure that ensued.

The Management Challenge of Managing Multiple Networks

The central organization's role in managing multiple network members that have resulted from various forms of partnering, ranging from strategic alliances to licensing of technology, has become mind boggling. The central organization's power over entrances and exits is always exercised with great care; if it were to be used in an arbitrary or self-serving way, the network could split. A tight network is stronger than its weakest member because weak members can be strengthened by training and coaching. Since no individual member can become stronger than the network, splits must be avoided at all costs.

The lack of interest that tight networks show in the "competence criterion" when selecting new partners is symptomatic of a general commitment to the sharing of skills, knowledge, and information. Apple worked with Adobe and Canon to develop a laser jet printer, and Corning linked its knowledge of glass making to BICC, Inc.'s cable-making expertise to produce optical fibers. Nike invites its partners to its Beaverton research site to show them new developments in materials, design, technology, and markets. And Toyota's subcontractors receive training from their central firm and are encouraged to develop their own problem-solving skills.

The Proprietary Information Battle

Proprietary information—a traditional source of corporate power which is jealously guarded—is anathema to the tight network. Members exchange not only hard data but also ideas, feelings, and hunches about market trends. Structure affects the quality of information. Within a hierarchical, integrated structure, knowledge is often power and tends to be transmuted as it is transmitted. In a tight network, knowledge is a common resource, less tainted by its role as a currency of power.

The central firm orchestrates information flows and directs them to where they are needed, but information flows between partners, as well as between partners and the central firm. There is democracy in information access, as well as the network's political and economic balance. But the development of an information-sharing culture is not easy. Lorenzoni and Baden-Fuller (1994) found a number of cases in which alliances failed because partners abused information-sharing privileges. In one case, the delinquent member used network information as an entry ticket to a rival alliance. It is risky for an individual firm to be open with this information, and it will be reluctant to take that risk in the absence of trust and of general commitment to reciprocity.

The Idea of Constrained Intelligence Sharing

Nintendo uses a special kind of "constrained" learning race to foster rapid innovation. For example, with its software designers, it limits the number of contributions each partner can make to three ideas a year. This constraint places the emphasis on the quality of ideas rather than the quantity.

In markets prone to violent, unexpected turbulence, caused by technological change or by shifts in fashion, the virtues of learning races and a culture of internal rivalry are obvious. Lorenzoni and Baden-Fuller (1994) have identified another "network learning" technique used by central firms. A key advantage of the "borrow–lend–develop" technique is that it sends a message to independent inventors that says, "There is no 'not invented here' syndrome at this organization. We are hungry for new ideas, we develop them fast and we pay top dollars."

All the central firms studied by Lorenzoni and Baden-Fuller (1994) have achieved dominance of their sectors by stretching and leveraging modest resources. They have won their battles of stretch and leverage partly by doing the obvious—developing lean production and being agile, flexible, fast, and technically innovative—but mostly by ignoring boundaries between firms and by using the power of cooperation within the value chain to arm it for the fight with rival chains. They have successfully challenged current management's wisdom and avoided many of the well-documented traps that lie in wait for less experienced and less wholehearted alliance markets. The central firm plays the role, not of the strategist, but of the orchestrator of the strategy-formulation process. It is the *glue* specialist, responsible for the creation and maintenance of a strong and energetic network culture that encourages both rivalry and cooperation between members.

STYLE/GROUP INTERACTION

When developing a GDSS it is important to take into account group style and manager interaction. This is shown in Table 4.2. Conflicts between a manager and groups can occur because of their respective decision styles. The Directive and Behavioral styles are most likely to encounter conflict. The Directive's need for power goes counter to the Behavior's need for affiliation or the Conceptual's need for independence. In general, the Analytic and the Conceptual styles will have fewer conflicts with groups. However, an Analytic manager will criticize a Directive group for incomplete work or not "doing their homework." The Analytic manager does not understand the Behavioral group because that group does not use a rational basis for decisions. By understanding style differences, designers of Intelligent Information Support Systems are in a better position to avoid some of these conflicts and can use the GDSS to improve communications.

THE TEAM APPROACH

Because formal organization structures inhibit communication and interaction among personnel, there is a tendency to develop subcultures which are less effective when implementing decisions. Teamwork has been found to eliminate artificial barriers and encourage an openness which

Table 4.2
Group Style Conflicts

Dominant Manager's Style	Dominant Group Style			
	Directive	Analytic	Behavioral	Conceptual
Directive	No conflict	Minimal	Conflict	Conflict
Analytic	Minimal	No conflict	Conflict	Minimal
Conceptual	Conflict	Conflict	No conflict	Minimal
Behavioral	Conflict	Minimal	Minimal	No conflict

improves with the use of formal information systems. Teams tend to share a common goal and to focus energy by emphasizing "self-control" on the part of participants. For example, Nabisco solved their labor problems when factory workers and management joined their efforts to solve a high-tech bakery problem. Also, teamwork produced meaningful results at Gould, where teams and the Total Quality Management approach, that was based on cooperation, were used. This required that management scrap traditional methods and management–labor roles. The results of sharing decision making have resulted in improved performance at Gould.

Many problems are best solved by teams. The questions that need to be answered are, What kind of information do teams prefer, and how will it be best to facilitate effective problem solving? In general, teams prefer verbal information rather than written reports, and are most effective when they are cohesive and interact cooperatively with members who have compatible personalities and decision styles. When they operate under mild-to-moderate pressure, they respond well. Patterns of communication, information available, and the style of leadership significantly affect performance.

Often, teams replace departments or divisions in the organization without boundaries, and they erase group labels. To be effective, however, teams require a leader who can balance the four elements described as authority, task, politics, and identity. In one example of team failure, the leader did not specify a clear authority boundary, and the team reacted by emphasizing an identity boundary. The strong identity boundary kept the team members from developing the task and political boundaries needed to do the job. While authority boundaries are needed, they are designed to define the limits rather than to control the effort.

When teams form cohesive groups, each member responds by being helpful in problem solving. Cohesiveness can be increased when team members feel that they are highly valued and that they work in a cooperative rather than a competitive relationship with each other. Team members prefer having an opportunity for social interactions in small groups. On the other hand, team cohesiveness is reduced when there are false expectations or when a few members dominate. This can lead to disagreement or reduced performance.

Personality or style compatibility is important when trying to achieve cohesiveness in a team. Successful teams seem to follow similar patterns of behavior. For example, it has been shown that airplane crews solve problems better in situations in which the team can make sense out of an initially unstructured, unclear situation. They communicate easily and have a meaningful goal toward which they work.

Teams develop creative collaboration because they communicate across divisions. Flexibility in team-member assignments helps to boost information flow and contribute to consensus decision making. Creative teams utilize computer-based tools such as the following:

1. Brainstorming software
2. IBM's Team Focus tool kit for organizing ideas
3. Electronic voting using Option Finder
4. Electronic Mail for group communication
5. Expert Choice that facilitates exploration of issues
6. Mathematical decision-support programs

Also, an increasing number of new computer programs, including expert systems, graphical-user interface, virtual reality, optical character recognition, voice recognition, semantic networks, and neural nets, are becoming available for use as support tools.

Margerison and McCann (1985) developed an approach to understanding team behavior called the Team Management Index (TMI) that has been used by Hewlett-Packard, Du Pont, Mobil, Shell, and others. The index covers four basic behaviors, including exploring, advising, controlling, and organizing. Research with over 4,000 managers using the TMI has shown that the typical behaviors in teams include the following:

1. *Advising.* Obtaining and disseminating information to others
2. *Innovating.* Being creative and willing to experiment with new ideas and pass them along
3. *Promoting.* Searching for new opportunities and ways to persuade others
4. *Developing.* Assessing how approaches can be applied to a problem pursued by the team
5. *Organizing.* Implementing means for making relationships work, assignments, and organization structure
6. *Producing.* Focusing on procedures that facilitate performance and can be done systematically
7. *Inspecting.* Evaluation of performance to assure it meets goals that have been set
8. *Maintaining.* Ensuring that processes and standards are used consistently

The TMI has been used for team building, as well as for individual development, and in assisting managers to carry out their functions.

For many years, Lincoln Electric has been considered one of the most efficient companies. They manufacture electrical welding machines and alternating current motors. In order to achieve economies of scale, they eliminated nonessential operations and reduced many of the functions that other companies accept as necessary for doing business. They are an excellent example of how a company can perform reengineering or restructuring. Their offices are plain, and there is no elaborate lobby or executive dining room. Paperwork has been eliminated ruthlessly (a goal often sought by information system designers). Jobs that require a great deal of labor but do not add value to the final product are changed or eliminated. The president of Lincoln believes that employees are the most important asset the company has. They search continuously for ways to save time or money, and reward workers on a very generous incentive program. Lincoln Electric is one of the few companies that have successfully kept the Japanese from taking over the electric welding industry in the United States.

HOW KNOWLEDGE IS USED FOR GROUP DECISION MAKING

An emerging concern in group decision making is how to use data and knowledge more effectively. The research on full-sized, knowledge-based systems reported by Silverman and Murray (1990) describes systems for solving problems to assist decision makers who relied previously on teams of experts. The full-sized systems contain multiple knowledge sources along with a modularity-designed architecture. These systems utilize diverse languages, various means for knowledge representation, heterogeneous hardware, and multiple styles of interface. Storey and Goldstein (1990) suggest that what is needed to improve the logical design of a data base is an expert system which elicits user views for the determining requirements for data storage. This approach helps to reduce inconsistencies, ambiguities, and redundancies. They claim that machine learning and knowledge mining will be the next areas that will have explosive growth.

Distributed computer processing allows people to work together more easily and provides room to grow because of greater flexibility and readily available information. Flexibility is becoming increasingly important for maintaining a competitive posture and for adapting computer systems to meet changing needs. New technology and new applications are needed for the implementation of changed structures or operating procedures. The question that is often asked is, How should new technology be introduced? Siegel (1992) recommends that it should be done in an evolutionary manner because of the need for organizational acceptance and the need to reduce the drain on scarce resources.

Groups use knowledge to make decisions in different ways. To design a GDSS, one needs to know what to look for in a given situation or pattern based on facts, criteria, structure, or kinds of judgment used. One must also understand how groups interpret the meaning of knowledge and data. When proposing solutions for groups, the proposals should be based on the experience, knowledge, or reasoning about alternatives, and there needs to be follow through on the implementation of the solutions to assure achieving goals.

There are a number of ways to add intelligence to knowledge and data used by groups. Powerful analytic representations and model-based reasoning can assist in decision making by analyzing and interpreting the significance of available data. Designing an intelligent front end to a knowledge base requires a system architecture that is based on users' decision-making needs. Analysis is required to determine whether information adds value for group decision making. Issues need to be addressed, such as how to integrate heterogeneous knowledge or data bases among groups and how to design an intelligent interface for the knowledge or data base. Where appropriate, natural language retrieval should be used to provide meaningful interpretation of the knowledge or data and to incorporate cognitive aspects of decision making. The speed of response can be enhanced by using patterns or templates to display information, or model-based reasoning can be applied to improve the usage of knowledge.

Intelligent design is critical to maintaining an adequate data base for all the requirements of analysis because transaction data are not always relevant. Event- and object-oriented knowledge bases are now beginning to replace massive storage that is difficult to maintain and that impedes interoperability. Maintaining massive data was precisely the problem that confronted American Express, and they were forced to use an expert system interface to the multiple data bases that they had for their customers.

Information technology will become a requirement for individual and group decision making. This includes problem recognition, formulation, analysis, solution, interpretation, and implementation. New systems will be required to provide all the technology needed by management to provide an integrated system so that individuals or group decision makers will have the best possible information to support their decisions. This technology will include all the various approaches and decision-aiding tools, such as simulation models, expert systems, or various kinds of economic and accounting models. In addition, hardware that will network computers and give access to the same data will also provide displays that will make information more meaningful.

SUMMARY

Groups are becoming increasingly important in today's rapidly changing organizations. Groups are often formed into teams that are being empowered to assume greater job responsibility and that require computer support to be effective in their decision making. In order to achieve the performance that is possible, managers need to understand group behavior, including issues such as cohesiveness and conformity. Because groups function in a different mode than individuals, models such as those proposed by Vroom and Yetton (1973) are helpful in knowing how best to interact with a group. Decision style is helpful in bringing together group members to form cohesive teams. The TMI index provides another measure of the potential effectiveness of teams. Groups and teams, like managers, need decision-support tools that can utilize available knowledge and data more intelligently.

A number of areas need to be improved, including natural-language interface, efficient query and search, and the logic of stored knowledge. Other considerations are the purpose for which knowledge is used and how to augment decision making reasoning power by using expert systems. A number of systems are currently in use that perform these functions. However, these can be enhanced by recognizing the difference between a methodologically efficient approach and intelligent usage. While experts have been the cornerstone for the development of expert systems, an opportunity for augmenting the reasoning power of nonexperts and groups exists which utilizes the expert's knowledge in a more intelligent way, would justify the effort, and would assure the best possible use of available knowledge and data base systems.

BIBLIOGRAPHY

AI + database = Personal Information Manager. 1988. *AIWEEK* (September 1): 9.

Argyris, Chris. 1991. Teaching Smart People How to Learn. *Harvard Business Review* (May/June): 99–109.

Baldwin, William. 1982. This Is the Answer. *FORBES* 130(July 5): 50–52.

Bartino, Jim. 1990. At These Shouting Matches, No One Says a Word. *Business Week* (June 11): 78.

Buss, Martin D. J. 1982. Managing International Information Systems. *Harvard Business Review* (September/October): 153–162.

Comaford, Christine. 1993. Expediting Development with Support Teams. *PC Week* (March 15): 68.

Coy, Peter. 1993. Two Cheers for Corporate Computing. *Business Week* (May): 34.

Dickinson, John. 1991. An Intelligent User Interface Should Possess Business Smarts. *PC/Computing* (May): 52.

Early, Michael D. 1993. Which Way to Client/Server Land? *Beyond Computing* (May/June): 45–48.

Floyd, Steven W. 1992. Managing Strategic Consensus: The Foundation of Effective Implementation. *Academy of Management Executive* 6(4): 27–39.

Griffith, Terri L. 1993. Teaching Big Brother to Be a Team Player: Computer Monitoring and Quality. *Academy of Business Management* 7(1): 73–80.

IBMP2P: Solid Base for Collaborative Computing. 1993. *PC Week* (March 22): 96–99.

Kantrowitz, Barbara. 1993. Eyes on the Future. *Newsweek* (May 31): 39–49.

Katzenbach, Jon R., and Douglas K. Smith. 1993. The Discipline of Teams. *Harvard Business Review* (March/April): 111–120.

Kenney, Ralph L., and Detlof von Winterfeldt. 1989. On the Uses of Expert Judgment on Complex Technical Problems. *IEEE* 36(2; May): 83–86.

Khoshafian, Setrag. 1991. Modeling with Object-Oriented Databases. *AI Expert* (October): 27–33.

Konsynski, Benn R., and F. Warren McFarlan. 1990. Information Partnerships—Shared Data, Shared Scale. *Harvard Business Review* (September/October): 114–121.

Lorenzoni, Gianni, and Charles Baden-Fuller. 1994. Tight Networks. *Transformation—The International Publication of Gemini Consulting* 4(Autumn).

Losee, Stephanie. 1994. Intellectual Capital. *Fortune* (October 3): 68.

Margerison, C. J., and D. J. McCann. 1985. *The Team Management Index*. New Berlin, Wisc.: National Consulting and Training Institute.

Morris, Charles R., and Charles H. Freemason. 1993. How Architecture Wins Technology Wars. *Harvard Business Review* (March/April): 86–96.

Moy, Sandy. 1992. Open Systems: How to Survive the Revolution. *Beyond Computing* (June): 62–63.

Nonaka, Ikujiro. 1991. The Knowledge Creating Company. *Harvard Business Review* (November/December): 104.

Pastrick, Greg. 1991. Brainstorming Software. *PC Magazine* (April 30): 329–333.

Ricciuti, Mike. 1993. Can CA Manage Open Systems? *Datamation* (January 1): 18–23.

Rock, Denny, Sandie Washburn, Dave Purdon, and Alex Houtzeel. 1993. Sharing Knowledge Bases in Industry. *AI Expert* (June): 25–31.

Siegel, William Laird. 1992. Distributed Processing Comes Out Swinging. *Beyond Computing* (May/June): 18–21.

Silverman, Barry G. 1992. Judgement Error and Expert Critics in Forecasting Tasks. *Decision Sciences* 23: 1199–1219.

Stevenson, Ted. 1993. Groupware: Are We Ready? *PC Magazine* (June 15): 267–299.

Storey, Veda C., and Robert C. Goldstein. 1990. An Expert View Creation System for Database Design. *USC Expert System Review* 1: 19–45.

Tapscott, Don. 1991. Open Systems. *Business Week* (October 14): 132–162.

Twombly, Steve. 1993. Client–Server Computing. *Datamation* (June 15): S.1–S.56.

Vroom, Victor H., and Phillip W. Yetton. 1973. *Leadership and Decision-Making*. Pittsburgh: University of Pittsburgh Press.

Walters, John R., and Norman R. Nielson. 1988. *Crafting Knowledge Based Systems*. New York: John Wiley & Sons.

Wreden, Nick. 1993. Regrouping for Groupware. *Beyond Computing* (March/April): 52–55.

Xenakis, John J. 1993. Videoconferencing: Smile, You're on Corporate Camera. *Corporate Computing*: 175–176.

Young, Jeffrey S. 1992. The Virtual Workplace. *FORBES* (November 23): 184–190.

CHAPTER FIVE

□ ❏ □

EMERGING INFORMATION TECHNOLOGIES FOR INTELLIGENT SUPPORT

Meaning of information is in the eye of the beholder.

From their inception, computer-based information systems have had an objective—to provide decision makers with information in a useful form. From the initial developments in management information systems to more current systems' efforts, there has been a constant migration toward the goal of intelligent information support. The development of information systems to support decision making has evolved in the following manner:

1. *Management-information systems.* These systems were used to analyze data based on the reporting of actual operations in a company. Trends, forecasts, or other analysis tools were used, as well as management reports. These could be provided as required, in graphic form or on terminals.

2. *Decision-support systems.* These systems provide the capability of continuous interaction with the computer. Decision makers are able to exercise judgment and insight when formulating problems. They are also able to tap into statistical, economic, and accounting data or models to help analyze data and to produce specific kinds of output.

3. *The automated office.* This application provides written and oral reports and group interaction, as well as teleconferencing and teleprocessing. Decision makers can obtain information from knowledge-based or data base systems. This application supports creative linking, which allows decision makers to exercise judgment on problems that confront them.

4. *Expert systems.* These systems store knowledge in a computer in a form that is readily available and can be retrieved. Decision makers can exercise judgment or utilize embedded rules that experts have previously supplied. Expert systems have been used as decision advisors for solving complex problems.

5. *Intelligent Information Systems.* These are the systems of the future which will provide continuous interaction and evaluation of the decision environment. They will be able to provide early warnings, timely information, and analysis for managers who are not involved with ongoing operations. Decision makers will have access to any level of details that exist in every organization and will be alerted to important events that require decisions. In these systems, reasoning and judgment will become increasingly important, as will understanding the cognitive style of the decision maker. Information and knowledge will be matched to the requirements of the decision maker. By adding intelligence to the information, these systems act as decision advisors.

Current information systems support decision making superficially—although efforts are underway to ameliorate this situation. Lotus Development introduced the personal information manager, which allows facts to be entered into an "Agenda" data base in natural, free-form units called "items," without the normal structure required in the typical data base system. Lotus "Agenda," as previously described, assists the user by applying intelligence to the expert's knowledge, based on contextual cues and historic information needed to perform logical inferences. Inference Corporation is using a self-learning approach that relies on case-based reasoning to derive rules for solving complex problems. Intelligent User Interfaces are moving in the direction of increasing the intelligent use of data and knowledge-based systems. One system, developed by Verity, uses haystack searching to facilitate target text retrieval.

THE IMPORTANCE OF TECHNOLOGY

Most industries have to stay abreast of the latest technology in order to stay competitive. Where consumers demand new technologies, that becomes the driving force leading to change. For example, three-dimensional virtual reality could revolutionize product design and manufacturing because designers can vastly improve products by visualizing change. The Boeing 777 was the first plane designed completely by Computer-Aided Design and Computer-Aided Manufacturing (CAD/CAM). Sony is a company where engineers develop four new products every day by turning generalists loose to work on advanced products. Their engineers and scientists work long hours, but they keep Sony a top technological company. To keep abreast of new technology, Sony spends $1.5 billion per year, which is 5.7 percent of their revenues. U.S. Surgical is another company that utilizes technology to maintain a competitive advantage. They rely on customers for many of their new product ideas. Their salespeople go to operating rooms or doctors' offices to find what new technology or new products are needed. U.S. Surgical was the first company to develop a user-friendly surgical stapler that has revolutionized closing wounds. They experienced a hundredfold increase in stock value from 1987 to 1992.

Companies such as IBM, Toshiba, and Siemens are working together to develop new technology for computer components. They expect to spend over $1 billion in order to develop advanced semiconductors and advanced manufacturing processes. They recognize that in the highly competitive computer market the way to sustain competitive advantage is to be in the lead for the next generation of advanced memory chips. Taking a note from these competitors, Fujitsu and Advanced Micro Devices have invested $700 million for development of new technology.

THE ROLE OF TECHNOLOGY

Where decision problems are too complex to solve because of their size, a computer, supported by an Intelligent Information System, can provide the manager with the necessary means for dealing with complex problems. The computer has had its major impact to date on an organization's internal environment. However, there are four other areas that need to be considered. They are the following:

1. Past data reflect the evolution of information systems. Historic data were used for data management as the principal input for operating management.

2. *Management Information Systems (MIS)*. These utilized current data that were stored in a data base to provide support for management decisions.

3. *Real-Time Data*. This is often considered synonymous with instant information and is available in time for current needs. It might actually be an hour, a week, or a month, rather than instantaneous. This kind of information is needed for adaptive response, which requires continuous modification to accommodate new needs or new requirements.

4. *Intelligent Information Systems*. Intelligent information is used as the basis for improving decision making by providing managers with projections, analysis, and forecasts of the probable impact of alternative decisions. They focus on the decision makers at the individual level (see Chapters 2 and 3), groups at another level (see Chapter 4), and the organization as a whole (see Chapter 6).

USE OF INFORMATION

Table 5.1 shows typical decisions that relate to management requirements. The external environment involves constant change, and there is

Table 5.1
Computer Support and Related Information Use

	Data Management	Management Information Systems	Real Time Information	Intelligent Informtation Systems
	Operating decisions	Company decisions	Adaptive decisions	Strategic decisions
External Information				
Unstructured environment (Turbulent conditions)	Program control, government regulations, competition	Production control, engineering design, spoilage	Research management, data storage, cash flow	New produ developme resource planning, investmen
Interface Information				
Semi-structured environment (Uncertain conditions)	Forecasts, market surveys, consumer analysis	Market analysis budget variance, resources	Inventory control, procurement control, logistics	Global competiti new prod developm research
Internal Information				
Structured environment (Certain/risk conditions)	Cost control, work order control, inventory	Performance measures, worker turnover, capacity	Quality control, production control, value	Total qu managen robotics, outsourci product
Organization Information				
Leadership and culture (Changing conditions)	Output, closeness, stability, trust, structure	Motivation, confidence, groups, change, development	Human resource management, team interface	Informat sharing, graphica interface flexibilit

a need for more rapid access to current information as well as a need to forecast external events. With rapid access to information, managers can have current information, (see MIS column). Management Information Systems provide managers the data and analysis needed to maintain control and evaluate performance.

Real-time information systems, which are required for adaptive response, reflect the needs of current operating decisions. As conditions change in production or quality and in cost or procurement, there is need for rapid, accurate, and appropriate response to the problems that arise. The data are required that can effectively deal with problems "in time," which is real time. "Instantly available information" does not imply instant response. On-line information is a better description. For example, when the telephone is used, we expect a dial tone when we lift the receiver. If a switch is flipped, we expect the light to go on. We want something that is continuously available on line. This is instant response because the dial tone is instantly available. If we should flip a switch for an information display, we would expect it to respond when we flip it. Rapid access information is often needed when purchasing an airline ticket. The person flying is unwilling to wait but wants instant response to an inquiry.

The IIS column deals with future projections, or determining the impact or consequences of decisions. It is concerned with strategic decisions. However, a real-time system also utilizes decision and simulation models which provide this capability. If we consider future strategies and projections as key ingredients determining the direction in which the company needs to move, then we see how important corporate models and other decision models, such as expert systems, are to the manager. Looking at some of the decisions in this column—new products, resource planning, investments, growth, mergers, market research, proposals, product life cycle, human resources, organizational development, motivation, automation, robotics, product mix, global competition—we see the very lifeblood of the organization. Each of these decisions determines the destiny of the firm because if the product is no longer competitive, if there is no growth, if the resources are improperly applied, if human resources are not used effectively, and if there is no motivation, then the organization cannot hope to be effective. These decisions are both critical and complex. They require considerable study and understanding when designing Intelligent Information Systems. The number of successful applications to date gives considerable credibility to the statement that future-oriented strategic forecasts will become a regular and important aspect of intelligent information support for managerial decision making.

An important design consideration is the cost of on-line and future intelligent systems. Typically, costs increase exponentially for rapid access systems, but the value contributed may not be sufficient. To be effective, information systems' design will have to be matched with the decision-making requirements and the need for rapid adaptive response in the situation. Walsh (1994) points out that being infallible is not the point because infallibility can be "paralysis by analysis." He recommends being quick and right more often than wrong.

Much has been said about the impact of the computer on management, the change of organizational structure, and the change in the way that decisions will be made. However, all the evidence to date indicates that although the organization structure is changing, it is becoming increasingly critical for decision making to have direct access to intelligent information. As this information becomes widely available, the concept of adaptive response, or the ability to meet new and continuously changing requirements in a more effective manner, will become as commonplace as today's management decision making.

Adaptive response is the emerging and most challenging aspect of decision making. Not only does it involve a change in the way that organizations respond to meet the continuous array of demands, but it requires the application of sophisticated technology, including the following: (1) intelligent data and knowledge-based design; (2) intelligent output displays (virtual reality) and terminal access using graphical-user interface; and (3) remote teleprocessing and sharing of computers from remote locations, such as in client–server networks. In many respects, these requirements will force a change in the way in which managers operate.

ADDING INTELLIGENCE TO DATA BASES

A knowledge-based design implemented at the UCLA Medical Center illustrates how a patient information system, located in many different data bases which were difficult to query from newly installed workstations, were integrated into a single, more user-friendly system. Applying a case tool, Integration Works, and a SUN computer, Chu and Cardenas (1993) were able to build communication scripts and data translators for interrogation of the multiple data bases. This allowed inquiries to be more efficient.

Considerable effort has been devoted to developing more effective means for utilizing stored knowledge. This includes knowledge mining, self-learning, and rule induction. However, while these efforts move the field forward technically, a key element that is not explicitly considered is how decisions are made and what is the most effective basis for storing knowledge so that it has direct applicability to improving decision making. Adding this requirement to knowledge bases and data bases requires knowing or "adding" intelligence to what is needed in the data base and how best to utilize existing knowledge.

Support for intelligent information requires access to available data. Intelligent retrieval is based on both context and relevance to the use under consideration. King (1995) developed an approach that relies on the following:

1. Structural relevance: Query is based on importance of the location. Rules can be developed that determine relevance and knowledge about a document.
2. Document linkage: Both internal and external document structures provide guidance for relationships among groups of documents that have similar information.
3. Glossaries of words: Glossaries provide input on the quality, completeness, and relevance or consistency of the desired application.
4. Searchable information: This creates a composite of the target documents and represents a network of the documents being searched. Browsing can be used to find the specific information desired.
5. Similarity assessment: Use of previous searches to determine future needs. Similarity measurements assist in matching and linking new queries to prior results.

The complex information superhighway will require intelligent search and query capability to successfully determine the context and relevancy of the information.

Data mining has become a useful approach for accessing valuable information that resides in a data base. In order to retrieve the information, however, clean data are needed, along with powerful warehousing strategies, parallel processes, and available hard disk space. Tools are available to cleanse and transform data into error free, consistently formatted data. Special servers or powerful parallel processors help both to store and access available information. Having this information readily available assists the decision maker in projecting sales, finding customers, determining capacity requirements, and other areas of interest (Krivda, 1995).

As new data base technologies emerge, it will become possible to integrate reasoning ability. For example, programming has been applied to rapid prototyping and specifying system behavior based on the use of expert systems. Knowledge engineering integrates reasoning by making information explicit and encoding it into a computer program or knowledge base. However, to reason intelligently about data, one will need to connect many different data bases. This is because relationships among data elements form a powerful means for examining declarative knowledge. Data-intensive expert systems require reasoning based on real-time access to existing data.

In order for Intelligent Information Systems to facilitate decision making and respond to new conditions, an understanding of causality between requirements and actions is needed. For example, the reason for deviations from current procedures must be determined so that appropriate corrective action can be incorporated. There is also a need to forecast the impact of decisions and their criticality upon economic success in order to know how to best implement a change. For example, farmers used to "guesstimate" the average yield of an entire field; but since Massey Ferguson, a Canadian farm equipment and machinery company, developed a yield mapping system, they can practice small-scale farming on a large scale and maximize the yield of each square yard in every field. The system links the farmer's tractor to a satellite-based Global Positioning System, which records the latitude, longitude, and yield of every square yard. Data are automatically sent to a farmer's desktop computer, which generates yield maps that show where variations are above or below target. The farmer can then investigate selected areas and pinpoint the reasons for the variations (e.g., soil compaction or nutrient imbalance), quantify them in financial terms, and find out if it is financially feasible to implement remedies. Today, this knowledge-based system is being used to provide a competitive edge. In the future, it may be worth more to Massey Ferguson's primary business. The basic requirement in the design of Intelligent Information Systems is to ensure that flexibility and variability in use of data are incorporated. This foremost requirement signifies a new approach to data gathering, data storage, and information retrieval. The data base design must become increasingly "intelligent."

An example of an intelligent data base design relied on an extended data base logic that could accommodate complex objects. This was accomplished by using a deductive data base to replace the current relational data bases in use. More recent applications, such as engineered data bases, use hierarchic structures, called "complex objects," because they allow direct representation of complicated structures. Deductive data bases contain facts and rules that allow for the derivation of other facts which yield important capabilities for extracting knowledge. Logic programming languages, such as Prolog, are closely related to what is incorporated in a deductive data base. There is also a direct connection between logic programming and complex objects.

Concepts involving deductive data bases, complex objects, logic programming, and data base logic represent an important advance in information technology. Extended data base logic is another approach that is suitable for use in hierarchic, network, and deductive data bases, and with complex objects. This capability is useful for the study of complex objects. Hypertext is also a powerful approach that has been used for interactive inquiry into text material in data bases. It can quickly follow documents without losing the original context. Hypertext software has four types of links: hierarchical, keyword, referential, and cluster. An extension of hypertext is hypermedia, which is more inclusive than hypertext. It incorporates other media, such as video, animation, and graphics.

In order to have an intelligent data base system, three thrusts are needed to accomplish the goal. First, the data base requires modeling power so as to be able to provide a richer and more accurate representation of the applications. The second capability is to enhance the data base so that it can handle expert systems' rule-based inference requirements. Finally, data bases should support interoperability of multiple, autonomous, and heterogeneous systems.

The attributes desired when adding intelligence to a data base would include natural-language inquiry capability, activity- or problem-oriented knowledge representation, and reasoning about the data or knowledge stored. A system called Front End for Data Bases (FRED) combines data base expertise with an intelligent user interface. The system supports query formulation and provides systematically correct dialogue. It allows queries on a conceptual level versus a factual level, such as values of objects, and automatically investigates the data base in a language that is independent of the logic used to store the data. FRED is a meaning-representation language that has a broad view of the data base domain that allows complex queries as well as grouped or nested queries.

In addition to developing an intelligent data base, the interface and storage logic, as well as ease-of-user applications can be significantly improved. For example, Jeffreys and Berger (1992) point out that one could apply Ockham's Razor, an heuristic that considers the "simplest" hypotheses which are consistent with the data, as a basis for search. Relying on a Bayesian analysis, they show that the intuitive notion of using simple explanations is generally better than complicated ones. When the "purpose" of using the data is known, the system can draw inferences related to the purpose from the data base.

Intelligence can be added to data in the form of activity hierarchies for more effective usage. This means that activities would be stored so that they become relational data–information–knowledge hierarchies. For example, project status could have embedded all the details necessary for reporting output. A user could point to an activity and "bring up" any details desired. When predetermined formats or templates are required, they can limit the ability to query data bases. When a system is required to support any type of decision without knowing what data may be required, the usability of these systems is limited again. An expert system acting as an assistant could evaluate data searches and use the decision maker's personal habits to come up with an assessment of the likelihood of the person requesting certain kinds of data. Over time and with learning, this could eventually provide an intelligent filter for data base queries.

Intelligent data base design provides meaning or significance to the information retrieved rather than merely providing data. Patterns among knowledge elements can be displayed in a form that adds meaning to the knowledge retrieved. Pattern recognition offers a meaningful alternative to having to interpret stored knowledge. The ability to reason with facts among many objects is called a *pattern*. Patterns are also used to describe what is contained in an object base. For example, one could determine whether there was only one active customer, and could refer to multiple sources of information to support this conclusion. A computer program could retrieve all active customers, and other subobjects of a global object, by using a specific characteristic or attribute of the objects.

To develop an intelligent data base, a number of support functions are needed. These include the following:

1. Query that can be done in a natural language dialogue mode
2. Query on a conceptual level which requires that stored knowledge be related to a specific problem
3. Automatic data base selection in response to a query
4. Automatic specification of data retrieval commands to achieve a specified objective
5. Portability in order to access different data base systems
6. The ability to integrate different data formats

Event-Oriented Data Base Design

A number of approaches can be used for adding intelligence to knowledge and data. The Pareto Law can be used to partition knowledge into "currently significant" information versus "archival information," needed only for reference or audit. Kandelin (1990) suggests that in order to have intelligence added to data one has to form an "events data base." As economic events occur, they are recorded in the data base. The intelligence component is based on updating reports automatically as new data–information–knowledge in the form of events is recorded. The key to this approach is the idea of predetermined report content, which is then updated as new information is received. This automated updating serves to "signal" the users of changes in activities that may be of interest and concern. Relevant data are quickly and efficiently put into use, while data that are not relevant (no predetermined report) are ignored.

In Kandelin's approach, it is necessary to determine where data information of lesser importance should be stored, if at all. Large-scale data bases could be scanned by using images. Images of data that were not relevant would be kept in permanent archival storage on devices such as optical disks. If such data were ever needed to support an audit or provide backup or other support, they would then be retrieved. For example, American Express processes all credit card transactions by image processing and stores all of these scanned images. What should be stored and how long they should be stored are the real issues for a large-volume transaction processor. An intelligent solution is required.

This approach includes the information needed to identify a transaction, economic information, resource information, and economic events. No inferencing is done at this level of processing. Facts about an event are recorded in the event data base in a way to facilitate their retrieval. The primary purpose of having an event data base is to be able to reports events to a knowledge-based system.

Using the event data base as an integral part of the knowledge-based system, Kandelin proposes a composite model of how intelligence can be added to knowledge and data prior to the storing of event data rather than use an expert system to manipulate the data after it is stored. This adds intelligence to data before it is stored.

Another issue in intelligent storage of data is that multiple agents or participants may have differing needs for a common set of data. Managers may only need exception data for making decisions but auditors may want to see all the data and the interrelationships among data for purposes of evaluating systems and data integrity. However, not all data are evaluated in the same way that they are used by managers. A framework or methodology for determining the relative merits of which data to retain or which to discard is where intelligence is added to data storage.

The problem of multiple uses of elemental data is explored by Essin (1993), who concludes that most present systems are "over specified." A broad range of applications utilizing data in an elemental form is required, which is deliberately "under specified" so that semantic information can be added at any time. Essin examines a number of medical data base applications and finds that they deal primarily with events, activities, and interactions concerning people. Over-specified data occur when the structures are represented in such detail that they cannot be used in multiple applications. He refers to this condition as "static binding" and proposes an entity-event model that separates semantic representations of reality from elemental data. This approach relates to case-based reasoning, which uses data for contract bid preparation and relationships among data which are not known in advance. By developing an appropriate algorithm, similarity between elemental data can be determined and applied for large data bases.

Adding intelligence to a knowledge or data base can be achieved by using powerful analytic representations and model-based reasoning to assist the decision maker in analyzing and interpreting the significance of the knowledge. Designing an intelligent front end to a knowledge base will require a system architecture that is explicitly based on user needs and on information that adds value to decision making. The logic of design will relate an intelligent interface to the knowledge-based structure and have the capability of integrating heterogeneous knowledge bases. Natural-language retrieval will assist in obtaining meaningful interpretation of the knowledge or data that incorporates the cognitive capability or orientation of the decision maker. With a constantly changing environment, flexibility and adaptability to meet new conditions and speed of response will be incorporated in information displayed.

Activity-Oriented Data Base Design

A system developed by Ensoft Corporation was designed to integrate logistics into a maintenance management system in order to assure a cost-effective approach that operated with a common data base. This system provided the capability for determining the status of schedules, reliability, quality, and maintenance at any point in the project lifecycle. The value of this approach is that it links users, contractors, subcontractors, and other responsible organizations with a data base that has full functionality integration.

This type of data base system incorporates a major shift that focuses on the "activities" performed rather than on entities, objects, or semantic nets. Activities have time-dependent, cumulative values based on other activities. This approach takes a problem-oriented perspective rather than a technical orientation, as used in object-oriented programming.

With front-end inquiry languages, such as Digital's Content-Based Retrieval Solutions, knowledge can be scanned based on text, numerics, images, and graphics, regardless of format or storage. The program searches by content or subject and extracts only the information required. The natural language data base connection becomes a process of moving from nonlinguistic representations of reality. A system developed in Quintus PROLOG allows multiple inferencing from a knowledge or data base. It searches for inconsistencies, patterns among entities, and relationships among a large number of areas of interest. The expert system front end, using natural language, gives the user summaries of the information in the data base, along with conclusions that can be inferred when using an expert system. Based on a set of "semantic concepts," Frost (1993) developed a scheme for representing abstract notions in various ways using syntactically different notations. This system requires automatic maintenance of the semantic integrity of knowledge represented, efficient methods of retrieval, and multiple uses of the knowledge by translating natural language into statements in standard form.

In a report on the full-sized, knowledge-based systems research workshop, Silverman and Murray (1990) describe systems that attempt to solve problems in large, multifaceted domains. Their purpose was to assist decision making that previously was performed by teams of experts. The full-sized systems contain multiple knowledge sources, along with a modularly designed architecture. These systems utilize diverse languages, various means for knowledge representation, heterogeneous hardware, and multiple styles of interface.

Knowledge discovery in real knowledge-based data bases is described by Shapiro and Hughes (1992), in which Michie predicted that machine learning (knowledge mining) will be the next area that will have explosive growth. Eliciting user views for the determination of requirements for storage eliminates inconsistencies, ambiguities, and redundancies which humans can readily detect and resolve. Building a knowledge base should be done prior to determining which search techniques to utilize. Initially, senior managers who are responsible for strategic decisions and for other managers will likely be involved in the design of storage systems. Where managers and professionals participate directly in the knowledge-based efforts, they are able to identify opportunities for improving usability of the stored information.

A more effective logic of data base design incorporates expert judgment that is needed in complex technical problems. Judgment is used to determine what is needed, to decide what data are relevant to interpret results, and how best to analyze the problem. Considering the importance of converting data to knowledge, the extension of data base logic to complex objects and deduction is a means for deriving meaning from facts and rules in order to obtain new facts. This is an example of how an expert advisor can help to augment the decision maker's reasoning power. Pacific Telesis, in San Francisco, and Nynex, in New York, have developed a management *flight simulator* to teach systems managers about the fast-changing telecommunications marketplace. The goal is to get managers to think differently, to focus on the marketplace, and to take a holistically integrated view of business. Pacific Telesis and Nynex are using the Telesim System for exploring and discovering the holistic meaning and implication of strategies, not for predicting what will happen with a particular strategy. Telesim displays its simulated world in the following three ways: (1) an interior view depicts the world inside a telecommunications company; (2) the landscape view presents the company's sales and service regions; and (3) the marketplace view emerges from the landscape to represent marketplace opportunities and vulnerabilities. The program presents conflict scenarios in a true-life form, with realistic details and surprises. The program does not resolve conflict but represents problems, tradeoffs, competitors, and regulations similar to those that managers face in the real world. Telesim enables managers to pilot a company through a simulated market by overseeing operations, maneuvering the business toward regulatory openings or away from technological threats, marketing new products, acquiring companies, balancing budgets, and negotiating competing interests within the organization. Managers are then able to watch the consequences of their actions on the computer screen.

Table 5.2 provides a comparison of a number of approaches that have been used with knowledge-based systems. Case-based reasoning uses stored knowledge to help formulate expert decision rules for use in expert systems. The disadvantage is that case-based knowledge represents historic information. Where conditions have changed, the decision rules would either require modification or no longer be applicable. Genetic algorithms can be used for a variety of problems and are more flexible than case-based reasoning because genetic algorithms are not limited to past decisions. These algorithms are fairly structured and do not incorporate judgment or model-based causality.

Multimedia introduces an entirely different dimension into the question of intelligent knowledge-based query. Using tools such as hypertext,

Table 5.2
Comparison of Knowledge-Based Systems Approaches

Knowledge based systems	Advantage	Application
Case-based reasoning	Based on prior experience, the system helps to formulate answers to comparable problems.	Helps to classify problems and provide useful answers for complex problems.
Genetic algorithms	Uses a sophisticated approach to formulate algorithms that facilitate finding answers.	Has been applied to financial/credit scoring and bio-technology analysis.
Multimedia	Integration of graphics, text, sound, and video which increases understanding of data or knowledge.	Used to maintain and document knowledge-based systems for training and marketing.
Virtual reality	Creates a 3-D environment that can simulate complex shapes and movement of objects.	Used for remote operations and process control and design of complex objects.
Neural Nets	A complex of nodes and layers of electrical connections where the network learns and provides responses to complex problems.	Initially used for pattern recognition, it is now applied to solve credit problems and provide financial analysis.
Fuzzy Logic	A means of treating information which allows a range of possibilities to be examined that are not simply zero or one.	A departure in the use of information for classifying interpreting results and design of efficient equipment.

FRED, or PROLOG, the decision maker relies on judgment and reasoning to determine the meaning of the knowledge retrieved. Graphics and sound enhance the user's ability to interpret the meaning and applicability of knowledge retrieved. Virtual reality extends the graphic capability of multimedia by allowing manipulation of the graphics retrieved.

Neural networks add learning to knowledge supplied. The problems do not need as structured an approach as genetic algorithms or case-based reasoning. On the other hand, neural nets are complex to program, and the output requires a well-defined approach to interpret the results. Nets have the potential of enhancing the knowledge they are provided. Fuzzy logic recognizes that all data and knowledge is imprecise and that conclusions drawn need to consider the reliability of the information that was retrieved. It adds another dimension to knowledge utilized.

It is not sufficient to access knowledge using powerful approaches such as objects or semantic networks. Representation schema are needed which have flexible control structures and which can deal with uncertainty, fuzzy logic, errors, incomplete knowledge, or even misinformation. A number of approaches have been tried, such as the Orion object-oriented data base developed by NCR, or the Mermaid program that allows modularity in object-oriented knowledge bases. These approaches can be used for knowledge bases where there are problems of concurrence, consistency, ownership, inheritance, connectivity, integration, and coupling. While these represent formidable technical advances, the question that remains is how to utilize knowledge more intelligently so that individuals or groups make better decisions.

MERGING KNOWLEDGE-BASED SYSTEMS
AND DECISION-SUPPORT SYSTEMS

Even though decision-support systems (DSS) and knowledge-based systems have evolved separately, there is now increasing impetus to merge the two into knowledge-based, intelligent decision-support systems. Decision-support systems are mechanisms for assuring that organizational decision making is consistent with overall organizational goals. The latest systems have been enacted in lower management as the new paradigms of management are being instituted. These systems are a check on lower management decision making, assuring that the decisions made match those of the organization. The automation of the office and the addition of decision-support systems in the organization have made today's businesses more efficient and interactive between offices (Houdeshel, Rainer, and Watson, 1992; Urban and Starr, 1991). Appendix A identifies potential application areas for knowledge-based decision-support systems (KBDSS). This process has been used mainly within the financial areas of an organization, but it has a promising future in aiding the intelligent decision-making processes in market-driven organizations that are flattening the pyramid (Burn, 1990).

Decision-support systems use facts and formulae which can give the *right* answers given appropriate input data. However, management most often has to deal with uncertainties and somewhat vague concepts. Intelligent knowledge-based systems can help by capturing, structuring, validating, and disseminating market knowledge, and, at a conceptual level, challenging their creators to understand and critically evaluate the elements of market-driven knowledge and their interrelationships. The objective in utilizing knowledge-based systems as a tool for strategic management is to build more effective, logical methods of applying heuristics, judgment, and intuition to resource allocation, new product and service development and evaluation, pricing, channel management, and competitive strategy. Knowledge-based systems can improve the odds for market-management success by deploying learned knowledge based on past successes, failures, and lessons learned. They have great potential to alter management practices, especially those involving recurring decisions. Development tools for knowledge-based systems are now available, making the widespread deployment of this technology very likely in the present decade.

CLIENT–SERVER NETWORKS

Enterprise-wide computing has propelled organizations forward in their use of new computer technology. With the changes comes a new set of architectural and organizational problems. If an organization is not yet sure of the need for client–server networks, the state of the art in enterprise-wide computing, it has only to consider the Integrated Management Information System (IMIS) of the United Nations. The United Nations struggled to get everybody in their building to connect electronically. It soon realized that it was time to connect the world with a client–server network. The IMIS was not an alternative communication technology to paper and telephones, but it involved the synchronization of multiple data sources and the linking of them to several mainframes. The mainframes using an IMIS will integrate human resources, budgeting, financial statements, and logistic operations at the United Nations. It involves the standardization of worldwide accounting systems, establishment of responsibility centers, and the standardization of procedures.

Client–server networks are not to be confused with monolithic architectures where a set of interrelated programs run requests on a single platform. Simultaneous processing of local data and networked file services of clients are often confused with client–server networks. Client–server networks segregate clearly the requester system or the client from the supplier or the server. The architecture is many-to-one, and data, as well as processing and presentation, are all distributed to appropriately-sized powerful platforms. The major advantage of client–server networks is the separation of production and operations, which require streamlined data, from decision support, which requires a great deal of processing, manipulation, and sharing of diverse data.

Client–server networks take into account the data needs of different parts of the organization and provide access intelligently to all who need information. An illustration is the analysis of warranty claim information in an organization. Corporate quality is interested in aggregate dollar amounts to predict and explain future costs. However, engineering requires detailed information on failure modes and components used. To handle this scenario intelligently, a client could request the appropriate information from the server, which would collect the data from its various sites. The actual processing and formatting of the information would be left to the client's platform, and requesters can customize the information according to their needs. Most organizations, like First Boston, have turned to distributing tasks in this manner; they have outgrown capacity and processing capability using their current technology. First Boston now has a client–server network that has resulted in their traders processing investments seven times faster than they did previously. The client requests a list of appropriate investments from a central server. Once the choice is made, the trader customizes the report on a workstation equipped with faxing capabilities.

Organizations, such as United Behavioral Systems (a medical enterprise), have realized the perils of physically dispersed sites carrying piecemeal and redundant data. They have linked their isolated clinics into a three-tier architecture with immediate feedback on insurance and patient history. While their preference was the proven capability of Unix networks, they were unwilling to replace the personal computers (PCs) in the clinics with expensive workstations. The relatively inexpensive solution was XWindows emulation software that provided the appropriate communication protocol. Now the local PCs do everything from statistical tracking and patient evaluation services to scheduling appointments. The ProvNet took an amazingly short period of nine months to develop. Unix was confined to engineering because it lacked desktop utilities, standardization, and portability. However, current standard software is available so that the speed, storage, and connectivity make Unix the best network platform. Unix is reliable and serves the large-scale networking for critical and core organizational processes. This is no longer an issue considering the platforms in use, such as Macintosh's in Design, Unix in Engineering, and IBM's Everywhere Else. All of these can communicate using client–server architectures.

Organizations that have ventured into client–server networks recognized that the costs, that may have created doubts as to the value of the technology, are not as great as the cost of programming, retraining, and man-hours of network management. Hidden costs occur when people who are not computer experts take over supporting their local networks, thereby reducing their own work productivity. Also, client–server networks most often provide only long-term savings. The key to controlling client–server costs is the decision to decentralize the architecture. Data base storage uses hierarchical management, where data that is used often is kept closest to the user. Where there are commonalties and data sharing, centralized architectures can be more effective because local data access and processing would merely slow down a centralized server. Good architectures do not necessarily have completely connected servers and clients. This can overload the Wide-Area Networks (WANs), while boundary routers which connect clients to many large centers allow decentralized architectures. Because over one-third of the cost is in WAN transmission, an appropriate network design can significantly reduce expenditures (Hurwicz, 1994).

Development costs can be kept within bounds by using available business applications, such as Object-Oriented Programming. The advantage of generic programming is that it is essentially vendor free, so that the entire business logic does not have to be redone when multimedia or 3-D Graphical-User Interfaces are implemented. Project management can also benefit from client–server because it facilitates the simultaneous tracking of tasks and the monitoring of project performance. Team effort is enhanced when using client–server, and individual productivity is improved when using Object-Oriented Programming because they help reduce development time and add value. Among the options that exist today, there is a tradeoff between the power of the tool and the ease of learning new programming languages.

The current era of computer usage could be characterized as being an "information utility," in which the use of super-fast Reduced Instruction Set Computing (RISC) architecture computers deliver enormous power at a low cost. Organizations such as Blockbuster use only Intel processors for maintaining their suppliers and providing consumers with in-store CD-ROM capability in order to listen to the music. Communication standards are providing unprecedented portability among vendors' products. Inadequate bandwidth, which in the past resulted in slow transmission on the utility of networks, has been rectified by fiber channels that significantly speed up WANs and Local-Area Networks (LANs). Powerful data base languages, expert systems, case-based software, and business reengineering are responsible for powerful computing capability at low cost.

These technical developments will give users the capability to shape their computer systems to meet specific needs. Ultimately, the success of a new client–server system depends on acceptance by the organization. The client–server tools should be selected "with the user" instead of the traditional "for the user" approach. This will ensure that the tools are cost effective in terms of the customization that the user will perform on the server. User familiarity can be encouraged by using telephone trouble-shooting personnel to walk users through network problems. Both technical and managerial issues need to be addressed when deciding on client–server operations. Successful implementation of the client–server systems can be achieved with the following steps:

1. Define the scope of the system and projected costs.
2. Identify performance measurements and define evaluation criteria.
3. Identify tangible benefits and value contributed.
4. Recognize the differences in business, management, and technical objectives and constraints.
5. Specify projected current and planned IT resources required.
6. Define organizational impact and a plan to manage the changes.
7. Define insourcing, outsourcing, hardware, software, and technology options by doing the following:
   - Identify the computing platform desired.
   - Identify the telecommunications technology to be used.
   - Identify the information and customization requirements of all clients.
   - Identify the use and frequency of cooperative processing.
8. Identify the support and training plans that will maximize the acceptance of the new system among internal users as well as customers.

The value derived from client–server networks will depend on how well the design fits the needs of the organization. An awareness that network complexity can jeopardize data integrity mandates the articulation and acceptance of the design by the organization. Also, security issues cannot be ignored, and new technologies developed for secure access need constant review. Users knowledge represents the lowest level of security. It can be augmented by electronic keys and biometric authentication, such as retinal and fingerprint scanners, which are flooding the market. Care must be exercised because security measures can be cumbersome to the user and extremely expensive for the organization.

As organizations move toward client–server architectures or enhance existing technologies, they should focus on not only what kinds of topologies are available but also on how users are capitalizing on their networks. It is a primary function of system management to avoid potential calamities where people use the wrong platform to run their applications in this shared and resource-restricted environment. Intelligent design and use of client–server occurs when we go beyond the traditional method of looking at what people need to do their jobs ad placing technology to meet that need. Intelligence comes with recognizing that technology will change how people do their jobs and what they need to do their jobs. Business processes and technology can no longer be treated in isolation of each other.

DOCUMENT MANAGEMENT SYSTEMS

Document handling has benefited from computer support and better technology. Most of the effort to date has focused on increasing the space available, the access, and the distribution of "codified" information. The requirement of "codifyability" has constrained what has been stored on a computer and what has been left as a paper trail. Organizations are now "uncovering the hidden 90 percent" cost of the information in their business by using current Document Management Systems (DMS). Law firms have been forerunners in the use of DMS because of the time savings, faster response, and lower staffing requirements gained by options such as full-text retrieval and document assembly programs. Sun Microsystems used an innovative approach in its DMS, called SunSolve, for its technical personnel who are bombarded by thousands of phone calls from users each day. Providing staff with the ability to look up the user's problem or solution with superior access and searches, and to troubleshoot efficiently with the user on the phone, is a competitive necessity when considering the service-quality dimension. The competitive advantage comes from allowing users direct on-line access to SunSolve, which has a rich text format. This has reduced the number of calls to the technical help and stopped many potential service-quality problems.

Documents articulate the intellectual capital of an organization. While they are produced in abundance, there are inadequate means of proper storage, retrieval, and sharing. Object linking, indexing, and secured access are some of the issues that have impeded the progress of document management software. The current emphasis on process improvement has pushed consumer demand for DMS because of the close link between processes and documents. Knowledge about processes exists within documents; they provide an indication of current procedures. Also, changes in documents often accompany changes in processes. Documents are now seen as dynamic, multimedia entities that need robust and flexible control. Document management will be the next user interface for mediated access, and it is what the Cairo system developments at Microsoft have promised.

Including a DMS in an organization is no small task. It has to be installed properly to interface with word processing and appropriate personnel. Many different word processing programs have created access issues. Also, off-the-shelf packages may not satisfy the varying document needs of an organization, and the net gain of building a DMS may consequently be unsatisfactory. In terms of cost, hardware can be a major deterrent because of the need to provide rich-access, mass-storage devices, scanners, and complete integration with other desktop technologies, like the fax and the internet. Many companies are laying the groundwork for an entirely new way of doing business—dealing directly with suppliers, distributors, industrial customers, and millions of on-line shoppers. Companies can use it as a tool for marketing, sales, and customer support, and as a low-cost alternative to faxes, express mail, and other communication channels. Even law firms are reacting to the communications power on the internet. Boston-based Hale & Dorr is using the net to speed up and cut the costs of some routine work. If a client company needs a contract for a foreign distributor, for example, it can fill out an electronic questionnaire and send it over the internet to a Hale & Dorr computer. Expert-system software then constructs a draft document from boilerplate text. A lawyer reviews the document, makes the appropriate changes, and ships it back over the net to the client (complete with a list of recommended lawyers in the other country).

An Enterprise-Wide Architecture (EWA) has to be devised for any DMS, especially where it has to fit into client–server environments which have very austere security, communication protocol, and bandwidth issues. Policing of the DMS is complicated, not only in terms of the hardware operability and software support, but in avoiding system overloading by users who attempt enthusiastically to eliminate all paper documents.

Considering the above issues, a DMS will provide obvious value if it includes the following intelligence:

1. The DMS must separate individual decision-maker needs that are specific to his or her responsibility. Documents should relate to core processes of the organization. The former should be under the authority of the decision maker, and the latter should be portable among various divisions of the organization. The latter requires predefined structure, protocol, and security access.

2. Ranking techniques in search procedures based on relevance is essential to avoid overloading the decision maker with either irrelevant or quasi-relevant information.

3. Unless an approach, such as Pareto, is used to separate current from historic data, becoming a paperless, fully automated office will simply transfer current bottlenecks to more expensive storage. The DMS must have the intelligence to positively correlate the frequency of use by the decision maker with the accessibility of the documents. This can be available at the enterprise level by being sensitive to the user's identity and role in the organization.

Although Graphical-User Interface has revolutionized the access to information, file input–output procedures have been essentially the same for at least a decade. Managers tend to place things not in hierarchical directories but in order of task and priority. Applications should be stored, viewed, and shared so that documents containing thousands of pages of simple reports are readily accessible. Graphical-User Interface has been built on the underlying concepts of objects and the desktop. It is used in client–servers that are widespread. Without a new structure that leads away from the notion of directories and files, document management systems may not provide information in as timely a fashion as some of the other technologies.

GRAPHICAL-USER INTERFACE

Graphical-User Interface (GUI) has fundamentally altered the human-computer interface and can be credited with being a catalyst for the interaction between the decision maker and the computer. Visual Basic (VB) supports GUI by providing object linking and embedding for easy construction of GUIs, and is selling 30,000 copies per month. It has an open architecture, multimedia facilities, and even accommodates third-party products as part of its tool bar. Never has the cliché that a picture is worth a thousand words come more to life than in the existence and use of GUIs. They are now routine, and users take their features for granted.

The popularity of this approach has led to a glut of objects crowding user interfaces. Each system and application uses different symbolism, which can be frustrating to a decision maker who has to use various programs. Consistency and comparison to real-world experiences are the cornerstones of good GUIs. Color has often been added to create a "Las Vegas effect" for GUIs. To provide an intelligent solution to removing ambiguity in interfaces, Microsoft Word provides short, pop-up translations of available objects when the user approaches an object with the mouse. Also, Word allows the user to decide which palette to use, which is another means of having unobtrusive objects and enhancing navigation among objects.

GUI can consist of screens, windows, menus, dialogue boxes, and cursors. However, the principles of GUI dictate the need to properly do the following:

1. Organize information using grids and studying screen layouts
2. Economize by emphasizing simplicity, clarity, distinctiveness, and salient objects
3. Communicate by legible, readable typography and color

The next technological landmark in visualization multimedia has only begun to achieve its application potential. The pioneers of multimedia were the entertainment industry and some art departments in organizations. Multimedia has had the largest impact for the teaching of specialized but not highly complex skills. The cost advantages and the increase in retention through computer-based or computer-supported training are phenomenal. Lawrence Martel of Integrated Learning Systems attributes this success to the fact that people learn differently; and by integrating multimedia, which is fast and easy to understand, learning can be achieved by the majority of people.

The U.S. Bureau of Census estimated that its costs of gathering information in 1990 were $2.6 billion. In spite of these costs, the data often were inaccurate or noisy. The bureau has now decided to equip its interviewers with laptops and to use video in the data collection procedure. Rover, in England, now allows customers to place on-line orders at deal showrooms by using multimedia to pick the vehicle of their choice. The system is directly linked to the production and inventory system at Rover. The Multimedia Tool Guide, from *NewMedia* magazine, lists over 750 products that are available. Point of sale and assembly kiosks providing just-in-time service are widespread. To aid organizations in developing multimedia, authoring tools, such as Macromedia's Authorware and Aimtech's IconAuthor, are now available and have passed customer satisfaction ratings for support and value with flying colors.

Given that organizations are now networked, a problem with multimedia is the effective transport of voice, data, and video. Transport has to be properly synchronized with unnoticeable time delays and sharpened accuracy. Active-matrix, liquid crystal displays are now considered the best hardware available for multimedia uses. Currently, Japan controls the market for manufacturing liquid crystal displays, while European and American companies are trying to break into the field by finding an easier manufacturing process.

Multimedia technologies will facilitate the integration of the decision maker with enterprise-wide, knowledge-based systems. Multimedia can enrich traditional modeling techniques by direct interaction with the experts. To facilitate early detection, researchers at Michigan University were looking for a certain anomaly in the chemical composition of human urine. The data on individual patients is hard to decipher because various chemicals interact and observations are taken over time. They used multimedia to map the normal level of different chemicals (an orchestra of chemicals) over several days (the notes in a song) to a familiar tune. Interestingly, the samples which were contaminated struck sour notes in the song. A time-consuming and often inaccurate procedure was reduced to the act of a technician listening for sour notes in the tune played by the computer. Matching the notes and detecting deviations is an example of an expert-system application.

Creative uses for multimedia can avoid having very interesting memos or data to be stored. The decision maker in today's world is juggling technologies like telecommunications, teleconferencing, and, at the least, personal digital assistants. One key to providing intelligent information is to integrate these technologies and establish their interoperability using advances in multimedia. As such uses are uncovered, the financial markets will evaluate multimedia companies as being able to meet customer demands and provide value on delivery.

VIRTUAL REALITY APPLICATIONS

Until recently, virtual reality was not taken seriously. Today, it is being applied in many places and for many uses, including in the movie *Jurassic Park* to show roaming dinosaurs. In a number of cases, virtual reality has been used as a tool for rapid custom design of new products. This capability can affect industry potential, just as the Sabre reservation system did in the airline industry. Because the brain uses about half of its capability to perceive and understand information, people feel comfortable when viewing computerized data in three dimensions and in virtual reality images. In Tokyo, Matsushita has developed a "virtual kitchen" as a selling tool because it allows the customer to move appliances around in the kitchen to get a feel for how they would look in a home. To illustrate the potential of virtual reality, Eastman Kodak has used it to demonstrate intricate interaction among the variables of temperature and pressure for injection molding.

Virtual reality has emerged as a critical tool for advanced decision support and systems analysis because decision makers can process three-dimensional data more efficiently than two-dimensional reports, such as spread sheets, and graphics are a natural direction in which the field is likely to grow. An extension of the ability to move objects and see them in three dimensions requires the use of tactile feedback devices which allow the human to feel the response to pushing the object. Eliot (1993) projects that these new devices can affect a person's sense of smell, ability to recognize speech, and other human activities.

Will these new capabilities be relevant to decision makers? Can we conjecture what the possible use might be? One recalls the introduction of the typewriter—nobody thought it would work. A promising application of high-powered microprocessor chips is to recognize patterns of data. Virtual computing is being used to design new chips that can verify whether a chip design is correct. Special purpose chips have the potential of speeding up computation while, at the same time, assuring consistency and meeting standard specifications. In another application of virtual reality, doctors use a three-dimensional model to illustrate the differences in veins, bones, and muscles.

Another example of where virtual reality has proven a useful technology for new product development is Boeing's use for the design of its aircraft. Currently, it uses augmented reality, where information is superimposed onto the real world. When a technician is connecting complex wiring, access to troubleshooting instructions are made readily available using multimedia. A virtual reality system that was built for Fujita, a Japanese construction firm, shows how to operate equipment where there is limited visibility and few expert operators. Virtual reality relies on human cognition because sensors are employed in its application. Although the visual system is the one used most by humans, motion sensing, auditory sensing, proprioceptive sensors, and olfactory sensors can also contribute to virtual reality because stimulus of the senses helps to create a more realistic environment. Perception thresholds and the modeling of sensor systems will become essential for creating a virtual environment. Perception of information from these cues determines how the brain will respond to the stimuli received.

Virtual reality systems can accommodate human requirements when interfacing with a cue generation system. For example, DARPA's SIMNET is an application of virtual reality that has been used for aural work and which can make up for a lack of visual or motion input sensory information. To increase effectiveness in space flights, perceived motion must be minimized to avoid induced sickness. DARPA's virtual reality includes metaphors for viewing, navigation, and manipulation. Two basic systems in use today include desktop and immersive virtual reality. Immersive virtual reality is referred to as "cyberspace" and uses a head-mounted display. Desktop virtual reality relies on a "window," or monitor, to view the physical world. When used for modeling assembly operations, the desktop metaphor was most appropriate, because people naturally manipulate objects.

Virtual reality is well suited for work-group communications. Users from a number of departments could be networked to view the virtual parts and fit subassemblies together. The users could then make changes in design in real time. Assembly modeling provides a common language and tools which are easy to learn. This allows technical groups to get involved while the product is in the preliminary design stage and the costs to change are minimal.

USE OF ARTIFICIAL INTELLIGENCE

The use of artificial intelligence (AI) for managerial decision making is gaining credibility. Although AI has been available for a number of years, it is now being used to tackle problems that were not readily solvable by inexperienced managers. It has been successfully applied in areas such as medicine, production scheduling, insurance, and banking. The extension to broader management problems, such as finance, are now beginning to appear.

AI systems are best applied to solve difficult problems which currently require professionally trained people to perform. In designing the transition from classical data processing to hybrid AI data processing solutions, the Mitsubishi Research Institute (MIRI) worked closely with the Mitsubishi Bank and Mitsubishi Trust and Banking. This joint effort placed special emphasis on the analysis of knowledge acquisition, as well as on graphic interfaces. A basic premise in the hybrid approach has been that no expert system will produce knowledge in a domain where there is no human expertise available. What expert systems do is to reflect and to generalize existing know-how among professionals. This basic premise cannot be ignored.

In order to reach its objectives, the joint effort between MIRI and the banks of the Mitsubishi Group developed an expert system called Solomon (solution-oriented systems design methodology). Solomon is based on AI technology but incorporates classical data processing. The implementation guidelines focus on analysis of the new requirements rather than on the restructuring of old programs. Solomon allows the integration of data processing and AI into hybrid solutions which can be shown to be cost effective. Also, the study showed that the bulk of the old programs would have to be phased out over time as the AI-enhanced information system was installed. Using this approach, the Mitsubishi Group's information technology implementation will be enhanced and at the same time will have distributed capability.

In a study of characteristics of experts, Shanteau (1987) found that experts have highly developed perceptual abilities and are able to simplify complex problems. He claims that they know when to avoid pursuing inappropriate strategies. They have a strong sense of responsibility and a strong sense of outward confidence in their decision-making ability. Interestingly, they reveal an unexpected degree of adaptability and responsiveness and seem to have a high tolerance to stress. The implication of these findings, according to Shanteau, is that preserving the role of the decision maker is as important as developing AI systems.

The ultimate potential of AI for management is the ability to augment the decision-maker's reasoning power. Implicit in such systems is the ability to capture the "expertise" of persons who have the experience or know-how to perform a complex, ill-defined task. This knowledge is represented in terms of heuristic rules and incorporated in intelligent systems. However, information on many specific expert systems is scarce because they are often used to solve specific problems buried deep within a company and are ubiquitous. For instance, a technician who is an expert at adjusting a certain multimillion-dollar boiler transfers his expertise to a computerized expert system so that other technicians can adjust it when he is not available. At one company, telephone operators are given expert systems to help them direct calls. The system tells the operator what questions to ask, what responses to expect, and where to send the caller. At another system, an expert system knows the airline flying preferences (e.g., window seats) of each person in a department and is able to schedule flight itineraries when requested. It obtains automatically the latest airline schedules by dialing the Official Airline Guide on-line service. AI has provided much of today's technology and continues to generate new and creative applications. It is currently described as "expert systems" due to the fact that earlier approaches to the development of AI focused on pattern recognition rather than problem solving.

SUMMARY

One should not underestimate the importance of high-performance computing to the survival of most companies. Because of the need to maintain a competitive position for survival, computer performance is a critical consideration. Management needs to review and update technology continuously in order to maintain competitive leadership. It is easy to lose a leadership position, and it is difficult to regain once it is lost. The time frame for implementing high technology often requires three to five years. Another three to five years is generally needed to assure that the change is fully accepted.

High technology is not a fad; it is a weapon. In the manufacturing industry, for example, advanced scientific research is impossible without supercomputers. Mechanizing will not be able to implement approaches, such as just-in-time inventory management, and the financial industry will not be able to move rapidly, without the use of high-performance computers in the global marketplace.

Massively parallel computers have been available since the mid-1980s and have become indispensable for developing new products, providing superior services, improving information processing, and exploiting markets. This is the hard reality, which those who stumble backward into the future are either unable or unwilling to accept. Thanks to high-performance computing, experimental processes, which would have been far too costly, too dangerous, and too slow, can now be executed in a fast and accurate manner. It is obvious that advanced technology is a critical driving factor in maintaining competitiveness in the computer industry. These advances portend better information systems to support management decisions.

APPENDIX: CURRENT KNOWLEDGE-BASED SYSTEM APPLICATIONS

The following are knowledge-based expert systems currently in commercial use or development:

Adcad. This expert system employs detailed, multifaceted, and substantial knowledge about advertising to help managers choose appropriate television campaign approaches. Adcad incorporates marketing and communications objectives, as well as audience category and brand characteristics, to provide detailed strategic recommendations. By asking management-oriented questions, the system forces the user to think about issues which are too often easily overlooked. Much of Adcad's value is its ability to steer advertisers away from inappropriate choices, no matter how enticing an agency's concept may appear. Rather than concede all expertise to an agency, managers can have informed opinions of their own with the help of the expert system's knowledge base.

Adduce. This is a frame-based expert system, built with Prolog, which predicts consumer responses to advertising on the basis of both theoretical and empirical knowledge. It was built to deal with unstructured problems.

Brand Managers Assistant (BMA). BMA represents a knowledge-based system approach to the brand management function. The four phases of brand management—analysis, planning, execution, and control—provide the framework for modeling the brand management process. The BMA was designed to augment a company's existing marketing management information system. The BMA provides a new architecture for supporting the key aspects of marketing management decision making: analysis, planning, and control. It contains data viewers for extracting and viewing data, analyzers for analyzing data, designers for designing marketing events and programs, and monitors for monitoring events and programs.

Business Insight. Business Insight is an expert system designed to help businesses find the best strategies for introducing a product. The program begins by interviewing the user in a question-and-answer format, asking hundreds of questions (both subjective and objective) that range from financial data to a description of the user's business and its market. The responses to the questions can be weighted on a one-to-ten scale to reflect the user's view of their significance. A simple spreadsheet is incorporated into the program for gathering and refining financial data. The objective of the program is to help a company pick the optimum conditions for offering a new product. After it analyzes the situation, the expert system generates a scorecard that rates the chances of success and suggests areas that can be modified. It identifies a company's strengths and weaknesses and points out inconsistencies in a product plan. As a guide for planning products and devising a competitive strategy, Business Insight uses an exhaustive checklist, imposing a logical pattern to the product-strategy process. The expert system is also used as a communications tool between product managers, giving insight as well as presenting different marketing management approaches. It may be utilized to assist marketing management in finding the best marketing strategies for positioning a product by answering questions such as, "Should the product be introduced now or should we wait for the market to develop? Should the product be priced low for market penetration or high for maximum cash penetration? What channels of distribution will be most effective? Should promotion employ a push or pull strategy?"

CASE. The computer-assisted sentencing (CASE) system has been developed in the United Kingdom to help sentencers choose an appropriate sentence to impose on a convicted offender. The system is aimed primarily at Magistrates' Courts. One of the advantages of such a computer system is that the sentencer does not have to struggle with the complexity of the statutes and can concentrate on the rational exercise of discretion.

CLINT. Met Life uses Checklist for Income Loan Transaction (CLINT) for loan-closing transactions for commercial real estate developments. A series of 400 rules about federal, state, and local laws and regulations are combined with Met's lending policies for loan-closing transactions.

Compushop. This is an expert system used by Builders Square, based in San Antonio, Texas, as part of its home-center operations. It notes prices at competing stores for key items in each market and then determines if prices need to be lowered to remain competitive. Their turnaround time for correcting a competitive market situation has been reduced to twenty-four hours or less.

CoverStory. One of the most promising expert-system applications for packaged goods marketing is CoverStory. This system automates the task of analyzing the vast quantities of scanner and other data received weekly by packaged goods companies. It utilizes "smart exception reporting" to uncover events and "intelligently" searches for possible explanations. The system has a natural-language front end so that it generates a one- or two-page written report (in English) of its major findings. Many service industries are also very data intensive, and managers using this system could benefit greatly from the rapid analysis of large quantities of data.

Design Center. Weyerhauser Company's Design Center is an expert system placed in hardware stores that allows customers to design home improvement projects interactively. The computer checks each design against the principles of structural mechanics and suggests needed changes. When the design is finished, the customer gets a detailed printout of the project, including a complete description of the lumber and hardware required. Stores with these systems report a 25 percent gain in sales of designed items and claim that 50 percent of the customers who use the Design Center place an order. In the first eight months of its operation, customers created $150 million in projects on the system.

Detector System. Novaction SA, in France, developed this expert system to support new product development. The system evaluates the permeability of a market by forecasting the sales potential of the next entry into the market before investing in a new product development program. Detector's forecast is based on the market structure and hypothesis on the mix performance—concept, advertising, product, and price—of the new brand (Harding and Nacher, 1989).

DOLRS. A special joint-venture development project between Target Stores and IBM resulted in a PC-based expert-system application for Distribution Center On-Line Receiving Scheduler (DOLRS). All seven of Target's distribution centers now have DOLRS. The project has improved the efficiency of the distribution centers. The scheduler decides which door to go to and how long it will take to unload based on the data compiled by IBM from interviewing Target's best schedulers. The DOLRS is linked with Target's Tandem network in order to access purchase information.

EICA. Employee or Independent Contractor Advisor (EICA) has been designed to save companies time and money. EICA costs $89 and uses a form of knowledge-based systems called case-based reasoning. The menu-driven application provides four modules to choose from: (1) common law tests; (2) statutory independent contractor tests; (3) safe haven independent contractor tests; and (4) statutory employee tests. The system asks a series of questions that require yes, no, or maybe answers. EICA is not a substitute for legal advice and research but is an excellent tool for "second opinion."

Exmar. This is an object-oriented expert system, developed with Smalltalk, and is intended to provide assistance for the marketing–planning process. The system should distribute knowledge and contribute to the understanding of how the multifarious factors of the market interact and serve to define the parameters of business activities. The development of the system has been funded by the British Department of Trade and Industry and by contributions from member companies of the Exmar club.

Infer. This expert system was designed because scanner technology has resulted in the problem of too much data. Infer helps translate large quantities of marketing data into meaningful insights for managerial actions. The system automates data interpretation by employing a knowledge base of simple data interpretation techniques often used by analysts. The system generates a summary report that is useful for management decision making. Marketing managers in packaging goods companies are inundated with 100 to 1,000 times more bits of data than what they had access to a few years ago.

Innovator. An expert system for new product planning, evaluating new financial services, screening of ideas, and provision of an approve, reevaluate, and reject recommendation. The system evaluates new product ideas in the financial services industry and provides a "go, no go, or reevaluate" decision to the user. The components of Innovator are (1) an inference control module; (2) a dialogue module; (3) the end-user profile; (4) the product profile; (5) a product evaluation algorithm; (6) a tracking module; and (7) a maintenance module. Innovator has been designed for screening new product ideas but can be extended to the subsequent stages of the development process. Innovator uses a rule base consisting of regular and fuzzy if–then rules and a backward chaining strategy to infer conclusions. Experts were used to develop a list of twenty attributes grouped in five logical factors: market, finance, product, corporate, and competition.

Insite. General Electric (GE) uses this expert system to troubleshoot customer's magnetic resonance imaging (MRI) machines by telephone from a central location. This technology serves as a marketing tool for GE, in that it can provide instantaneous service that gives the customer a high confidence level in GE.

MAGIC. The Merced Area Global Information Communication (MAGIC) was developed by the County of Merced, California, to reduce social worker's time per case by up to 40 percent for over 200 social workers. MAGIC addresses legal issues regarding eligibility requirements and amounts for entitlement programs, such as disability and unemployment.

Manufacturing Process Planner. This system was developed by Northrop Corporation (Fiegenbaum, 1988). It aids in the planning process for the manufacture of approximately 20,000 parts that go into a fighter plane. The system develops a plan that identifies the operations that need to be performed on a piece of raw material for transforming it into a finished item, as described in the engineering drawing or mode. The plan includes specifications of the equipment to be used on the shop floor, any additional tooling needed, and the sequential routing of the parts and their associated material through the factory.

Mesa-1. This system helps in the selection of engines for merchant ships. The selection of engines is based primarily on a customer's requirements for specific tonnage and performance. In addition, customer's concerns about fuel costs, payment schedules, costs of dampening the engine vibration, engine costs, power plant requirements, and any special requirements are considered. It used to take four to five days to process two to three engines and two power plants. With Mesa-1, it takes between ten to fifteen minutes to process ten engines.

More/2. The system is commercially available through Persoft, Inc., and is designed to be used by service bureaus and large direct-mail companies. It serves direct-mail marketers by ranking customers according to their likelihood of response to a mass mailing. It runs on an IBM mainframe and can process one million names in forty-five minutes. The knowledge base is built around the results of previous mailings, using standard statistical models based on rules developed by direct-mail experts. The user provides lists and financial information and defines objectives for the mailing. The system ranks each name and determines the size of the mailing to accomplish the stated objectives. More/2 has the ability as an expert system to learn how to improve subsequent mailings based on the experience gained with earlier ones. It can also modify and change its underlying model, setting it apart from conventional analytical software.

Negotex. This expert system is designed to help international marketing negotiators prepare for a negotiation. The system is designed to assist in developing a priori strategies for international business negotiations involving two parties. It is not intended for use concerning problems of arbitration or negotiations involving more than two parties. During the course of consultation, the system asks a series of questions regarding the context of the negotiations, the philosophical approach of the user to negotiating, and the nature of the other party to the negotiation. Negotex then makes recommendations concerning several aspects of the negotiation. Confidence factors may also be scaled if the user is unsure of an answer. The system is designed to map the user inputs to recommended strategies based upon the following six fundamental, intermediary concepts: (1) the context in which the negotiation takes place; (2) prior evaluations of self, other party, and the upcoming negotiation; (3) negotiation philosophy, style, and goals; (4) recommended negotiating strategies including guidelines on preparing for a negotiation (e.g., whether to have an agenda, who should set the agenda, whether minor issues should be discussed before major issues, etc.); (5) team composition (number of members, the skills of members, etc.); and (6) communication strategies and behavioral responses during the negotiation.

Packaging Advisor. This is an expert system designed by Du Pont for the product design of rigid plastic food containers, helping Du Pont break into the highly competitive barrier resin market. They have also developed the Maintenance Finish Advisor for use at trade shows to answer questions on high-performance paints and to obtain sales leads.

Pricing Strategy Advisor. This expert system aids pricing decisions by applying well-established pricing principles, successful strategies, heuristics, and firm-specific information. The Advisor has three sections. The first section evaluates the company's strategic position based on industry attractiveness and the firm's competitive market position. The second section suggests an overall pricing strategy, as well as the tactical elements necessary for its implementation. The third section, a bidding strategy module, recommends preliminary and initial bids based on the outcome of the last bidding attempt, the number of bidders, the importance of the account, the variable cost of providing the goods or service, and the full cost of the product.

Promoter. This is a system for evaluating sales promotions and for helping marketing managers design, select, and schedule promotion programs. A growing body of evidence says that the majority of sales promotions are unprofitable and that many are actually harmful to the long-run prospects of a brand. For example, Abraham and Lodish (1987) found that only 16 percent of the trade promotions they studied were profitable. Promoter examines statistics, such as shipments, warehouse withdrawals, or store-level scanner data, according to the expertise of managers and analysts. It isolates the impact of promotions and calculates their profitability.

Scan*Expert. Scan*Expert, from A. C. Nielsen Company, seeks unusual changes in sales and attempts to explain them according to marketing variables. In spirit, as well as structure, this application is quite similar to CoverStory.

Shanex. This prototype expert system is used for market-share analysis of a consumer brand. It makes human-like judgments based on how managers solve marketing problems using their experience, judgment, and belief.

SMART. Compaq Computer Corporation has installed a large-scale, help-desk automation system that draws on case-based reasoning. Currently in production, the Support Management Automated Reasoning Technology (SMART) system automates the process that customer-support personnel use to resolve product-related problems and systems integration issues experienced by customers, dealers, and national accounts.

STRATEX. Strategic Decision-Making for Expert Firms (STRATEX) is a knowledge-based system for strategic market planning, supporting the choice of marketing segments, and is used in the export trade of raw and manufactured fish products in Norway. The expert system was developed at Nordland Research Institute in Norway, and uses the XiPlus expert-system shell by Expertech.

Stratmap. The Stratmap knowledge-based system's shell has been developed to assist managers in the design and implementation of their competitive marketing strategy. This knowledge-based system prototype is designed to help managers decide which strategic, competitive marketing alternative is more appropriate for their company, given the position of their product within the industry and within the company, as well as the position of the product relative to the customer and the competition. The system uses if–then rules and forward chaining to reason with information provided by the users in order to reach its recommendations. The dialogue with the user covers four sets of variables: the industry, the company, the product, and the consumer. Within each of these sets of variables is a sense of heuristic decision rules that are used by the expert system to provide a management framework for the development of a competitive strategy (Davis and Sisodia, 1992).

XCENCAL. The Expert Sentence Calculator (XCENCAL) was developed at the Ministry of Correctional Services in Ontario, Canada, for the sentencing of a criminal. XCENCAL contains the expertise of attorneys, administrators, and other experts from the Ministry. Relevant information about a convicted person, collected during presentencing, is maintained in a separate computer file, including prior arrests, convictions, sentencing, probation, parole, and length of time for past incarceration. The system reviews these factors to ensure the sentence is consistent with a host of statutes, rules, regulations, country-specific policies, and other variables.

XSEL. Expert Selling (XSEL) is used at Digital Equipment Corporation. It conducts a structured interview with a salesperson, asking fifteen to twenty multiple choice questions about the customer's needs and characteristics. Combining that information with stored technical and product data, XSEL generates a report recommending a specific sales system. Also, it explains the reasons for its choice and alerts salespeople to any inconsistent information they entered. Digital uses XSEL to fill about 70 percent of its orders. XSEL serves as a valuable training tool, also.

BIBLIOGRAPHY

Abraham, Magid M., and Leonard M. Lodish. 1987. Promoter: An Expert Evaluation System. *Marketing Science* 6: 101–123.

Borch, Odd J., and Gunnar Hartvigsen. Knowledge-Based Systems for Strategic Market Planning in Small Firms. *Decision Support Systems* (May): 145–157.

Burke, Raymond R. 1991. Reasoning with Empirical Marketing Knowledge. *International Journal of Research in Marketing:* 75–90.

Burn, Janice. 1990. *Management of Information Systems Technology.* New York: Van Nostrand Reinhold.

Carrabine, Laura. 1990. Plugging into the Computer to Sense Virtual Reality. *Computer-Aided Engineering* (June): 18–24.

Charniak, Eugene, and Drew McDermott. 1985. *Artificial Intelligence.* Reading, Mass.: Addison-Wesley.

Chu, Wesley, and Alfonso Cardenas. 1993. Utilizing Integration Works in the UCLA Medical Center. *IEEE* Data Engineering Bulletin: April.

Davis, Sue Anne, and Rajendra Sisodia. 1992. *Knowledge-Based Technology & Experience-Based Marketing Decision Making: An Expert System for Strategic Marketing and Competitive Strategy.* Proceedings at the AAAI-92 National Conference on Artificial Intelligence, July, San Jose, Calif.

Depompa, Barbara. 1993. Waging War on the Applications Backlog. *Beyond Computing* (July/August): 41–44.

DiLorenzo, Jim. 1994. SimCity Creators Simulate Life in the Telco Fast Lane. *Telephony* (March 28): 20.

Donovan, John J. 1988. Beyond Chief Information Officer to Network Manager. *Harvard Business Review* (September/October): 134–140.

Dorsey, Jean Green. 1992. Xerox's Visionary CIO. *Beyond Computing* (October/November): 22–24.

Eliot, Lance B. 1993. Analogical Problem-Solving and Expert Systems. *IEEE Expert* (Summer): 17–28.

Essin, D. J. 1993a. The Electronic Medical Record: A Challenge for Computer Science to Develop Clinically and Socially Relevant Computer Systems to Coordinate Information for Patient Care and Analysis. *Information Society* (April/June): 157–188.

Essin, D. J. 1993b. Intelligent Processing of Loosely Structured Documents as a Strategy for Organizing Electronic Health Care Records. *Methods of Information in Medicine* 32: 335.

Fiegenbaum, Edward, Pamela McCorduck, and H. Penny Nii. 1988. *The Rise of the Expert Company*. New York: Times Books Random House.

Flax, Steven. 1992. Global IT without Tears. *Beyond Computing* (August/September): 18–26.

Fox, Bruce. 1992. Expert Systems Help Builders Square. *Chain Store Executive* (April): 41–42.

Francis, Bob. 1993. Client/Server Integrators—Is BIGGER Better? *Datamation* (July 15): 24–28.

Frost, M. 1993. It's a Matter of Semantics. *Computing Canada* 19(August 16): 25.

Ganz, Jonathan. 1988. Artificial Intelligence: Man's Question to Duplicate Human Thinking. *Professional Careers Magazine* (January/February): 5–8.

Goul, Michael. 1992. A Dyed-in-the-Wool Tool Builder Sings the Blues for DSS and Becomes Somewhat Excited about a New Romance with "O" DSS. *Decision Line* (October): 14–16.

Govoni, Stephen J. 1992. Practical Solutions in Optical Storage. *Beyond Computing* (August/September): 30–31.

Haeckel, Stephan H., and Richard L. Nolan. 1993. Managing by Wire. *Harvard Business Review* (September/October): 122–132.

Harding, Carlos, and Bernard Nacher. 1989. Simulated Test Markets: Can We Go One Step Further in Their Use? *Applied Marketing Research* (Spring): 21–32.

Hertz, David B. 1983. Artificial Intelligence and the Business Manager. *Computerworld* 17(October 24): 19–26.

Houdeshel, George, R. Kelly Rainer, and Hugh Watson. 1992. *Executive Information Systems: Emergence, Development, Impact*. New York: John Wiley & Sons.

Howles, Les. 1993. Designing Instructional Multimedia Presentations: A Seven-Step Process. *T.H.E. Journal* (June): 58–61.

Hurwicz, Michael. 1994. WANs: How to Add Branches without Going Bankrupt. *Datamation* (March 15): 42–46.

IntelliCorp. 1988. Data Is Data. Knowledge Is Power. Advertisement in *AI Expert* (September): 55.

Jakobson, G., C. Lafond, E. Nyberg, and G. Piatetsky-Shapiro. 1986. An Intelligent Database Assistant. *IEEE Expert* (Summer): 65–79.

Jeffreys, William H., and James O. Berger. 1992. Ockham's Razor and Bayesian Analysis. *American Scientist* (January/February): 64–72.

Kandelin, Nils. 1990. An Event Database Approach to Object Oriented Representation. University of Southern California, School of Accounting, Dissertation.

Kenney, Timothy P. 1991. Search and Love. *AI Expert* (March): 52.

Keyes, Jessica. 1992. Living in Parallel. *AI Expert* (February): 42–47

Kleinschrod, Walter A. 1992. Outsourcing: Weighing the Issues. *Beyond Computing* (October/November): 44–50.

Klempa, Mathew J., Ph.D. 1993. Management of Information Technology Innovation: A Heuristic Contingency Paradigm Research Perspective. *ACM* (April): 56–74.

Koslov, Alex. 1988. Rethinking Artificial Intelligence. *High Technology Business* (May): 18–25.

Kurzweil, Raymond. 1985. What Is Artificial Intelligence Anyway? *American Scientist* 73(May/June): 258–264.

Levinson, Marc. 1992. IBM, Please Call AT&T. *Newsweek* (December 28): 44.

Lewis, J. 1986. How Smart Is Artificial Intelligence? *Microtimes* (February).

Linden, Eugene. 1985. Intellicorp.: The Selling of Artificial Intelligence. *High Technology* (March): 22–25.

Lipkin, Richard. 1988. Making Machines in Mind's Image. *Insight* (February 15): 8–17.

Littman, Jonathan. 1993. Breaking Free. *Corporate Computing* (June): 104–111.

Longbottom, B. W. 19XX. Artificial Intelligence Means Business. *ICP Business Software Review* 20–21.

McCann, John M., William G. Lahti, and Justin Hill. 1991. The Brand Manager's Assistant: A Knowledge-Based System Approach to Brand Management. *International Journal of Research in Marketing* (April): 51–73.

McCune, J. 1992. Consultant in a Box. *Success* (February): 46.

McDonald, M. H., and H. N. Wilson. 1990. State-of-the-Art Developments in Expert Systems and Strategic Marketing Planning. *British Journal of Management* (1): 159–170.

Mehler, Mark. 1992. CIOs Plot Strategic Moves. *Beyond Computing* (October/November): 27–31.

Michals, D. 19XX. The Brains Behind Artificial Intelligence. *Fortune* 96–103.

Mitchell, Russell. 1990. Can Cray Reprogram Itself for Creativity? *Business Week* (August 20): 86.

Mitchell, Russell, Gary McWilliams, John Carey, Neil Gross, and John W. Verity. 1991. Where No Computer Has Gone Before. *Business Week* (November 25): 80–88.

Moad, Jeff. 1993. Does Reengineering Really Work? *Datamation* (August 1): 22–28.

Moad, Jeff. 1993. How ISO 9000 Quality Programs Affect IS. *Datamation* (August 3): 65–66.

Moad, Jeff. 1993. New Rules, New Ratings as IS Reengineers. *Datamation* (November 1): 85–87.

Morton, Michael S. 1967. Interactive Visual Display Systems and Management Problem Solving. *IMR* (Fall): 69–81.

Needleman, Raphael. 1992. Enlightened IS. *Corporate Computing* (August): 13.

Nolen, Troy. 1992. Parallel Processing for Problem Solving. *AI Expert* (February): 35–40.

Olesen, Erik. 1993. Mastering CEO's Secrets for Exploiting Opportunity. *Success* (October): 44–45.

Parsaye, Kamran. 1988. Acquiring and Verifying Knowledge Automatically. *AI Expert* (May 19): 48–67.

Piatetsky-Shapiro, Gregory. 1990. Knowledge Discovery in Real Data Bases: A Report on the IJCAI-89 Workshop. *AI Magazine* (Special Issue): *Technology* (Spring/Summer): 11–21.

Ram, Sudha, and Sunderesan Ram. 1990. Evaluating Financial Service Innovations: An Expert Systems Application. Presented at the American Marketing Association, George Mason University Workshop on Expert Systems in Marketing, August, Fairfax, Virginia.

Rhines, W. 1985. Artificial Intelligence: Out of the Lab and into Business. *Texas Instruments, Journal of Business Strategy* 6(1; Summer): 50–57.

Robins, Gary. 1992. Target Stores, IBM Develops Expert Receiving and Scheduling System. *Stores DC Scheduler* (March): 33–35.

Rock, Denny, Sandie Washburn, Dave Purdon, and Alex Houtzeel. 1993. Sharing Knowledge Bases in Industry. *AI Expert* (June): 25–31.

Rowe, Alan J. 1988. Management Use of Artificial Intelligence. In *Applied Expert Systems—Trends & Issues*. New York: Elsevier Science Publishing.

Rowe, Neil. 1988. *Artificial Intelligence Through Prolog.* New Jersey: Prentice-Hall.

Schmitz, John G., and John D. Little. 1990. CoverStory—Automated News Finding in Marketing. *Interfaces*.

Sedlock, David. 1988. The Natural Language–Data Base Connection. *AI Expert* (July): 26–36.

Shanteau, James. 1987. Psychological Characteristics of Expert Decision Makers. Kansas State University, Department of Psychology, Manhattan, Kan.

Shapiro, Jeremy, and Shelley K. Hughes. 1992. Network Information Resources in Distance Graduate Education for Adults. *T.H.E. Journal* (June 11): 66–70.

Silverman, Barry G., and Arthur J. Murray. 1990. Full-Sized Knowledge-Based Systems Research Workshop. *AI Magazine* (Special Issue): 88.

Simon, H. 1982. *The Science of the Artificial.* Cambridge, Mass.: MIT Press.

Stewart, S. D., and G. Watson. 1985. Applications of Artificial Intelligence. *Simulation* (June).

Storey, Veda C., and Robert C. Goldstein. 1990. An Expert View Creation System for Database Design. *USC Expert System Review* 19–45.

TenDyke, R. P. 1987. Outlook on Artificial Intelligence. *Journal of Information System Management* (Spring): 10–16.

Trelease, Robert B. 1987. The Fourth Wave in AI. *AI Expert* (October): 48–67.

Urban, Glen L., and Steven Starr. 1991. *Advanced Marketing Strategy: Phenomena–Analysis–Decisions.* Englewood Cliffs, N.J.: Prentice-Hall.

Varhey, Sarah E. 1993. IBM Outlines Parallel-System Plans. *Servers & Databases* (November): 61–63.

Verity, John. 1994. The Internet, How It Will Change the Way You Do Business. *Business Week* (November): 80–88.

Verity, John. 1993. The Parallel Universe Grows. *Business Week* (August 16): 32.

Verity, John W., and Evan I. Schwartz. 1991. Software Made Simple. *Business Week* (September 30): 92–100.

Vogelgesang, Peter. 1990. Drowning in Data. *Byte* (February): 251–256.

Wakin, Edward. 1993. Managing to Win: Harnessing the Power of Teams. *Beyond Computing* (July/August): 27–32.

Walsh, Bill. 1994. Managing the Big Idea. *FORBES ASAP* (June): 19.

Weber, Jack. 1993. Visualization: Seeing Is Believing. *Byte* (April): 121–128.

Wickham, Robert F. 1988. Supercomputers: America's New National Resource. *Professional Careers Magazine* (September/October): 9–12.

Williamson, Mickey. 1989. User Developed Expert Systems—Expert Systems for the Rest of Us. *AI Magazine* (March/April).

Wohl, Amy D. 1993. Anywhere, Anytime Computing. *Beyond Computing* (July/ August): 19–23.

Wohl, Amy D. 1993. Multimedia: Toy or Tool? *Beyond Computing* (January/February): 57–59.

Xenakis, John. 1995. Create an Office "Expert" That Has All the Answers. 1610 Worcester Road, Suite 629 A, Framingham, Mass., Interview.

Zenios, Stavros A. 1992. Parallel Computing. *OR/MS* (August): 44–49.

CHAPTER SIX

❑ ❑ ❑

ORGANIZATION TRANSFORMATION AND INFORMATION

Advice begins where information ends.

To achieve a future edge in decision making and to succeed in tomorrow's turbulent and unkind global environment, a major organizational paradigm shift is required. Not only will the way business is being conducted change, but many of the old rules that were successful in the past will have to be thrown out. What is this new direction and how will it work? Incrementally changing the old bureaucratic structure and rules will no longer suffice. What is being proposed is a "quantum" shift in ideas, products, services, and organizational structures that will help businesses relate more effectively to customers. Experience has shown that major paradigm shifts rarely take place without significant organizational upheaval. However, Hewlett-Packard (HP) was able to achieve a radical organizational change when they set out to develop a new desktop laser printer. HP went about interdicting change in the right way. Today, they are the leaders in the laser printer field, which has contributed $1.5 billion in additional sales beyond the base product line.

Many analysts have projected that a new strategic architecture for organizations will be required to compete in the next decade. Although external factors such as industry structure, competition, or changing customer requirements are important, the real potential for strategic competitiveness will focus on improving, reframing, or reengineering internal capabilities. Internal factors that focus on organizational learning, innovation, experimentation, constructive contention, empowerment, improved value potential, sustainable competitive advantage, and strategic reframing are the requirements for a new strategic architecture of the firm.

THE ORGANIZATION PARADIGM SHIFT AND ITS INFORMATION MANAGEMENT IMPLICATIONS

If we examine the crisis that faced General Motors (GM), we can see how difficult it can be to make a major paradigm shift, and we can see the implications for information system design. GM had hoped that introducing a team approach for their new Saturn car would bring about a significant change in performance. For a number of years, GM built new plants, hired many new workers, and introduced the "J" car, the "L" car, and the "A" car. However, the overlap among the divisions forced a day of reckoning which led Chief Executive Officer Stemple to eliminate 74,000 jobs and close a number of facilities. This was, in part, what led to the revolt by the board of directors, resulting in Stemple losing his position. The board's signal was clear: "Stodgy old bureaucratic order was dead" (Taylor, 1992). An Intelligent Information System would have identified the potential conflicts and possible alternative actions that GM could have taken. By itself, information systems do not correct organizational deficiencies.

The new organization paradigm focuses on identification of opportunities, anticipates problems, and rapidly adapts to new conditions. To accomplish these goals, managers will shift from using retrospective data to proactive information generation. Information systems that ignore this reality will not be effective in assisting managers to survive in highly competitive environments.

A new style of leadership that recognizes the importance of people and computer-based information support will emerge. Ann Morrison (1992) described the new style of leader as one who is concerned with assuring a broader market share and improving employee satisfaction, leading to increased productivity. Increasingly, strategic decisions employ information that can project the impact of changes in markets, products, and operations. For example, Japan utilizes a flexible manufacturing approach which allows rapid change and the ability to adapt to new marketing conditions. Robotics devices are more easily reprogrammed than fixed equipment, and they facilitate the retraining of workers. Flexibility and adaptability are both information dependent.

Information systems will need to deal with diversity in the workforce because of the changing mix of employees. The high-potential manager will have to know how to link the diverse goals of individuals with rotational assignments that require computer literacy. Internal worker networking and mentoring will be needed to assure that high performance and equitable pay systems are achieved. These influences will mandate a behavior twist to future information systems in organizations.

Industry continues to search unabatedly for the ideal organization that can create future growth and profitability. Because the new organization focuses on performance, it will need to integrate information as a critical element of the strategic imperative in order to achieve competitive advantage. It has been predicted that this new organization will virtually eliminate corporate staffs and will replace the traditional vertical–hierarchical structure that has impeded information flow. In its place, a horizontal structure will be used which empowers the worker. Horizontal organizations are considered to be able to leverage their core capability and be more responsive because they utilize cross-functional work and information flow. The horizontal organizational has generally resulted in reduced cycle time, reduced cost, and performance that focuses on continuous improvements. The horizontal structure focuses on key core processes as the primary locus of control. These core competencies include information and material flows rather than the specific tasks that need to be done.

A NEW ORGANIZATION PARADIGM

Fundamental changes are occurring in the economy that place a special value on knowledge workers—professionals who have special skills to solve expensive business problems. Because businesses today cannot always afford to employ a wide range of specialists, they are moving quickly toward becoming "virtual" companies that are working together in a networked economy and are finding new ways to tap into the expertise of knowledge workers who may be available outside the company. As knowledge work (as opposed to manual skills) becomes increasingly important, it is predicted that there will be an emergence of these virtual corporations with no fixed identity, workforce, or geographic base and that knowledge jobs will account for one-third of the workforce by the end of this decade—surpassing industrial workers as the largest work group. Lester Thurow, economics professor at the Massachusetts Institute of Technology, feels that "We are entering an era of organizational change as profound and as pervasive as that caused by the Industrial Revolution. Survivors will be the companies that invent and embrace new possibilities brought on by technological, social, and economic change as well as those companies who are concentrating on their core competencies, the flexible skills that allow them to produce a stream of distinctive products or services that cannot be easily imitated by the competition."

Firms also need to take a close look at the flow of information within their organization by removing internal barriers to the flow and sharing of information. No amount of capital investment can make up for poor communications. In the 1980s, GM spent nearly $80 billion for new factories and equipment to reduce its dependence on its workers, yet its productivity gains were minuscule. In contrast, Ford Motor Company concentrated on knocking down internal barriers, and their productivity accelerated rapidly (Helms, 1995). Yet, no matter how open their organizations are, firms need to pay special attention to the design of the information flow processes, to the appointment of gatekeepers to keep employees up to date with what is going on in their industry, and to the notion of empowering mentors to train young and inexperienced workers. Many companies are looking for knowledge workers with deep expertise in one discipline and enough breadth to contribute across functions. In alignment with the approach, many companies are forming teams with individuals who have different levels of expertise, skills, or personalities. However, if technology is important in tying together geographically disparate and often temporary organizations, so too will be the hard-to-define people issues such as trust, loyalty, and culture.

It may be that people who resist or are afraid of information technology may have good reason to feel that way. Corporations concerned with effective information management must begin thinking about how people use information, not how people use machines. Some organizational dynamics that you may want to consider when you are designing and implementing information sharing and knowledge management systems include the following:

- People do not share information easily. As an example, Davenport (1994) has stated that "At one large pharmaceutical company, IT managers tried to implement shared databases and other new technologies to speed up research and development, only to have their efforts foiled by significant cultural barriers." In this case, managers assumed that researchers involved in the development of a drug would pass along all information about it to the people conducting its clinical trial; if researchers had found early on that, say, the drug's effect diminished when taken with certain foods, then patients in the clinical trial could be instructed not to take the drug at meals. Such early release of data rarely happened at this company causing clinical trials to be redone, delaying the drug-approval process, possible for years. Instead of implementing new technologies, top management should have designed and implemented a program of cultural change to convince highly competitive scientists that they would not be penalized for sharing early or incomplete results.

- Changing a company's information culture requires altering the basic behaviors, attitudes, values, management expectations, and incentives that relate to information sharing. The solution that most reliably leads to successful IT implementation is also the hardest one to carry out—changing an organization's information sharing culture.

- Most of the information in organizations is not on computers, and a majority of managers prefer to get their information from face-to-face or telephone conversations or from documents that come from outside the organization. How people in the organization use and obtain information must be addressed.

- Rather than forcing employees to simplify information so that it will fit into a computer or a "sanitized" report, a human-centered approach to knowledge management calls for preserving the rich complexity required in our quest for information. The format and standards guiding how information is presented and saved becomes critical to understanding its use.

- One of the primary principles to be addressed in information management centers on the need for a clear owner of each major piece of information and clarified responsibilities and priorities for supplying information to other parts of the organization. An information map that describes the location and availability of the most widely used pieces of information in the organization is most valuable.

- Along with maps that portray the flow of information sharing, information users need people and training to guide them to the right kinds of information in the first place. Using new kinds of human support for information technology management can help toward enhancing the organization's information culture.

- Information data bases will have to be managed and restructured on an ongoing basis, which will require individuals managing this effort who have judgment and wisdom plus content expertise regarding which documents to delete, restructure, and so on.

- The issue of the need for power, or power plays, as a result of technologies that promote information sharing can end up controlling employees rather than empowering them if the information sharing culture that evolves creates a management culture of micromanagement.

- From a legal perspective, as information becomes more structured and available to the organization, systems will need to be designed to protect intellectual property from theft.

- Executives must decide which aspects of their organization's information are to be accessible and shared on a global basis.

An example of where a flat organizational structure used information sharing systems to improve performance was at the GE plant in Salisbury, which had five management levels and separate departments for design and manufacturing. After restructuring, the management levels were reduced to three, and self-managing teams replaced the previous workforce. Cross-functional communication was supported by computers that were used in the weekly meetings. The result of the new organization structure was a 10 percent reduction in cost, delivery in three days instead of three weeks, and only one-tenth the previous number of complaints. There have been over 400 companies since the early 1980s that have introduced this form of organizational structure.

When redesigning a corporation, a critical consideration is determining how to encourage change at the middle-management level. This appears to be the major obstacle to flattening organizations. Because organizational change can be a wrenching and time-consuming process, especially when trying to retain critical skills, managers who are currently responsible for worker performance will also have to change.

THE "BOUNDARYLESS" ORGANIZATION

Bossidy, Chief Executive Officer of Allied Signal, predicts that there will be a corporate revolution in the structure needed to cope with the dramatically new competitive environment. He predicts that the hierarchic structure of the past will wither away and be replaced by one that fosters high involvement, self-managing teams, and information technology which will support persons who are held accountable for their actions and who depend on useful knowledge. The key is an integrated activity flow, supported by knowledge, that enhances performance.

In the past, the hierarchic form of organization dominated in most companies. The matrix structure was one of the first changes that was made. This form of organization required crossing classic organizational boundaries and became a transitional step to the "boundaryless," or open, organization, where formal lines of authority lose their importance. The matrix form was concerned with building an organization that focused on strategic innovation. A successful matrix form required a clear statement of goals and objectives in which each individual identified with the organization and worked to build a shared vision.

Today, rigid organizational relationships are an impediment to effective information flow, decision making, and strategy formulation. In the "boundaryless" organization, individuals can question what is being proposed. Hirschhorn and Gilmore (1992) consider the following as critical to the success of this form of organization:

1. *Authority boundary.* Defining who is in charge of which key decisions
2. *Task boundary.* Identifying who has the responsibility for carrying out the decisions
3. *Political boundary.* Determining who receives support and major resource allocation
4. *Identity boundary.* Establishing a feeling on the part of individuals that they are critical to the organization

Teams are the dominant structure in a "boundaryless" organization, and department labels are erased. Teams develop creative collaboration because they communicate across divisions. Flexibility in team-member assignments helps to boost information flow and contribute to consensus decision making.

Following his tenth anniversary, Jack Welch is still reinventing GE. Although he is considered one of the most controversial and most praised Chief Executive Officers, he has created an organization that is "boundaryless." He has done this by transforming GE so that definitions of internal divisions are blurry. This allows everybody to work as a team. GE considers that it is a partner with its customers. The results have shown an annual growth of 8 percent and profits of 11 percent per year, leading to a total of $4.3 billion in 1990. This is despite the fact that the workforce was reduced from 410,000 to 300,000, and the return on equity reached approximately 19 percent per year. His goal was to fix, close, or sell businesses that were not "number one or two" in their industry. Recently, he has sold $10 billion worth of GE companies and bought $25 billion worth in others. "Neutron Jack" has the reputation of being arrogant and ruthless, but he claims he is "hard headed but warm hearted."

In an interview with Tichy and Charan (1989), Welch commented that insecure managers use complexity and clutter to distract others. He maintains that self-confident leaders use speed and simplicity to achieve a transformation of attitudes that releases "emotional energy, encourages creativity, and creates a feeling of ownership and self-worth." GE has consistently relied on decision-support systems to evaluate and back up its strategic decisions. The results of a combined understanding of the organization with a strong computer-support system has shown a handsome payoff.

THE ENTREPRENEURIAL ORGANIZATION

An entrepreneurial organization structure requires a more aggressive posture that focuses on increasing value and customer satisfaction. For these organizations to be successful, a new corporate vision is required that relies on a flat, flexible structure which can utilize teams, provide the freedom needed to achieve innovative solutions, and allow the empowerment of workers so as to assure shared values. Where these organizations create an adaptive and responsive culture, they can assure that customers will receive superior value.

Because they are under extreme pressure, entrepreneurial organizations need to provide clear guidelines for the redesign process, introduce rewards that challenge performance improvement, simplify systems, and ensure that appropriate training and support are given in order to accelerate the change process. By loosening control procedures, they can emphasize shared values and worker satisfaction, and are more likely to achieve their objectives. They are also holding teams accountable for introducing change, which helps to eliminate the bottlenecks resulting from hierarchic structures and can encourage participative decision making.

Obviously, this entrepreneurial approach would not apply to all organizations. Depending on the leadership, the organization culture, and the shared values, some organizations would readily adopt this mode of introducing change. Those that are inflexible, such as IBM or GM, have found that they are losing their competitive position and even their survivability. The challenge is to develop intelligent decision-support systems that help to facilitate the change process, which can become an accepted part of operating procedures.

In the past, entrepreneurial organizations have used a "hip-pocket" approach to running the operations. For example, after Apple Computers began to grow, the fun was gone and Wozniak took his money and left. On the other hand, Jobs did not want to run a large organization, and he brought in John Scully, a friend and an organization man from Pepsi Cola. The chemistry seemed to be good at the beginning, but eventually power and control became an issue between the two, and Jobs was forced out. Apple reflected Scully's analytic decision style, which he used to develop systems, procedures, rules, and the discipline essential to continued growth in a large organization. Perhaps Apple will revert to becoming a more entrepreneurial organization in order to maintain its competitive edge.

INTRODUCING ORGANIZATIONAL CHANGE

As global pressures mount, the need to redesign U.S. businesses becomes critical. A radically new approach to management change is required that utilizes information technology and careful planning to fit the varied organizational pieces back together in a new pattern. Heygate (1990) cites the case of a major bank that had three years to cut costs by 30 percent and increase its profits by 100 percent. The bank wanted to remain competitive and increase productivity by restructuring the branch network, which meant bringing new skills to 20,000 staff members. The organization redesign would result in a 50 to 80 percent reduction of the remaining jobs which were being changed. To accomplish this task, new information support processes had to be introduced which could easily have been sabotaged. The change required a massively parallel front-line effort to achieve an accelerated new design.

The bank had to overcome many obstacles to achieve its objective. To accelerate the change, they required an enhanced-information, technology-program management effort. However, what they found was that there was resistance from middle management. Also, they would have to have a massive training effort for skill building and would have to eliminate an existing inflexible information system and inflexible change program. The bank decided to take the steps needed. The introduced precise definitions of all the new tasks and roles, and they used computer workstations to support the training effort. They managed to sidestep the current inflexible approaches to redesign of the computer system by using an incremental approach to introducing improvements. Using a modular approach, they introduced a parallel design, which relied on program management that changed from the sequential approach normally taken. Continuous communications and worker empowerment was a hallmark of their efforts. They were able to obtain improvements using a disciplined release of new updates. Key team leaders were kept informed of progress, and senior management was kept involved at every stage of the changed design. A central logistics unit was established to assure appropriate delegation of the line and functional operations. Implementing a massively parallel, accelerated change requires new approaches and new support tools because conventional approaches are much too slow and do not assure meeting overall design objectives.

MOBILIZING ORGANIZATIONAL CHANGE

To introduce new intelligent technologies and change an organization, it is not enough to dream grand dreams and plan to realize them. The passions and enthusiasms of the employees must also be engaged. There can be no business transformation without people transformation. Some dispute this fact and insist that if the analysis is correct and the plan is good, change will occur. They believe that reason and clear thought need no advocates but themselves, and they see emotion as friction loss. Others dislike the implication that psychology has a role to play in change programs because it strongly implies covert manipulation. Although it is right to appeal to reason, it is dangerous to assume people always behave rationally. It is not unethical or manipulative to try to manage the irrational. Explaining the emotional cycle of change can be helpful. If people know what sort of emotional roller coaster they will be on, they are more likely to hang tough.

Mobilization has two prongs: (1) a top-down, leadership development and large-scale mobilization-driven prong; and (2) a bottom-up prong consisting of work teams and the encouragement of individual change. Both are needed; neither is sufficient by itself. The need for leadership is clear, but top-down programs on their own are readily rejected by the company's informal organizational and communication systems.

REFRAMING THE CORPORATION

Today's complex environment is leading more companies to reinvent themselves to take advantage of the opportunities for change that exist. Many basic procedures have been around for many years, even though the workforce is better educated, new communications media exist, and economies of scale are decreasing in importance. One insurance company estimated that it took almost twenty-two days to approve a policy, even though the actual work took only seventeen minutes. By sharing information, new technology highlights showed that most insurance policies need only consultation with specialists. When specialists can be consulted quickly, most policies can be handled by a single person, which is a result of reengineering or reinventing the work.

How should a company go about reinventing or reframing itself? Simply creating new products, without the support of an organization structure that emphasizes continuous innovation, will leave management in an organizational miasma. Xerox is an example of a company that reinvented their Palo Alto Research Center (PARC) to pursue advanced research in the areas of computers, electronics, and materials. As a result of this effort, the center has contributed a significant number of fundamental innovations in computer technology through the development of bit-mapped computer screens. They improved on the fundamentals of local area networks and developed mouse editing using an object-oriented programming language. Probably their most important contribution was the first prototype laser printer, which is a major product for Xerox today. PARC now focuses on the relationship of technology to work and how information technology can support group collaboration.

It is now imperative that organizations be capable of change, but how should the change be carried out? One approach that has been brought forward is to create a learning organization. Global competition requires strategic learning in order to do things "differently" than in the past. The advantage gained by introducing radical change far outweighs the problems that such change engenders. A major difficulty that must be overcome is that large organizations need to learn how to cross functional lines. While this is no trivial matter, the real impetus for change often comes from the people in the organization, rather than from the reflecting of a concern with problem solving that may emanate from the outside. The central task of management is to continuously build a knowledge base that contributes to the learning process.

According to Nonaka (1991), Japanese companies create knowledge by changing organizational roles, structures, and practices in order to guide continuous innovation. These companies recognize that knowledge is typically generated by individuals who have an insight about a problem. However, developing new knowledge requires a supportive culture and one in which the organization values innovation. To be successful, a knowledge-creating organization must recognize that knowledge creation affects all managerial roles and responsibilities.

Creative organizations are able to relate a company's values and norms to performance expectations. Leadership has been identified as the single most critical factor that separates successful change from that which fails. Because leadership styles are highly correlated with decision styles, it is possible to identify which style best fits a given environment and to predict which managers have the personality that can accomplish this difficult task. Typically, managers who are a combination of the conceptual and analytical styles are best able to utilize the right approaches in given situations so that the objective of introducing creativity into the organization is readily achieved.

An ability to sense environmental change and whether it carries threats or opportunities is essential for survival because the anatomy of today's corporation is always evolving. Reward systems are changing, work architectures are being redefined, and visions are being refreshed. We once assumed that corporate evolution consisted of long periods of stasis, punctuated by periodic adaptations; but the pace of change is too fast for that now. The company needs to adapt every day. To that end, or beginning, an organization's ability to learn and change takes on new meaning. The learning required in becoming a learning organization is transformational learning. Such learning is about who we are as an organization. It is not an individual task, and it demands a shift that goes all the way to the corporate culture, value systems, flow of information, reward and recognition systems, and—most important—to the human relationships, managerial practices, and underlying sense of integrity that constantly renew and support the knowledge bases and corporate intelligence.

RESTRUCTURING AND DOWNSIZING

Organizational change is also accomplished by restructuring or downsizing. This has brought new life to many troubled companies because it abandons obsolete products and focuses on innovation and new business. The Williams Company of Tulsa exchanged a pipeline business for fiber optics, and has MCI Communications as a major customer. Goodyear was the number three tire maker in the United States, but because of severe competition and limited growth, they left the tire business and shifted to the production of plastics, specialty chemicals, and aircraft parts. Although Goodyear initially lost money, they felt that it was better than the tire business. Although restructuring is not easy, it is better than remaining in a declining business, or in a business where competition is severe.

Business reengineering leads inevitably to organizational change. Effective analysis and implementation have been found to require involvement of both senior management and information technology professionals. At the same time, any program that introduces change should be able to show tangible payoffs, while being able to obtain commitment from those involved or to find outside expertise when needed. A number of Business Process Reengineering (BPR) tools have begun to emerge to help automate the analysis, design, and implementation processes. These software tools include the following:

1. *Program planning*—contributes to the overall planning for carrying out the BPR program.
2. *Organization analysis*—examines the cost of changes in the organization and helps to decide which to keep and which to eliminate.
3. *Modeling analysis*—helps to identify and map nonvalue stages in the process and the cost associated with each step.
4. *Activity costing*—relates cost and time to each step in the process and helps to evaluate the desirability of changes.
5. *Graphic simulation*—facilitates the review of the overall process and communication with upper management.
6. *Business analysis*—tracks productivity, quality, market penetration, inventory, and backlog of demand.
7. *Benchmarking*—provides comparisons with other processes in the same or other comparable organizations.

Although tools are now available for BPR, the analysis and design of a new system is time consuming and costly. The most successful programs are a combination of technology with a behavioral approach, which creates the environment where change is accepted (The, 1995). For example, Xerox has relied on ReThink, a software program developed by Gensym Corporation. They estimate savings of $150 million in their BPR. The BPR team started by mapping the existing purchase order flow and quickly identified the potential bottlenecks using intelligent software which was able to refine the process. The intelligent software relied on a simulation program that represented the purchase orders and graphically traced the flow of items in the process. Feedback was provided to the reengineering team, who were able to correct the design to take advantage of the information. This is an excellent example of how an intelligent information system was able to help the system designers make better decisions than they could alone (Blanchard, 1995).

Discontinuous Thinking

To make radical changes, reengineering implies discontinuous thinking. System designers have to break away from the outdated rules to avoid rearranging current operations. Breakthrough performance requires eliminating many existing processes. Old assumptions need to be discarded to get away from what had made the business fail to reach goals. The key is to design jobs around the objective or the outcome instead of the task, and to design work in which one manager is responsible for an entire operation.

Reengineering involves process innovation and redesign leading to radical change in business. Reengineering starts by asking, What would we do differently if we were a new company? Reengineering creates problems and possibilities. AT&T's Global Communications Systems Business, with sales of $3.4 billion, embarked on rewriting hundreds of job descriptions, prepared new reward systems, updated the computer system, retrained massively, and made extensive changes in financial reporting, proposals, and contracts.

The following steps highlight what is required for successful reengineering:

1. *Involve top management.* Reengineering is cross-functional and requires someone with authority to take charge.

2. *Avoid political infighting.* Create a sense of urgency by making reengineering compelling.

3. *Start with a clean slate.* Create designs based on what the customers want in order to satisfy their needs.

4. *Reengineer.* Work with Total Quality Management, using teams to implement the program.

Despite all of the difficulties associated with reengineering, results can be startling. Union Carbide saved over $20 million in their industrial chemical division by applying the reengineering approach.

However, the problems associated with reengineering, downsizing, restructuring, or outsourcing include potential loss of qualified personnel, frustration, and resentment. Management can deal with these problems by utilizing transformational leadership developed by Tichy and Charan (1989). This approach helps people to handle change. Widespread layoffs should be comparable to a loss due to death or divorce. Tichy suggests a period when employees can openly discuss their thoughts so they are better able to cope with the new situation.

Michael Hammer currently admits that 70 percent of all the reengineering projects wind up in disappointment. One of the major reasons for the large number of failed projects is the attempt to use the wrong software. Companies such as Chevron, Intel, and Microsoft feel that they have found the missing link to reengineering. It is a software program called SAP that was developed in Germany. The SAP software allows companies to standardize their software systems. Large software systems are difficult to install because they also require a change in attitude on the part of the IT staff. For example, Border has been implementing SAP, and it has taken over three years and cost millions of dollars. SAP provides the equivalent of a road map that systems designers can use. The objective is to put information into the computer only once. SAP consolidates warehousing with worldwide order processing and integrates the information received by linking data base servers to various sales offices, the factory, the warehouse, accounting, and headquarters, where they monitor operations. Although the initial cost is high, implementing SAP will generally pay for itself within a few years (Jaynes, 1995).

When management contemplates a drastic change, it is important that employees understand what is being proposed, how it affects them, and why the change is needed. If some employees must be let go, they need to be treated properly and be given an opportunity to transfer to another job or have outplacement services available. For the others who are kept, management needs to provide a clear description of their new roles and what they might expect in the future. The organization becomes responsive to employees' needs, while enhancing the chances for survival by being able to cope with new conditions. Although this may be difficult, the Chesapeake Corporation, known for production of wood pulp, had to restructure because of severe competition and a declining market share. The result of the reengineering was that they became the leading producer of customized paper products. The conversion was not easy, but it was the better alternative to staying in a declining business where the competition prevented growth and profitability (Hage and Geier, 1992).

By using a humanistic approach, management can avoid many of the problems associated with restructuring or reengineering. To be effective, change requires a careful analysis of the business, the organization structure, and the information system requirements. Operating improvements and tangible benefits need to be estimated along with a plan specifying the costs involved. Using this information as a base, the overall strategy for the organization reengineering can be determined.

The majority of jobs and organizational structures were introduced long before the advent of the computer. Their orientation was efficiency and control. What is needed is innovation, speed, service, value, and quality. Hammer and Champy (1993) recommend that when companies reengineer, they should not automate first, but they should obliterate unnecessary work. The sad history of automation is that it has not yielded dramatic improvements and has generally required large investments. Speeding up existing processes does not achieve desired results, because fundamental performance deficiencies are ignored. Instead of embedding outdated processes in silicon, they should be eliminated. Applying the power of information technology, companies can easily redesign business processes. As an illustration, Ford's top management wanted to cut the costs of accounts payable, which had more than 500 people. By comparison, Mazda had only five people in its accounts payable organization. The difference was so astonishing that Ford concluded that its accounts payable organization was five times too large.

In addition to organization restructuring, businesses must explore the reengineering of information systems that replace outmoded systems so that they can meet the needs of future business requirements. Old approaches to software development need to be undertaken in order to save the many hours of analysis that would otherwise be required to change poorly maintained systems. Users gain substantial benefits from information systems reengineering because it helps to achieve state-of-the-art applications without incurring enormous costs of new hardware and software (Turban, 1993).

THE ORGANIZATION LIFE CYCLE

A major reason for organization change is the need to cope with the forces that cause change, such as the following:

1. An aging organization
2. Cumbersome size of the organization
3. Meeting competitive challenges
4. Declining growth potential
5. Regulatory or stakeholder demands
6. Impact of new technology and the need for new products and processes

From an information and decision-support perspective, decision-making requirements change at each stage in the organization life cycle. For example, the entrepreneurial stage requires a manager who is a combination of the conceptual and directive decision styles. The entrepreneur has ideas, drives, and the willingness to take the risks.

During the start-up phase, the organization is under intense pressure from competition, seldom has adequate resources, and faces the possibility of failure. The culture is typically cohesive, and excitement contributes to the high involvement of a start-up. Communication is face-to-face, and there are few written procedures. Timely status information is vital and contributes to the success or failure of the organization. Ninety percent of all start-ups fail because they cannot meet cash-flow requirements.

Typically, entrepreneurial organizations have only two levels. One level focuses on the ideas and the other on operations. Large organizations can behave in an entrepreneurial mode, such as the case of Lockheed's Skunk Works, which produced advanced avionics.

New product development is a critical aspect of the organization life cycle. Innovation is needed to avoid obsolescence when the product reaches the saturation state. In the past, the product life cycle averaged seven years. In today's merciless technological environment, products can last as short as three to six months, especially in software or computers.

Tracing the typical life cycle of an organization, there is a change in each of the activities that are normally carried out. This is shown in Table 6.1. The classic paradigm of the organization life cycle will have to be adapted to fit new environmental forces. Today, organizations reengineer, restructure,

Table 6.1
Changes Associated with the Organization Life Cycle

Management function	Organization structure	Performance control	Crises prevention
Innovation	Informal	Creative	Leadership
Transition	Functional	Direction	Autonomy
Growth	Decentralize	Delegation	Control
Consolidation	Groups	Coordinate	Red Tape
Adaptation	Teams	Collaborate	Survival

and reinvent themselves almost continuously. The life cycle model that has persisted for many years has changed to a continuous process of innovation and invention in order to stay competitive. Although organizations do go through phases, they no longer have the luxury of time to change in the way that the classic life cycle implies.

DECISION MAKING AND THE ORGANIZATION LIFE CYCLE

Each phase of the life cycle requires a different style of decision making. The start-up phase is generally characterized by considerable openness and high risk taking. Individuals who are best suited to start new organizations are not necessarily the ones who are capable of handling the growth phase, in which more structure is used. During the growth phase, management tends to overcontrol and overreact to situations. To correct this situation, delegation and empowerment should be used to distribute decision making to continue the growth. Following this phase, managers have reverted to control, coordination, and centralization, which is now recognized as having a deleterious effect on organization performance. What is described as the final phase—adaptation—takes place continuously as the organization grows.

If the mode of adaptation is not appropriate and action is not taken in time, the organization may not survive or enter a new growth cycle. Lack of adaptation leads to a decline, and the organization is eventually taken over or goes bankrupt. This can be very painful, as evidenced by the kinds of desperate actions taken by companies when attempting to restructure for growth to avoid the trauma of a takeover.

The information requirements for each phase of the organization life cycle are shown in Table 6.2, which recognizes that change and coping with competition are continuous processes and not separate or distinct phases. Each phase shown in Table 6.2 suggests a different information emphasis to meet the organizational requirements. In a start-up situation, openness and involvement of personnel are important in order to overcome the many problems encountered. Information needed at this phase is current, accurate, and timely so as to meet rapidly changing conditions.

IMPROVING ORGANIZATIONAL PERFORMANCE

Performance evaluation is needed to assure that an organization is achieving its goals and objectives. No matter how well decisions are made, results depend on acceptance by the individuals involved. Increasingly, management recognizes that a decision is, at best, only a guide to what is

Table 6.2
Organization Life Cycle and Information Requirements

Phase	Management Style	Information Requirements
Innovation	Openness	Accurate and timely status
Transition	Flexible	Competitive position
Growth	Strategic	Real-time decision support
Consolidation	Creative	Intelligent decision support
Adaptation	Participative	Network processing

needed. As conditions change, this gives rise to new requirements and a change in the way that a decision is implemented. When changes in tasks are not predictable, managers cannot simply rely on formal procedures and performance measurement. If tasks change continuously and are highly uncertain, then problem solving or innovative approaches using Intelligent Information Systems are most appropriate. Worker participation in decision making and empowerment determines effectiveness of performance.

Because decisions effect the future and involve uncertainty, it is difficult to predict precisely what changes are likely to take place and how people will respond. Expert systems are increasingly being used for complex problems that build on the knowledge and expertise of managers. Expert systems will not replace approaches such as team effort or empowerment; rather, they will facilitate effective decision making so that effort is not wasted in pursuing wrong directions or improper execution of a task.

There have been five approaches used to measure and evaluate performance. These include the following:

1. *Historic.* This approach used past data or performance standards to measure output.

2. *Real-time.* This method relies on computers to provide information that is as current as possible to determine what has actually been accomplished.

3. *Adaptive.* This approach attempts to respond to the changes that are occurring by determining the best course of action. Expert systems can have a significant impact in this area.

4. *Predictive.* This is an attempt to anticipate future events or to develop strategies to achieve desired outcomes. Predictive systems typically involve computer models, simulation, or similar approaches to forecast future conditions.

5. *Organizational.* These measures attempt to achieve goal congruence, commitment, acceptance of decisions, empowerment, and organizational transformation. Group decision sharing and teamwork contribute to more effective performance.

Performance evaluation is multidimensional and involves many organizational factors. Organizational learning and strategic reframing are used to determine where the company is uniquely well equipped to dominate a market segment. Future information systems will need to consider the impact of current performance evaluation and the impact on workers.

PERFORMANCE DETERMINATION

Determining performance is never an end in itself; it is only a means toward the end of achieving an objective, such as more innovation. For example, quality control does not build quality into a product, it merely identifies whether the quality is satisfactory, which is useful information needed to change the manufacturing process or process reengineering. In a similar manner, if performance does not meet the level desired, measurement itself cannot change that performance. A fundamental consideration in designing Intelligent Information Systems is to recognize that data and information are only indicators that identify when a change is needed, but not how it might be done. Expert systems are increasingly being used to assist in determining how much change is needed.

Another consideration in performance is determining the effect of interactions and dependencies that exist in any organization. Where operations overlap, disruption is the result. Dependencies and interactions, along with continuous change, need to be tracked. It is virtually impossible to predict the exact course any decision will follow. Computer monitoring of results, using a trend analysis, can forecast possible outcomes. These form an integral part of an intelligent performance evaluation system.

Occidental Petroleum is an example of how one company dealt with improving performance when it decided to change its approach to IT operations. Rapid growth had forced a reevaluation of whether to insource or to centralize IT. They made the decision to insource and bring the computer back in-house. This is contrary to what many companies have done when they used outsourcing as a means of reducing costs. After three years, insourcing has resulted in reducing Occidental's three data centers to one. The budget was reduced by 40 percent, and the staff was reduced by 60 percent. Also, consolidation of hardware, software, and personnel reduced the number of changes to the production system. This has made data processing easier to manage and significantly improved performance.

USE OF INFORMATION TECHNOLOGY
FOR PERFORMANCE EVALUATION

Performance evaluation requires accurate information that describes output. Hertz (1983) points out that information is only relevant within a general frame of reference, and that information needs a theoretical framework to distinguish "facts" from randomly structured data. Simon (1982) makes it clear that in complex, real-world situations, numbers are not the name of the game. He says, "Representational structures that permit functional reasoning, however qualitative that data may be, is what is required." The question then is, "What information is needed in order to identify changes in relationships, and what conditions will produce desired results and with what risks?"

An important concern in performance measurement is that the mere gathering of data can create dysfunctional behavior in an organization. McGregor (1957) points out that the manner in which performance evaluation is applied, as well as criteria used for performance review, often induces dysfunctional and unintended consequences, such as widespread antagonism, resistance, noncompliance, unreliable performance, need for close surveillance, and high administrative costs.

STAGES IN PERFORMANCE MEASUREMENT

There are five basic stages used to understand problems in performance measurement. The first stage is to identify that something significant has occurred. The second is how to measure the event. The third is recording the information. The fourth is making decisions based on an evaluation of the information reported. And the fifth stage is making any necessary changes needed. At the fourth and fifth stages, Intelligent Information Systems can provide more effective support for decision makers than merely reporting data.

Each stage of measurement can severely impact performance. For example, when something happens, accurate information is needed to describe the situation. After a change has been identified, the next step in measurement is to determine what needs to be done with it. Basing measurement on historic data is like examining something after the fact; as a consequence, any proposed change which is based on historic data is comparable to driving a car using the rearview mirror.

Another problem in measurement is that, in general, there is no provision for variability in the data. Rather, absolute measures are used: The equipment is busy only 50 percent of the time, or 20 percent of sales quotas have been missed. In the past, management reports were not only notoriously late but they were generally used with averages of the data which hid or eliminated variability. Improper or arbitrary allocations of overhead or general and administrative expenses pose a problem when one attempts to evaluate performance. It is almost axiomatic that, because of the inherent problems in measurement, potentially dysfunctional behavioral effects will occur.

ORGANIZATIONAL PERFORMANCE

An important consideration in determining overall performance rather than department or division performance is that there is inevitably a bias in performance measurement when dealing with only one division, area, or product. For example, where profit centers have a high degree of interdependency or joint sharing of cost among divisions, poor evaluation is inevitable. To avoid this problem, information should be based on assigning cost allocations based on where they are incurred. At Lincoln Electric, all new designs are prepared jointly by engineering and manufacturing, which eliminates the possibility of conflict between the two departments.

When units operate independently, total organizational costs are higher than where there is cooperative effort. Group decision-support systems and open information systems can help to avoid some of these difficulties.

Another consideration is recognizing that using only one factor for performance evaluation will generally lead to suboptimization. For example, a company's cash reserve can be reduced by relying on a line of credit. This approach proves cheaper for the few times that there are heavy cash demands. Using a probabilistic approach, one can readily establish the "float" or reserve required. A real-time information system can continuously monitor cash flow, and an expert system then can recommend actions needed to avoid overdrafts.

USE OF BENCHMARKING FOR INFORMATION MEASUREMENT

Benchmarking has been used to evaluate performance of a company by comparing it with what other companies do. Computer performance has been evaluated using picture-level benchmarks and layered graphics to assess performance. A picture-level benchmark measures the speed with which an image can be displayed on a system. There are four basic levels of evaluation used: primitives, pictures, system, and applications. A primitive-level benchmark measures points or lines drawn on a screen; this type of benchmark reports pixels, vectors, or polygons per second. A primitive-level benchmark requires little effort or investment and provides a "first pass" for evaluating graphics performance. A system-level benchmark measures the whole graphics system. Application-level benchmarks are the most accurate measure of computer performance but require the most time and effort to perform.

San Dover, president of Dover & Associates, claims that too much effort is focused on improving the process rather than the usefulness of the information product. To improve product quality, he maintains that companies need information standards or benchmarking. IT systems are notoriously inconsistent among applications. The problem transcends specific methodologies, platforms, or technology.

MEASURING EFFECTIVENESS OF PERFORMANCE

The effectiveness of an information system can be judged by how well performance meets a specified goal. Effectiveness can be defined as:

$$\text{System effectiveness} = \frac{\text{Total resources employed}}{\text{Value received}}$$

The resources used include both organizational and financial factors. Value represents the performance in terms of quantity, quality, cost, and service.

Effectiveness can also be considered at three levels rather than as a single overall measure. Effectiveness can be considered at the individual level, the managerial level, and the organizational level. Obviously, these three levels interact and influence one another, but their separate evaluation is needed to determine how best to design an information system. Starting with the individual decision level, effectiveness is concerned with the technical or analytical soundness of the system. For example, doubling capacity does not increase twofold output, where there are random effects that create delays. Using resources in the "hope" of doubling output would not be an effective technical decision, and performance would not reach the level desired without additional costs to the organization in terms of overtime or reduced morale because of the increased pressure and stress to meet the desired goal. At the managerial level, effectiveness is concerned with the decision process used. Decision styles, control styles, and the exercise of power are all ingredients of managerial effectiveness.

Organizational effectiveness is associated with overall performance, such as profitability or growth. Because of the interaction with the other two levels—the individual level and the managerial level—organizational effectiveness cannot be treated separately. Too often, poor performance is a result of dysfunctional organizational behavior rather than the technical aspect of a system.

APPROACHES TO MANAGING PERFORMANCE

Keeley and Roure (1990) propose a framework for performance evaluation based on the level of detail required, the compatibility with organization stability, and the consistency or importance of the data. To avoid some of the problems with performance management, the following factors are suggested for examination:

1. *Behavioral.* Define performance in observable, physical actions which take into account the motivational requirements of the employee.
2. *Objectives.* Use of measures which are specific and can be related to actual results achieved. Recognize variability in data and allowance for changes.
3. *Evaluators.* Utilize persons who are knowledgeable and who rely on multiple approaches to measurement. They recognize that measurement can cause dysfunctional behavior and that standards are often arbitrary.

Each of these is related to given conditions, such as individual differences in the workers. These behavioral-based measures work best for structured tasks where workers do not desire autonomy. Objective measures fit where the organization is moderately structured and workers have a moderate desire for autonomy. Judgmental measures fit best for those situations where there is considerable uncertainty and where workers have a high desire for autonomy. Fitting this framework into intelligent information poses a challenge to the designer of such systems.

Why has performance measurement not been effective in the implementation of decisions? Often, management is reactive to situations which create a negative atmosphere. What is needed is a proactive, responsive, and anticipatory approach. Often, organizations require behavior which they cannot reward, such as switching jobs to meet an emergency. There are a number of substantive issues concerned with having adequate information to understand the reality of a situation. Furthermore, because of perceptual bias, what is observed may not be what has actually happened.

Cost reduction, by itself, is a misconception concerning improving performance. For example, if sales are dropping, larger expenditures might be warranted to increase sales rather than reduce the sales force. An approach taken by International Rectifier during the period when transistors flooded the marketplace was to shift their engineering workforce to sales engineers. They actually increased their sales rather than following the downward forecast and downsizing, which is undoubtedly overused by organizations.

When people cooperate, they can make any organization work effectively. The converse is also true: Workers who have a poor attitude can foul up the best system or organization. The human element needs to be considered when making significant changes. For example, the assembly-line methods used by many automobile manufacturers do not achieve the same performance as the team approach used by Volvo in Sweden. Job specialization is yielding to job enrichment. The concepts of common goals, participation by workers, appropriate recognition of performance, and sharing of rewards have openly and fairly improved performance in many companies.

To improve performance in an information system, organizational factors, such as quality, inventory, or finance, must be taken into account. Drucker (1966) has succinctly stated that in a social system, goal setting and value setting are important but they are not objective. Excessive controls in a system become meaningless or become mere noise, which leads to chaos. Because something can be quantified, it does not mean it should be measured. What needs to be determined is what the manager considers important, what a manager should focus on, and what is needed to achieve effective direction with maximum economy of effort. An Intelligent Information System should be able to support the decision making by matching information with the manager's cognitive style. Knowledge and data can be dealt with more intelligently where there is natural-language interface, efficient query and search, use of knowledge based on activities or objects, and augmenting of the decision maker's reasoning power by use of expert systems.

SUMMARY

The effective leader will have to possess technical, human, and conceptual skills in order to see that the organizational systems and structure reinforce the vision and desired state of their business. This builds teamwork and legitimate empowerment that permeates the organization. A company committed to this approach, GE, is attempting to run the company as a group of small businesses. This has boosted the growth of their productivity. In 1990, the company's sales growth was $3.8 billion, more than the total sales of all but the largest U.S. companies. With $4.4 billion in profits, it was second only to Exxon in earnings.

Most industries have to stay abreast of the latest technology to stay competitive. Where consumers demand new technologies, these become the driving force. As an example, three-dimensional virtual reality could revolutionize product design and manufacturing. With the ability to easily visualize reality, designers can vastly improve products. The Boeing 777 was the first plane to be designed completely by computer-aided design and computer-aided manufacturing. Sony is a company where engineers develop four new products every day, turning generalists loose to work on advanced products. Their engineers and scientists work long hours, but they keep Sony a top technological company. To keep abreast of new technology, Sony spends $1.5 billion per year—5.7 percent of their revenues.

"Information is power" is perhaps just a slogan in many organizations, but its real test is how to convert information into intelligence to be used as a powerful management tool. When we say that giving information to workers will empower them, what is meant is that information will make them more competent to reach their own decisions. The challenge for management is whether they will be given the authority—the power—to make those decisions and become more productive. One of the most significant and dramatic developments in recent years has been the role of technology in significantly expanding the capacity of the value-added chain as a communication channel to store, process, and transmit information. The effects of this expansion in channel capacity generally involve an increase in the speed with which intelligent information is transmitted and an increase in the amount of information that can be stored and processed. The result is the creation of new types of patterns

to organize intelligent information, with quantitative changes giving rise to qualitative changes. The results in the speed and amount of processing are functions of technology, but the emergence of new ways of packaging and organizing intelligent information suggests the importance of considering the information itself, above the technology, as the key variable for analysis.

Taking this one step further, information turns into knowledge and becomes the key variable for analysis within Intelligent Information Systems. From this significant trend emerges the following: (1) the recognition of knowledge itself as an asset, with significant marketplace value; (2) a redefinition of categories between the organization (internal) and the outside (external) world; and (3) knowledge is displacing the traditional factors of capital and labor as a basis for achieving competitive strategy. It is obvious that advanced technology is a critical driving factor in maintaining competitiveness in the computer industry. These advances portend better information systems to support management decisions and corporate strategies.

Successful strategies for the 1990s will be based more on core capabilities that are difficult for competitors to imitate. Intelligent strategies can assist the organization to be more responsive, innovative, and understanding of customers' needs. They can also develop organizational flexibility and make more extensive use of information technology. In short, responsiveness is a key factor in being competitive.

Capability-based strategies require identification of core competencies. This begins with an evaluation of a company's capability profile and helps to determine the company's strengths and weaknesses in four key areas: managerial, marketing, financial, and technical. The very nature of the development of intelligent knowledge-based systems (drawing from the expertise within the organization) and the use of Intelligent Information Systems (disseminating that expertise throughout the organization), makes Intelligent Information Systems a catalyst for change in the organization.

Beginning with the integration of knowledge and expertise from within the organization, decision making and problem solving have now a common base of knowledge for action. This common base of knowledge may lead, depending on the former decision-making processes used, to centralization of decision making, or it may create a decentralized decision-making process with confidence. In either event, decision trails for intermediate and final recommendations will tend to be shorter, more trustworthy, and better defined. An important result will be that the speed of complex task accomplishments will be increased.

The effect of Intelligent Information Systems on organizational structures could be profound, as knowledge supplants task as a criterion for organizational development and utilization. As expert knowledge permeates the organization, the number of organizational levels involved will certainly increase. Therefore, it may be found that fewer (and more knowledgeable) organizational levels are equally productive. A change in physical organizational boundaries is inevitable as common knowledge permeates the organization. Knowledge is not bound by task; the opposite is true, and this will be reflected in the knowledge-directed organization. Changes in organizational levels and boundaries must change management's perspective of workflow and procedures of the organization. Simpler procedures can be developed to direct work and speed the introduction of tasks into and through the organization.

Organizational communications will be aided by Intelligent Information Systems. This is because the knowledge-based systems are drawn directly from the organizational memory, intelligence, and expertise, and because this expertise is then infused back into the organization as commonly useable knowledge. Because of this common baseline, the quality and timeliness of organizational intelligence is upgraded. The improved effectiveness of communication is an important product of quality and timeliness, as is the communication and effectiveness patterns between departments.

Just as Intelligent Information Systems change the organization structure, so they will create a change in work tasks and processes. These will now be based on common knowledge, better intelligence (information), and its more effective flow. Central to this change is the economization of scarce human expertise. Management will jealously guard their knowledge possessors as they now guard their patents and proprietary products. With expert knowledge infused throughout the organization, work quality will improve, since the worker has been drawn into the scheme of things and not left to watch from the outside. Specialization of skills can be easily disseminated, spreading management's risk of skills loss and improving the quality of the workforce. The physical and temporal boundaries of work for the individual employee should be expanded enormously, making for a more satisfied and loyal workforce. Improved quality, satisfaction, and loyalty in the workforce will have its ultimate effect in better service offered to clients and customers.

A knowledge-directed organization will alter the usual methods for monitoring and controlling work. What an employee knows and how that knowledge can be applied effectively will become a challenge for management; knowledge is harder to judge or direct than task accomplishment. Fortunately, an organization working from a common knowledge base can be urged toward standardization in work accomplishment, never in the sense of rote, but in the sense of initiative, imagination, and learning.

Perhaps most important to the success of Intelligent Information Systems in any organization is training. Management must not only accept and trust the knowledge-based systems born of their organization's own intelligence and expertise, but they must also strive for an increased capacity for the organization to learn and apply the knowledge gained to continually improve the organization, its management, and its products.

BIBLIOGRAPHY

Alter, Steven L. 1976. How Effective Managers Use Information Systems. *Harvard Business Review* (November/December): 97–105.

Apiki, Steve, Stanford Diehl, and Howard Eglowstein. 1990. Not Just Numbers Anymore. *Byte* (February): 148–165.

Argyris, Chris. 1991. Teaching Smart People How to Learn. *Harvard Business Review* (May/June): 99–109.

Armstrong, Larry. 1992. Software that Can Dethrone "Computer Tyranny." *Business Week* (April 6): 90–91.

Arnst, Catherine. 1993. Faith in a Stranger. *Business Week* (April 5): 18–21.

Babcock, C. 1987. Programmer Power. *Computer World* (January 5): 51–53.

Bartholomew, Doug. 1995. Shooting Checks Off-site. *Information Week* (October 2): 88.

Bauer, Roy A., Emilio Collar, and Victor Tang. 1992. *The Silverlake Project*. New York: Oxford University Press.

Bauerschmidt, Alan, and James J. Chrisman. 1993. Strategies for Survival in the Microcomputer Industry. *Journal of Management Inquiry* (March): 63–82.

Baumohl, Bernard. 1993. When Downsizing Becomes Dumbsizing. *Time* (March 15): 55.

Bicket, Jock. 1992. *Adventures in Relevance Marketing*. Denver: Briefcase Books.

Blanchard, David. 1995. Xerox Saves $150 Million with Intelligent Information. *OR/MS Today* (December): 10.

Boone, Mary E. 1991. *Leadership and the Computer*. New York: St. Martin's Press.

Bowen, William. 1986. The Puny Payoff from Office Computers. *Fortune* (May 26): 20–24.

Brown, John Seely. 1992. Research that Reinvents the Corporation. *The McKinsey Quarterly* (2): 78–96.

Buday, Robert. 1991. Observations of an Influential Bystander. *Insights* (Fall).

Budiansky, Stephen, Bruce A. Auster, Joseph L. Galloway, and Peter S. Green. 1993. New Weapons of War. *U.S. News & World Report* (May 31): 30–33.

Business and Information Systems Re-Engineering. 1993. *Decision Line* (May): 7.

Can He Make an Elephant Dance? 1993. *Newsweek* (April 5): 46–47.

Carroll, Paul. 1992. IBM to See PC Clone Made by Asian Firm. *Wall Street Journal* (March 11): B1.

Cascio, Wayne F. 1993. Downsizing: What Do We Know? What Have We Learned? *Academy of Management Executive* 7(1): 95–104.

Cecil, John, and Michael Goldstein. 1990. Sustaining Competitive Advantage from IT. *The McKinsey Quarterly* (4): 74–89.

Cecil, John L., and Eugene A. Hall. 1988. When IT Really Matters to Business Strategy. *The McKinsey Quarterly* (3): 2–26.

Chorafas, D. N. 1987. *Applying Expert Systems in Business*. New York: McGraw Hill.

Cochrane, Charles B. 1991. Defense Acquisition Policy: A New Set of Directives for "A Disciplined Management Approach." *Program Manager* (May/June): 29–34.

Comaford, Christine. 1993. Are You Object-Based or Object-Oriented? *PC Week* (June 14): 56.

Corey, John. 1993. The Light. *Business Week* (May 10): 44–50.

Davenport, Thomas. 1994. Saving ITs Soul: Human Centered Information Management. *Fortune* (March/April): 120–131.

Davenport, Thomas H. 1989. How Executives Can Shape Their Company's Information Systems. *Harvard Business Review* (March/April): 130–134.

David, Bernard. 1993. Building a Business Case. *Beyond Computing* (March/April): 46–48.

Davis, Sue Anne, and Rajendra Sisodia. 1992. Knowledge-Based Technology and Experience-Based Marketing Decision Making: An Expert System for Strategic Marketing and Competitive Strategy. Proceedings at the AAAI-92 National Conference on Artificial Intelligence, San Jose, Calif.

Davis, Tim R. V. 1991. Information Technology and White-Collar Productivity. *Academy of Management Executive* 5(1): 55–67.

Dealy, Michael F. 1992. Changing Organizational Structures. *Fortune* (July 13): 49–51.

Dickinson, John. 1991. An Intelligent User Interface Should Possess Business Smarts. *PC/Computing* (May): 52.

Dobrzynski, Judith H. 1993. I'm Going to Let the Problems Come to Me. *Business Week* (April 12): 32–33.

Downsizing or Rightsizing the Information Resources. 1993. *Decision Line* (March): 7.

Drucker, Peter. 1966. *Leadership and Motivation*. Cambridge, Mass.: MIT Press.

Dumaine, Brian. 1993. The New Non-Managers. *Fortune* (February 22): 80–84.

Eager, William. 1993. CIO Survival Skills. *Corporate Computing* 1: 37.

Edelstein, Herb. 1995. Faster Data Warehouse. *IW* (December 4): 77–78.

Ensoft Corporation. 1992. *Executive Summary* (March).

Fillon, M. A. 1992. Systems in Sync. *Corporate Computing* 1(1): 265–270.

Fisher, Anne. 1988. The Downside of Downsizing. *Fortune* (May 23): 42–52.

Fitzgerald, Thomas H. 1971. Why Motivation Theory Doesn't Work. *Harvard Business Review* (July/August): 37–44.

GE Keeps Those Ideas Coming. 1991. *Fortune* (August 12): 41–49.

Glazer, Rashi. 1991. Marketing in an Information Intensive Environment. *Journal of Marketing* (October): 1–19.

Hage, David, and Thom Geier. 1992. Corporate Reincarnation. *U.S. News & World Report* (June 15): 43–50.

Hamel, Gary, and C. K. Prahalad. 1991. Corporate Imagination and Expeditionary Marketing. *Harvard Business Review* (July/August): 81–92.

Hammer, Michael. 1990. Reengineering Work: Don't Automate, Obliterate. *Harvard Business Review* (July/August): 104–112.

Hammer, Michael, and James Champy. 1993. The Promise of Reengineering. *Fortune* (May 3): 94–96.

Hampden-Turner, Charles, and Alfons Trompenaars. 1993. *Seven Ways of Creating Wealth*. New York: Doubleday.

Harrar, George. 1993. Outsource Tales. *FORBES* (Special Edition ASAP): 37–42.

Heintz, Timothy J., and William Acar. 1992. Toward Computerizing a Causal Modeling Approach to Strategic Problem Framing. *Decision Sciences* (23): 1220–1230.

Helms, Leslie. 1995. Workers Brave a New World. *New York Times* (December 10): D1, D11.

Hertz, David B. 1983. Artificial Intelligence and the Business Manager. *Computerworld* 17 (October 24): 19–26.

Heygate, Richard. 1990. Nerve Centers for IT. *The McKinsey Quarterly* (4): 59–73.

Higgins, Steve. 1992. Decision-Support Package Opens Up to SQL Data. *PC Week* (November 20): 82.

Hirschhorn, Larry, and Thomas Gilmore. 1992. The New Boundaries of the "Boundaryless" Company. *Harvard Business Review* (May/June): 104–115.

Holbrook, Dave. 1991. Stereo Viewing: Looking "Into" Manufacturing. *Manufacturing Systems* (January): 30–31.

Hsieh, Tsun-Yan. 1992. The Road to Renewal. *The McKinsey Quarterly* (3): 28–36.

Huber, Richard L. 1993. How Continental Bank Outsourced Its "Crown Jewels." *Harvard Business Review* (January/February): 121–129.

IBM Multimedia Education. 1993. *T.H.E. Journal* (June): 33–35.

IntelliCorp. 1988. Data Is Data. Knowledge Is Power. Advertisement in *AI Expert* (September): 55.

Izzo, Joseph E. 1987. *The Embattled Fortress*. San Francisco: Jossey-Bass.

Jack Welch Reinvents General Electric—Again. 1991. *The Economist* (March 30): 59–62.

Jaynes, Madeline. 1995. Here Comes SAP. *Fortune* (October 2).

Kay, Emily. 1992. Strong Medicine. *Corporate Computing* (August): 153–158.

Keeley, Robert H., and Juan B. Roure. 1990. Management, Strategy and Industrial Structure as Influences on the the Success of New Firms: A Structural Model. *Management Science* 36 (October): 1256–1268.

Kelly, James. 1994. Mobilization for Change. *Transformation: The International Publication of Gemini Consulting* 4(Autumn).

Kiechel, Walter, III. 1988. Corporate Strategy for the 1990s. *Fortune* (February 29): 34–42.

Kiernan, Matthew J. 1993. The New Strategic Architecture: Learning to Compete in the Twenty-First Century. *Academy of Management Executive* 7(1): 7–22.

The Knowledge. 1995. *The Economist* (November 11): 63.

Koselka, Rita. 1992. Distribution Revolution. *FORBES* (May 25): 54–61.

Kosinar, Patricia T. 1987. A Proactive Approach to End-User Computing. *Sim Spectrum* 4(2; April): 1–7.

LaPlante, Alice. 1993. The Big Deal about Thinking Small. *FORBES* (Special Edition; March 29): 22–38.

LaPlante, Alice. 1993. Rightsizing Angst. *FORBES* (Special Edition ASAP): 93–104.

Lederer, Albert L., and Vijay Sethi. 1991. Critical Dimensions of Strategic Information Systems Planning. *Decision Sciences* 22: 104–119.

Main, Jeremy. 1992. How to Steal the Best Ideas Around. *Fortune* (October 19): 102–106.

McCaskey, Michael B. 1982. *The Executive Challenge: Managing Change and Ambiguity*. Marshfield, Mass.: Pitman Publishing.

McFarlan, F. Warren. 1981. Portfolio Approach to Information Systems. *Harvard Business Review* (September/October): 141–150.

McGregor, Douglas Murray. 1957. Adventures in Thought and Action: Proceedings of the Fifth Anniversary Convocation of the School of Industrial Management, April 9. Cambridge, Mass.: Technology Press.

McNamee, Patrick B. 1985. *Tools and Techniques for Strategic Management.* Pergamon Press.

McWilliams, Gary. 1993. Data General: Here a Niche, There a Niche. *Business Week* (April 26): 91.

Michaelsen, Robert H. 1985. The Technology of Expert Systems. *Byte* (April): 303–311.

Miller, Michael J. 1993. The Next Software Revolution. *PC Magazine* (March 30): 81–82.

Minicucci, Rick. 1986. Managing a Melange of Media. *Today's Office* (August): 29–34.

Mitroff, Ian I. 1974. On Management Information Systems. *Management Science* 21(4; December): 371–382.

Mockler, Robert J. 1989. *Knowledge-Based Systems for Strategic Planning.* New Jersey: Prentice-Hall.

Moeller, Gerald. 1991. Templates and Best Practices Used in the Army. *Program Manager* (May/June): 10–13.

Morrison, Ann. 1992. *The New Leaders: Guidelines on Leadership Diversity in America.* San Francisco: Jossey-Bass.

Morrison, David. 1993. Corporate Marriages: Tying the Technology Knot. *Beyond Computing* (May/June): 35–40.

Morton, Michael S. Scott. 1991. *The Corporation of the 1990s.* New York: Oxford University Press.

Negroponte, Nicholas. 1995. *Being Digital.* New York: Vintage Books, Random House.

A New Vision of Application Development. 1993. *Beyond Computing* (May/June): 51–52.

Nonaka, Ikujiro. 1991. The Knowledge-Creating Company. *Harvard Business Review* (November/December): 96–104.

Nunamaker, Jay F., Jr. 1992. Corporate Consciousness: In Search of Group Memory. *Corporate Computing* (1): 203–206.

Ostroff, Frank, and Douglas Smith. 1992. The Horizontal Organization. *The McKinsey Quarterly* (1): 148–167.

Pearl, Judea. 1984. *Heuristics.* Reading, Mass.: Addison-Wesley.

Peters, Barbara H., and James Peters. 1993. Corporate Renaissance: Restructuring for Global Competitiveness. *Business Week* (April 5): 75–78.

Peters, Tom. 1989. *Thriving on Chaos: Handbook for a Management Revolution.* New York: Knopf–Random House.

Pfeiffer, Eckhard. 1993. *FORBES* (Special Edition ASAP): 88–89.

Porter, Michael E. 1980. *Competitive Strategy.* New York: The Free Press.

Quinn, James Brian. 1992. The Intelligent Enterprise: A New Paradigm. *Academy of Management Executive* 6(4): 48–63.

Rash, Wayne, Jr. 1993. Six Ways to Begin One Company's Migration. *Corporate Computing* (June): 113–116.

Rebello, Kathy. 1993. Is Microsoft too Powerful? *Business Week* (Special Report; March 1): 82–90.

Reinhardt, Andy, and Ben Smith. 1990. Sizzling RISC Systems from IBM. *Byte* (April): 124–128.

Reinventing Companies. 1991. *The Economist* (October 12): 67–68.

Rhind, C. Ridley. 1968. Management Information: The Myth of Total Systems. *The McKinsey Quarterly* 5(1): 3–13.

Rifkin, Glen. 1993. Reengineering Aetna. *FORBES* (Special Edition ASAP): 78–86.

Rothfeder, Jeffrey. 1993. Is Big Iron Good for You? *Beyond Computing* (May/June): 23–27.

Rothschild, Michael. 1993. The Coming Productivity Surge. *FORBES* (Special Edition ASAP; March 29): 17–18.

Rowe, Alan J., Richard O. Mason, and Karl E. Dickel. 1993. *Strategic Management*. Reading, Mass.: Addison-Wesley.

Saporito, Bill. 1989. Companies that Compete Best. *Fortune* (May 22): 36–44.

Scheler, Robert L. 1993. Sales-Force Shakeup Will Be First Major Action of the Gerstner Era. *PC Week* (July 19): 1, 11.

Schurr, Amy. 1993. Storage by the Gigabyte. *PC Week* (July 19): 111.

Schwartz, Evan I. 1993. IBM: A Work in Progress. *Business Week* (August 9): 24–25.

Schwartz, John, Dogen Hannah, and Anthony Duignan-Cabrera. 1993. The Revolution Starts Here. *Newsweek* (January 18): 42.

Sedlock, David. 1988. The Natural Language–Data Base Connection. *AI Expert* (July): 26–36.

Senge, Peter. 1992. Building Learning Organizations. *Journal for Quality and Participation* 15(2; March): 32–39.

Senge, Peter, and Fred Kofman. 1994. Communities and Commitment: The Heart of Learning Organizations. *Organizational Dynamics* (Autumn): 15, 19.

Shapiro, Jeremy, and Shelley K. Hughes. 1992. Network Information Resources in Distance Graduate Education for Adults. *T.H.E. Journal* 19(11; June): 66–70.

Sherman, Stratford. 1993. The New Computer Revolution. *Fortune* (June 14): 56–80.

Shim, J. P. 1992. Living Up to the "Hype." *OR/MS Today* (February): 34–43.

Simon, H. 1982. *The Science of the Artificial*. Cambridge, Mass.: MIT Press.

Simpson, David. 1995. Switch on the New Computer. *Datamation* (November 15): 40–43.

Smart, Tim. 1992. How Jack Welch Brought GE to Life. *Business Week* (October 26): 13–14.

Solomon, Jolie. 1993. The Fall of the Dinosaurs. *Newsweek* (February 8): 42–51.

Stewart, Thomas. 1992. U.S. Productivity: First but Fading. *Fortune* (October 19): 53–64.

Tapscott, Don, and Art Caston. 1993. *Paradigm Shift*. New York: McGraw Hill.

Taylor, Alex, III. 1992. The Road Ahead at General Motors. *Fortune* (May 4): 94–95.

Tazelaar, Jane M. 1991. The Office of the Future. *Byte* (September): 205–210.

The, Lee. 1995. Now You Can Automate BPR. *Datamation* (March 1): 61–63.

There's No Substitute for the Real Thing. 1992. *Corporate Computing* (August): 76–80.

Tice, Steve E., Mike Fusco, and Paul Straley. 1988. The Picture Level Benchmark. *Computer Graphics World* (July).

Tichy, Noel, and Ram Charan. 1989. Speed, Simplicity, Self-Confidence: An Interview with Jack Welch. *Harvard Business Review* (September/October): 112–120.

Tully, Shawn. 1993. Can Boeing Reinvent Itself? *Fortune* (March 8): 66–72.

Turban, Efraim. 1993. Business and Information Systems Re-Engineering. *Decision Line* (May): 7.

Turban, Efraim, and Paul R. Watkins. 1988. *Applied Expert Systems*. New York: Elsevier Science Publishers B. V.

Verity, John, and Russell Mitchell. 1995. A Trillion Byte Weapon. *Business Week* (July 31): 80–81.

Verity, John W., and Evan I. Schwartz. 1991. Software Made Simple. *Business Week* (September 30): 92–100.

Vitalari, Nicholas, and Robert Savoia. 1993. It's Becoming the Object of Much Attention. *Insights Quarterly* (Fall): 76–80.

Vogelgesang, Peter. 1990. Drowning in Data. *Byte* (February): 251–256.

Von Ernest, M. 1990. The "Centrally Decentralized" IS Organization. *Harvard Business Review* (July/August): 158–162.

Waterman, Robert. 1987. The Renewal Factor. *Business Week* (September 14): 104.

Webber, Alan M. 1993. What's So New about the New Economy? *Harvard Business Review* (January/February): 24–42.

Weber, Jack. 1993. Visualization: Seeing Is Believing. *Byte* (April): 121–128.

Wohl, Amy D. 1993. Multimedia: Toy or Tool? *Beyond Computing* (January/February): 57–59.

Wohl, Amy D. 1992. Is Downsizing Right for You? *Beyond Computing* (August/September): 10–11.

Wreden, Nick. 1992. The Ups and Downs of Downsizing. *Beyond Computing* (August/September): 12–15.

Yang, Dori Jones, and Andrea Rothman. 1993. Reinventing Boeing, Radical Changes Amid Crisis. *Business Week* (March 1): 60–67.

Yip, George S. 1982. *Barriers to Entry*. Lexington, Mass.: D. C. Heath.

Yourdon, Edward. 1986. What Ever Happened to Structured Analysis? *Datamation* (June 1): 133–138.

Zuboff, Shoshana. 1989. IT and Authority: The Case of Tiger Creek Mill. *The McKinsey Quarterly* (Winter): 44–56.

□ □ □
INDEX

ALAN J. ROWE is Professor Emeritus, Management, at the University of Southern California. He has had extensive experience in applying simulation and information technology at G.E. and Hughes Aircraft, and was the Director of Industrial Dynamics on the Corporate Staff of Hughes Aircraft Company. He has published twenty books on management, managerial decision making, and related topics along with over 150 journal articles including leading articles in *Artificial Intelligence.*

SUE ANNE DAVIS lectures in the fields of information technology integration and strategic marketing at the University of California, and is Vice President of Market Research with Entre International, Inc. She combines international business experience with a research background in the utilization of technology in organizational development and design. She has published many articles on knowledge-based systems emphasizing the use and application of information technology.

ISBN 0-89930-912-7

HARDCOVER BAR CODE